REVELS IN JAMAICA

THE NOTORIOUS TERESA CONSTANTIA PHILLIPS, MISTRESS OF THE
REVELS, FIVE TIMES MARRIED, THRICE IN JAMAICA

REVELS IN JAMAICA
1682 - 1838

Plays and Players of a Century, Tumblers and Conjurors, Musical Refugees and Solitary Showmen, Dinners, Balls and Cockfights, Darky Mummers and Other Memories of High Times and Merry Hearts

By

RICHARDSON WRIGHT

ILLUSTRATED

BENJAMIN BLOM  New York/London

For

BRIAN O. B. NATION

and

J. H. HARVEY CLARK

First Published 1937
Reissued 1969 by
Benjamin Blom, Inc., Bronx, New York 10452
and 56 Doughty Street, London, W.C. 1

Library of Congress Catalog Card Number 78-81202

PREFACE

THIS meandering into the past of Jamaican social life, and particularly as to its theatre, was first begun out of curiosity. It has led over so many roads that now, after nine years of leisurely research, the story of its progress has become a journal of travel. Such an outcome is sure to be the experience of those who choose to write on the history of the stage and kindred amusements. Showmen are by nature wanderers. They continually seek new and fresher fields. And we who would record their venturings must follow the same vagrant trails.

Time makes no effort to keep those trails open. The roads soon go to "ruinate," as the natives down here say of fields abandoned. One must use a mental machete to hack away the undergrowth and strangling creepers that in the tropics spring up out of the ruins of every ancient foundation. In many instances even the vestiges of such foundations are gone.

Retracing these trails has demanded the intimate reading of the several histories of the island, the records of parishes, the acts and minutes of the Assembly and the Legislative Council; searching the tax rolls, death and birth records, and the wills preserved in the Island Record Office at Spanish Town, and such published and manuscript diaries and memorandum books as remain; and the careful scanning of all Jamaica newspapers printed in the eighteenth century and the first third of the nineteenth—at least of such copies of them as have survived fire, earthquake, flood, hurricane, the devouring worm, and just plain common neglect.

The study began and has centered in the West India Reference Library of the Institute of Jamaica at Kingston. I cannot express adequately my gratitude to Mr. Frank Cundall, the learned historian and curator of that institution for the past forty-six years, and to his able assistant, Miss Violet Nash, for their scholarly direction, untiring help, and patience in the face of my insistent exactitudes. They have walked all the way with me "foot by foot."

The trails have also led to the stack rooms of the American Antiquarian Society at Worcester, Massachusetts, and the Historical Society at Philadelphia; to public libraries at Bristol, England, and New York, and those at Harvard University, the New York Historical Society, the John Carter Brown Library at Providence, the British Museum and Colonial Institute and Public Record Office in London; and to the libraries of the Players in New York and the Historical Society in Barbados. I am also indebted to Professor Allardyce Nicoll of Yale for many suggestions and much assistance.

Up to the present, the only study of the theatre in Jamaica has been that contained in one chapter of George O. Seilhamer's *History of the American Stage before the Revolution,* published in 1888. From the paucity of his findings, it is evident that his research was limited to data then available in the United States. Consequently, his chapter left many sources unexplored. He reported finding records of 54 performances and 86 plays; whereas, up to the year 1785, I have been able to record 141 performances and 120 different plays. The Montego Bay seasons were totally unknown to him. And, of course, he did not record the activities of the theatre beyond the period of which he wrote.

Seilhamer's chapter, also, since he was writing strictly of the theatre, offers nothing of the background before which the ladies and gentlemen of the Jamaica stage strutted and read their lines. Since the stage is not an isolated phenomenon, I have tried to make the picture more intelligible by supplying contemporary history and local color.

My studies have stopped at 1838, the year of the final freeing of the slaves. Beyond that point, the whole of Jamaican life was cast in a different mold; the island went into economic and political doldrums, from which it did not emerge until the late eighties of the past century.

"But why," ask some of my fellow disporters on the white sands of Montego Bay, "do you bother to do it?"

Well, because of a persistent sense of *noblesse oblige*. Fragmentary though it may be, this study of high times and merry hearts in Jamaica is, in some poor measure, a return for the happiness, health, and friendship that well-nigh twenty winter vacations in the island have given my wife and me. It is a bread-and-butter note for a hospitality as wide as the island is long, as high as Blue Mountain Peak, as clear and unruffled as the waters that lap upon the shores, as constant as the thousand springs and waterfalls which are among the glories of the island, as fragrant in memory as the flowering logwood. Yes—and more: as sustaining as the bananas and cocoanuts and breadfruit and akee and yams of the woods and fields, and as conducive to the making of high times and a merry heart as good old Jamaica rum.

RICHARDSON WRIGHT

Montego Bay,
Washington's Birthday,
1937

CONTENTS

PAGE

PREFACE vii

CHAPTER I . . . . 1682–1752 I
"From the Theatre in Jamaica"—Spaniards and Pirates at Play—
The First "Publick Theatre"—Tony Ashton—Early Life in
Kingston—The Notorious Mrs. Phillips—John Moody and Players
Arrive

CHAPTER II . . . 1755–1774 31
Early Theatrical Troupes—Face Paint and Printer's Ink—Thes-
pians in Barbados—We Meet Delightful Stage Folk and Journey
Back and Forth with Them to Jamaica

CHAPTER III . . . 1775–1777 59
Theatres at Kingston, Spanish Town, and Montego Bay—Some of
the Plays That Delighted the Genteel Populace in These Towns

CHAPTER IV . . . 1779–1780 88
The Backdrop of History—A Rush of Plays—Mr. Hughes Departs and so Does a Valuable Wardrobe—Military Thespians

CHAPTER V 123
Morals and the Lack of Them—Houses and the Manner of Living
and Entertaining—The Pace of Life—The Coming of Art

CHAPTER VI 1781 141
Our Servants Precede Us to the Playhouse—We Enjoy an Un-
interrupted Run—Montego Bay Has a Lecture—Some Portentous
Doings in the States

CHAPTER VII 1782 165
A Busy Year for the Comedians—Jamaica Is Saved by Rodney—
Feelers for American Theatrical Support—Three-Fingered Jack

CHAPTER VIII . . . 1783–1785 193
Montego Bay Enjoys a Third Season and Mr. Henry Publishes
His Play—The Company Departs for the States and We Follow
Them—Solitary Showmen Appear

xi

PAGE

CHAPTER IX 228
Hilarious Market Days—Sable Venus and Sooty Adonis—Maroon
Fun—Negro Dances and Picturesque Musical Instruments—Christ-
mas in Town and Country—Koo-Koo and John Canoe—The Set
Girls

CHAPTER X . . . 1786–1790 248
The Stage Rests—Kingston and Montego Bay Diversions—Frances
Barret Woollery—Terpsichore and the Creole—A New Company
on the Island

CHAPTER XI . . . 1790–1808 281
Troubles in Santo Domingo Bring an Invasion of Foreign Talent
—The Last Decade of the Century Drags on in a Welter of
Singers, Tumblers, and Nondescript Showmen

CHAPTER XII . . . 1808–1838 314
The Theatre Returns in Earnest—Kingston's Later Playhouses—
Freedom Comes to Jamaica, and to the Reader

FOOTNOTES AND BIBLIOGRAPHY 339

INDEX 359

ILLUSTRATIONS

Teresa Constantia Phillips . . . . *Frontispiece*

The Destruction of Port Royal. 1

John Moody 2

Lewis Hallam the Younger and Mrs. Hallam. 3

Harbour Street 4

King Street 5

Mrs. Owen Morris and Frances Barnett Woollery . . . 6

Kingston's Early Theatre and Governor's Ballroom . . . 7

The Parade Ground, Kingston 8

Governor Henry Moore and Thomas Wignell 9

General Ogle, Cujoe, Henry Morgan and Mary Carleton . 10

Theatre Royal up to 1900 11

Spanish Town Square 12

Montpelier Estate 13

Rodney and Nelson 14

Drs. Moseley and Dancer 15

Montego Bay 16

John Henry and later Theatre Royal, 1907 17

Koo-Koo 18

John Canoe 19

John Canoe and Band 20

Queen of Set Girls and Set Girls 21

French Set Girls. 22

The Ward Theatre 23

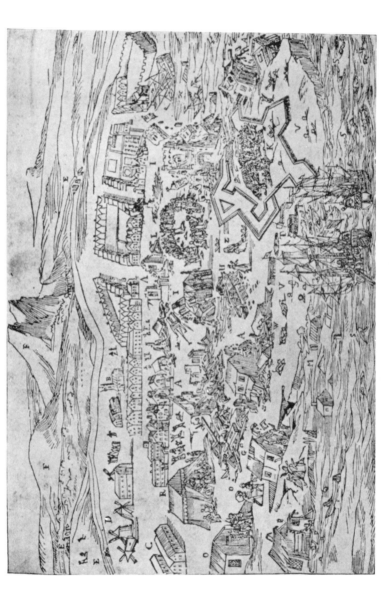

1   THE DESTRUCTION OF PORT ROYAL, PIRATE HAVEN, IN 1692. AFTER THIS CATASTROPHE, KINGSTON
WAS FOUNDED ACROSS THE HARBOR

2 JOHN MOODY, WHO MANAGED THE FIRST THEATRICAL TROUPE
TO PLAY IN JAMAICA

3   LEWIS HALLAM THE YOUNGER AND MRS. HALLAM. HALLAM WAS MASTER OF THE REVELS AND A THEATRICAL MANAGER BOTH THERE AND IN THE STATES. MRS. HALLAM, HIS SECOND WIFE, WAS MISS TUKE, ACTRESS

Courtesy of the Players

4 HARBOUR STREET, KINGSTON, ON WHICH JAMAICA'S FIRST THEATRE WAS LOCATED ABOUT 1750. A VIEW MADE OVER A CENTURY AGO

5 KING STREET, KINGSTON. AT THE FARTHER END IS THE PARISH CHURCH AND BEYOND THAT THE
PARADE WHERE THE SECOND JAMAICA THEATRE WAS BUILT

FRANCES BARNETT WOOLLERY, A JAMAICAN-BORN
ENGLISH ACTRESS

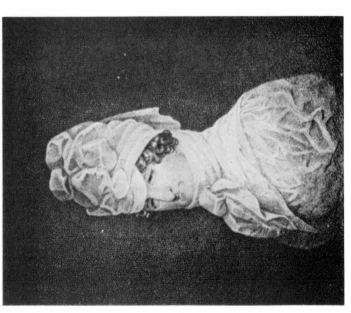

6 MRS. OWEN MORRIS, ACTRESS ON BOTH THE JAMAI-
CAN AND AMERICAN STAGE

THE EARLIEST JAMAICAN THEATRE OF WHICH A PICTURE EXISTS WAS
THIS BUILDING, LOCATED ON THE PARADE

7 BALLROOM AT KING'S HOUSE, SPANISH TOWN, THE SCENE OF MANY
ROUTS AND DANCES

8　THE PARADE, NOW VICTORIA PARK, KINGSTON. TO THE LEFT THE BARRACKS AND TO THE RIGHT THE THEATRE, SEPARATED BY KING STREET

THOMAS WIGNELL, COUSIN OF LEWIS HALLAM AND
AN ACTOR IN JAMAICA AND THE STATES

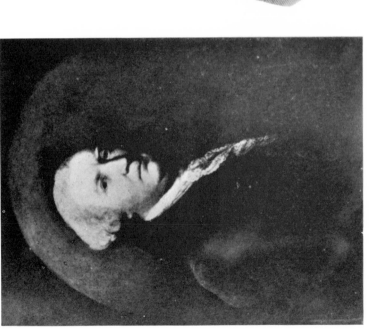

9 LIEUTENANT GOVERNOR SIR HENRY MOORE, WHO
BROUGHT A BAND OF MUSICIANS TO JAMAICA IN
1743

SIR CHALONER OGLE, WHO AS-
SAULTED A GOVERNOR

CUJOE, A STUBBORN LEADER OF MAROON
INSURRECTIONS

S.ʳ HEN. MORGAN

o HENRY MORGAN, LIEUTENANT GOV-
ERNOR AND REFORMED PIRATE

MARY CARLETON, PLAY-GIRL OF PORT
ROYAL IN PIRATE DAYS

11 THEATRE ROYAL AT KINGSTON, AS IT STOOD ON THE PARADE FOR A CENTURY UNTIL PULLED DOWN IN 1900

12 THE SQUARE AT SPANISH TOWN, THE OLD CAPITAL. AT THE FARTHER END IS THE RODNEY MEMORIAL, TO THE RIGHT THE LEGISLATIVE ASSEMBLY AND TO THE LEFT KING'S HOUSE, THE GOVERNOR'S RESIDENCE

13 MONTPELIER ESTATE, ONE OF THE IMPORTANT PLANTATIONS IN THE 18TH CENTURY, SHOWING THE GREAT HOUSE, DEPENDENCIES AND SUGAR WORKS

NELSON, WHOSE VICTORY AT TRAFALGAR WAS AN-
OTHER CAUSE FOR ISLAND REJOICING

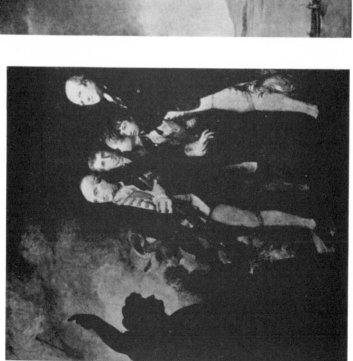

14 RODNEY, WHOSE VICTORY OVER DE GRASSE IN 1782
WAS CELEBRATED FOR MANY DECADES

DR. THOMAS DANCER, BOTANIST AT THE FASHION-
ABLE SPA OF BATH IN THE EAST END OF THE ISLAND

15   DR. BENJAMIN MOSELEY, WHO WROTE THE
PROLOGUE FOR THE COMEDIANS' FIRST JAMAICA
PERFORMANCE

16 MONTEGO BAY, NOW A FASHIONABLE WINTER RESORT, ONCE A CENTER OF LIVELY THEATRICAL INTEREST

JOHN HENRY, ONE OF THE EARLY COMEDIANS

17   THEATRE ROYAL, DESTROYED BY THE 1907 EARTHQUAKE

18 KOO-KOO, ONE OF THE MUMMERS WHO PARADED THE STREETS OF
KINGSTON AT CHRISTMAS

19 JOHN CANOE, A POPULAR CHRISTMAS MUMMER IN KINGSTON AND
OTHER JAMAICA TOWNS

20 JOHN CANOE WAS ACCOMPANIED BY A BAND OF MUSICIANS PLAYING
NATIVE INSTRUMENTS

QUEEN OF THE SET GIRLS

21 THE SET GIRLS WHO DANCED THE STREETS AT CHRISTMAS AND
NEW YEARS

22   THE FRENCH SET GIRLS FROM SAN DOMINGO DANCED MORE DECOROUSLY THAN OTHERS

23 THE WARD THEATRE, KINGSTON'S PRESENT PLAY-HOUSE

REVELS IN JAMAICA

CHAPTER I

1682–1752

"From the Theatre in Jamaica"—Spaniards and Pirates at
Play—The First "Publick Theatre"—Tony Ashton—Early
Life in Kingston—The Notorious Mrs. Phillips—John
Moody and Players Arrive

A YOUNG buck, eager for diversion, flicks a speck of dust
from his buckled shoes, sees that his black silk stockings
are taut, pulls down the corners of his embroidered waistcoat, pats the flaps of his stiff-skirted coat, sets his three-
cornered hat at the prevailing angle of swagger on his
powdered wig, takes his gold-headed cane in hand, and
strolls down to the theatre.

Down John Street in New York, or Cedar Street
in Philadelphia, or Queen in Charleston, or Duke of
Gloucester in Williamsburg, or the dusty and rutted main
street in Annapolis, or Providence, or even Albany. If he
is lazy, he might save steps by dropping into the nearest
tavern. There the playbills are sure to be found. As his
eye runs down the list of actors for tonight's performance,
he notes that some of them are advertised as being "From
the Theatre in Jamaica."

In those days Jamaica did not seem so far away from
the States as it does today, even with our swift steamers
and swifter airplane service. There it lay, just south of
Cuba, stretched out upon the blue waters of the Caribbean,
like a crocodile sunning itself. True, a good round month

—sometimes six weeks, if head winds off Hatteras were high, or a hurricane swirled up from the Gulf—might drag along before a merchant's shipload of timber, mules, salt fish, and flour out of Boston or New Haven finally crept past the tip of Port Royal and tied up to a Kingston wharf. Then, Jamaica was one of us—part of the same Colonial family. It sent us slaves and sugar and rum and molasses and allspice and ginger and indigo and dyewood; and, once in a while, a bride, a gallant soldier, a brilliant civil servant, and, quite often, ladies and gentlemen of the theatre.

Would the tavern's playbills puzzle our pleasure-seeking buck? Would he snap his snuffbox and stutter, "What? What? Damme eyes, a theatre in Jamaica? That infinitesimal scrap of Christendom crawlin' with lazy niggers and rum-jiggled planters?"

Not he. Since Jamaica was so close and one of us, his newspapers quite often carried columns of "West Indies Intelligence." Like as not, his mother or father had a cousin down there or business connections. He would have *known* there was a theatre in Jamaica.

Anyone looking up the family tree of the American theatre soon finds what the young buck knew—that one side of its lineage stems from Jamaica. There in Jamaica it was reared. There it sought refuge and support when times grew hard and when restrictions clamped down by the impending Revolutionary War threatened its life. And from Jamaica it slowly and cautiously crept back when the peace of 1783 brought the Revolution to a close. It is possible to draw, if not a straight line, at least a comfortable, meandering curve from Harbour Street, Kingston, to Broadway, New York.

There is no use starting too far back, no use trying to

push aside the veils of the improbable past. We can glance at a rumor, then pass on to the safer ground of a footnote to early Jamaican history and finally encounter a lively character.

Spaniards and Pirates at Play

Spaniards had been in the island since that day in 1494 when the caravels of Columbus anchored in a safe haven somewhere along the corrugated north shore. Settlers dribbled in. Troops that came with the earliest settlers slaughtered great numbers of the native Arawaks and enslaved the remainder.

The newcomers settled in two main sections. They developed their *hatos* or cattle pastures along the flat coastal plain on the south side and in the midst of it they eventually built a capital, St. Jago de la Vega, the present Spanish Town, thirteen miles from where Kingston lies today. But even before this, at advantageous spots on the north shore, facing Cuba, they established little trading posts. Near the existing St. Ann's Bay they began building an extensive city called Sevilla Nueva. This they abandoned before it was finished. Some say buccaneers drove them off; others claim that they found "their armour, their daggers and their fine speech as naught before a most terrible visitation of innumerable ants."

Due to the island's isolation, raider attacks and lack of trade, the Jamaican Spaniards were soon corrupted into a slovenly and spiritless populace. The island was an easy target for any well-armed force. Twice it was raided by an English adventurer, Sir Anthony Shirley, and in 1643 by Colonel Jackson, whose men fought their way to Spanish Town and "plundered it to their no small enrichment." Then in 1655 the British under Penn and Venables, with a ragamuffin army of eight thousand soldiers and sailors, blundered into the island, fairly blundered.

Cromwell, urged by a lusty Elizabethan hatred of all things Spanish, had sent them out to snatch Hispaniola, the present Haiti–Santo Domingo. In this assault, due to disagreement between the two commanders, they failed. Next they headed their ships toward Jamaica, which they took from the slack and incapable Spaniards with as little effort as we took Porto Rico in 1898. Most of the Spaniards capitulated. Some fled to the north coast, eventually making their way to Cuba. Many of their negro slaves disappeared into the hills and became the forerunners of the Maroons, who for years harried the countryside, just as savage Indians disturbed our own frontier settlers. Fever and tropical sickness soon decimated the English ranks, but to such as survived and wished to stay, bounties of land were granted.

Cromwell offered seductive acreages to any English venturer who was white, free, and Protestant. English, Irish, and Scotch arrived—quite a number of them indentured servants. Although the entirety of Newgate was not poured upon the island, many who came well deserved the gallows. Fortunately, all did not last long; the island was "rather the Grave than the Granary to the first English Colonists." [1] The small landholders having failed to accept this challenge to adventure, when the Restoration arrived in England, the capitalist planter, who counted his Jamaican acres by the thousands and his slaves by the hundreds, eventually came into control. Almost from the beginning, England was determined to make Jamaica the finest sugar colony in the world.

All signs of the Spanish occupation were soon erased. The British retained only a few of the place names, which they proceeded to corrupt into something wonderful to hear. On the north shore they helped themselves to the stones of Sevilla Nueva to build their houses, and at Spanish Town they set up their government offices and solemn courts of justice and their rowdy Assembly. By 1670, when the island was finally ceded to England, Jamaica was well started on to being the thoroughly British colony it is today.

Vague rumors have persisted about the Spaniards having a theatre at Sevilla Nueva.[2] What kind of theatre, who played there, and what they played and for how long are all questions over which a heedless past has drawn a veil.

From the accounts that remain of this city, it might well have supported a place of amusement. Planned on the grand scale, its palace stood at quite a distance from the cathedral, with the town evidently intended to grow up between. Sir Hans Sloane described its ruins. A fledgling physician, he came over with the Duke of Albemarle and his lady to the island in 1687. Albemarle was a new governor. Sloane remained fifteen months, collecting plants and exploring the island, including the jungle-grown ruins of Sevilla Nueva. When the governor died, he accompanied the mourning widow back to England. Out of this experience he wrote two stout volumes—*A Voyage to the Islands Madera . . . and Jamaica.*

It would be pleasant, were there time and space, to play with this notion of a theatre lightening the existence of those three thousand grandees, soldiers, and servants who started to build a city on the lush hillsides of what is now the Parish of St. Ann's.

No one has taken the trouble to tell us, about it, not even Sloane, so we must push along.

The First "Publick Theatre"—1682

We begin to find safer footing in a note dug out of "Mr. Francis Hanson's Account of the Island and Government of Jamaica, which was wrote in or about the year 1682." [3] It runs:

All gentlemen's coaches (which are there very numerous) go with six Horses apiece; we have also several Hackney Coaches. The Manner of living there for Gallantry, Good Housekeeping and Recreations (as Horse-Races, Bowls, Dancing, Musick, Plays at a Publick Theatre, etc.) sufficiently demonstrate the flourishing condition of the island.

Mr. Hanson does not tell us in what town the theatre was located. Since his date of 1682 was only twelve years after the island was ceded to the English and ten years before the frightful destruction of Port Royal (for its sins, they say) by earthquake and tidal wave, we presume this "Publick Theatre" was either at Spanish Town or Port Royal. Spanish Town gay and gallant while the Assembly met; Port Royal wallowing in the high life and gaudy vices brought it by the fabulous wealth of the buccaneer trade.

Francis Hanson was quite correct about the gay and merry living in the seventeenth century. And he is supported by three charming bits of evidence.

The first is a letter that Henry Egleton, Clerk of the Council, wrote on November 6, 1681:

At the Council's rising on the 13th October, the Governor reminded them that the next day was the King's birthday, which was duly celebrated. The Governor reviewed the regiment, many of whom were in scarlet, which they had provided expressly for the day. The Governor entertained all the principal gentlemen and officers with a very sumptuous dinner; and in the evening the Governor's lady, being waited upon by all the gentlewomen of quality, gave them a very fine treat, and afterwards entertained them at a ball, composed of a suitable number of masqueraders, very curiously habited, and a variety of music, all managed with that admirable order as gave great beauty and grace to it. They continued dancing very late, but the streets shone with bonfires to light them home.[4]

What a lovely sight the gallants and their ladies must have made walking home in the flare of those bonfires and how musical their laughter in the night!

We read, too, of the will of the Earl of Inchiquin,[5] governor, who died at Spanish Town on January 16, 1691, which contains, among other legacies, all his plate "made up in Jamaica," indicating that goldsmiths and silversmiths were already working there.

Then there was the request that Du Casse, the French governor of Santo Domingo, sent in September, 1693, to the authorities at Spanish Town. He asked that his agent, la Plass, be permitted to come to Jamaica and purchase the following:

Eight Barrells of fine flower, four pipes of Medera Wine, two dozen of Hamms, three hundred weight of Butter, two hundred weight of Pewter dishes or plates, Six Small Skillets, Six Spitts, Six frying pans, Six three-legged Skillets, Six Ladles, one peice of silk, Some Stuff for a Suite of Cloaths, a little Ribbin, one dozen pair of

Shoes, one Necklace of Pearle and Emeralds, six Cheeses, Some Garden Seeds, and some dozen of Beer.[6]

This list reads as though Madame Du Casse had made it out. The casual order for a "Necklace of Pearle and Emeralds" slipped in with such household items as skillets, beer, shoes, cheese, and flour, indicates that one could purchase almost anything in Jamaica in those days. We hope Madame Du Casse received all her order; and with a bow and a sweep of our hat, we shall leave her checking over the parcels, and return to our major interest—amusements.

We have now repeated all there is to be said about the rumored Spanish theatre at Sevilla Nueva, and given prominence to Mr. Hanson's note about what we believe to be the first theatre of record in Jamaica. Let us now glance at our first character. Or, better still, the character might introduce himself.

Tony Ashton, the First Playboy

My Merry Hearts, you are to know me as a Gentleman, Lawyer, Poet, Actor, Soldier, Sailor, Exciseman, Publican in England, Scotland, Ireland, New York, East and West Jersey, Maryland, Virginia (on both sides Cheesapeek) North and South Carolina, South Florida, Jamaica, Hispaniola, and often a coaster by all the same.[7]

This picturesque introduction presents Mr. Anthony Ashton commonly called Tony Ashton, and Mat Medley, as amusing a ne'er-do-well as ever trod boards or chased the butterflies of vicarious avocations.

Tony, we find from his own account, was born about

1682, son of Richard Ashton who, "tho' a Lawyer, liv'd and dy'd an honest Man." He compiled a valuable work, published in 1661, which staggered through three editions under the handicap title of *Placita Latine Rediviva.* His son, Tony, following a course at Tamworth Grammar School, was articled to the Six Clerks' Office. Shortly afterward he was transplanted to the more legal environment of the office of a Mr. Paul Jodrel. There, after dreary weeks copying bills, he decided that the law was not his vocation. He would much rather see plays—and he did see them. Thus it came about that he abandoned the law altogether. He sets the year 1697 as the date when he finally forsook briefs and took to Drury Lane to serve Mimos.

Three years of barnstorming proved that the stage was the life for him. Mind you, he was only in his sixteenth year and entering on a romantic adolescence. At the time privateering was a lusty trade in West Indian waters. Rumors of the exploits of Sir Henry Morgan and the high life at Port Royal still thrilled the youth of England, even though Sir Henry had settled down this quarter of a century and had given his huge ale stein—the silver one with the whistle on the handle that brought the pot boys running—to the local church for a Communion flagon. But Tony didn't know this, didn't know that pirates were now hanged at yardarms and the strumpets, such as the notorious Mary Carleton, "the German Princess," had been driven from the streets of Port Royal. His head filled with lurid dreams, toward the close of 1701, he set sail for Jamaica in the brigantine *Diligence.*

We hear no more of his dream of becoming a privateer; he gave us, however, an account of the voyage. They

buried no passengers. Evidently, it was a calm crossing
even though it did consume eleven weeks. As the *Diligence*
was small and the arrangements did not admit of isolation
or much privacy, the passengers were certain to have become intimate. But Tony could not keep his lusty self in
hand all those serene, long sea days. He reports, "Captain Walters . . . put me in Irons, because of one Betty
Green (who went by the name of Pritchard and was married to a gentleman of Lincoln's Inn and had a thousand
pounds given her to quit him) who would not remember
or take notice of me, because she had a great cargo
aboard."

With what became of Betty Green Pritchard and her
£1000 and her "great cargo," we need not bother our
heads. Tony evidently didn't let them bother his. Landed
in Jamaica, he "took to the Law, having a good friend
there, who help'd me to a Study of Books of Mr. Scarlett's [8] of King's Town. I got money, kept my Horse, liv'd
gay, boarded at my Widow's, pay'd all off."

Kingston had been settled then only ten years. The destruction of Port Royal in 1692, when half the town slid
into the sea, was still a vivid memory. The Colony fathers
thought it wiser to make their permanent settlement on
the mainland, on the Liguanea Plain across the bay. There
Colonel Christian Lilly, the Island's surveyor, laid out
the new town like a checkerboard.

Tony's memoirs continue:

Governor Selwyn invited me to bear Arms in his Regiment as a Cadet. I had my own frank Practice of the Law
and Quarters and, as is well known, kept Company with
the best of the Island. The Governor's death made me quit

the same; because altho' it is known to the surviving Officers I should have had the first vacant Commission, yet the succeeding Governor, Mr. H-d-e, neither lov'd me, nor Mr. Keyting, both Cadets and Gamesters. I had my certificate from Mr. Nichols.[9]

Thwarted in his ambition for an army grade, Tony "embarqued on board the Diligence of London, Capt. Wild, and altho' we came to the Windward Passage, was cast away in the Gulph, on the South Land off Port Royal Harbour, twenty Leagues Southward of the Harbour of Charles-Town in South Carolina." He and his mates arrived there "full of Lice, Shame, Poverty and Nakedness," despite which, he adds, "I turned Player and Poet."

It may seem extravagant to devote so much space to Anthony Ashton for, so far as I can find, he never lifted even a provocative eyebrow to amuse an audience in the year or so from 1702 to 1703 he was on the island. And this is a matter for wonder, because, once he set foot on Carolina soil, he reverted immediately to his Thespian ways: wrote a play, acted drolls up and down the Atlantic seaboard, in fact is the earliest recorded figure in the long history of American amusements. He apparently returned to England—penniless as usual—in 1704. He is believed to have died sometime after 1749,[10] before which date he had probably appeared before more audiences in the American Colonies and the British Isles than any man in the theatre. Nevertheless, so far as the Jamaican theatre goes, he left absolutely no mark that we can find. Probably at this time there were no amusements of the stage variety to attract his talent. After all, Kingston and Spanish Town in this era were nothing more than villages.

Early Life in and around Kingston

Production of sugar and cattle raising were the main occupations of the countryside around Kingston at the opening of the eighteenth century, and in the town itself were merchants who handled the increasing shipping and slave trade and conducted the shops. By 1702 the Assembly was figuring how it could raise funds to build the barracks for three thousand soldiers that had been ordered to be erected in various parts of the island. Spanish Town had one or more companies assigned to it and Kingston four. Uniforms of these troops and of the sailors of the men-of-war in the harbor gave the drab Kingston streets a needed touch of color. The streets were colorful, too, with cries. Merchants employed negroes to proclaim the catalogues of their wares through the streets.

There were well-established amusements in these early days. Writing of Spanish Town, a contemporary historian says:

Here being several fair and well-built Houses; and the Inhabitants live in great pleasure, where they have their Havana, in which the better sort recreate themselves every evening in their Coaches, or on horseback, as the gentry do here in Hide Park. . . . All commodities that are necessary and useful, either for the Back or Belly, are here Vendible. And it is observed that the better the Commodities are (especially Apparel and Ornaments for the Back) the sooner and better are they vended.[11]

Horse racing appears to have been transplanted early by the English settlers. In 1687 the autocratic governor, the Duke of Albemarle, dissolved the Assembly "because one of the members, John Towers, in a debate repeated

the old adage *salus populi suprema lex,* in protesting
against the speaker's refusal to grant him permission to
attend a race meeting." [12] The races were held every
March on the savannah to the west of Spanish Town.
Breeders along the south shore competed with one another in raising the standard of horses for the track.

Music, too, added a cultural flavor to the life. We find
the printer of the *Weekly Jamaica Courant* advertising in
his issue of June 28, 1721:

Just come from England and to be sold at the Printer's,
a choice collection of Newest Songs, with Notes, engraved
on Copper Plates: also Instruction Books of Lessons for
the Violin, Harpsichord and Flute; New Sets of Minuets,
Rigadoons and Country Dances; likewise good Violins
and Flutes

In November five years later, the *Courant* was reporting "the monthly Consort at Kingston."

Another diversion in these early days was Bath.

Toward the east end of the island, in the Parish of St.
Thomas, and inland a few miles from the present Morant
Bay, is a thermal spring. Its healing properties, so legend
says, were discovered by a runaway slave. Sir Hans Sloane
believed that the waters bathed in and drunk would cure
"the dry Belly-ach with great success." This affliction, according to him, came (although it may seem strange)
from an overindulgence in rum punch.[13]

In 1699 Colonel Stanton, owner of the land, sold his
right in the spring to the public and an act of the Assembly
that year vested the land in "The Directors of the Bath
of St. Thomas the Apostle." Soon a bathhouse for the
accommodation of the sick was built and a village sprang
up around it. Lots were laid out, villas erected, slaves pur-

chased to look after the roads and vegetable gardens that were planted for supplying the hospital. Wealthy people began building houses and they brought their amusements with them—music, cards, dancing. Life at the spa ran a giddy pace at times, and so it continued until the middle of the eighteenth century. Then the social set began quarreling, grew tired of the place, and ceased going there. Bath went into a decline as a fashionable Jamaica resort, and became merely a botanical garden under the watchful care of Dr. Thomas Dancer.

A May Day Fair of 1719

Reaching down into the misty grab bag of those far-off days we bring up one prize. It is an extract from the *Weekly Jamaica Courant* for April 15, 1719, a paper that boasted it contained "News Foreign & Domestick"—or, as we would put it, all the news there is to print. On that April day the Captain General and Governor in Chief, Sir Nicholas Lawes, Kt., granted a patent to one Thomas Spencer of Kingston, a bricklayer, to hold a Fair on May Day and three days thereafter

in the precincts of Littleworth in Kingston, and for the Benefit of the Inhabitants thereof, and for the Promotion of Trade . . . to be kept in the Front of the King's Store-Houses next the Sea; where also there will be all manner of Sports and Pastimes, as Horse-Racing, Cockfighting, Bull-baiting, Cudgelling, Playing for Hats, Wrestling for Belts, Dancing for Knots, Troll Madam, Coits, Leaping, Pitching the Bar, Raffling for Plate and all other Recreations used at such Times.

Just a little corner of Merry England set down on Kingston's water front! We hope Tom Spencer was well patronized. May is a rather sticky month for Troll Madam and Pitching the Bar. However, the populace seems to have patronized the Fair. The Mayor of Littleworth (this is believed to have been a section to the west end of the present Kingston) was chosen on May Day, "as usual, with all the solemnity on that occasion," and "a very fine repeating Gold Watch, with a Gold Hook and Chain, value—100 Pistoles" was run for by "5 Horses, Mares or Geldings." A near-by merchant tried to lure the populace into his shop by advertising that during the Fair he would offer a special line of "Glass Sconces, fine Dressing Glasses of the best and newest fashion, made in England."

What more can we find to give us a cross section of the state of Jamaica in general and life around Kingston, Port Royal, and Spanish Town in the first third of the eighteenth century?

Troubles and High Times

Severe storms, hurricanes, and earthquakes in 1711, 1712, 1722, and 1726 brought destruction to crops and houses. In 1718 the first printing press was set up and the first British West Indian newspaper, the *Jamaica Courant,* issued. The government in 1723 purchased thirty thousand acres of land in the northeastern section of the island for settlers. The parishes of Portland and Hanover were formed in the same year, indicating that the settlements were going deeper into the island and farther away from the three big towns on the south shore. Coffee was introduced in 1728 by Sir Nicholas Lawes and planted at Temple Hall in St. Andrew's, on the road to the present Castleton Gardens. Troubles with Maroons and runaway slaves distracted the people from 1731 on until, in 1734, the situation required the declaration of martial law. Thus the years rolled on through the reigns of Queen Anne, George I and George II.[14]

Yet with troubles inside the island and troubles outside, among them the War of the Spanish Succession which had lively repercussions in the West Indies, Jamaica was on its way to prosperity for the planters. For instance: when Peter Beckford died in 1735, he left £478,000 and an equal value in lands. Fifteen years later Simon Taylor, who left behind him the greatest fortune any West Indian ever acquired, casually paid £100,000 for Holland, a sugar estate in the Parish of St. Thomas. By treaty with Spain, the slave trade for the Caribbean and North America was centered in Jamaica. Vast sums were being made in "black ivory." Money was made, too, in privateering. Scarcely a planter, a merchant, or even a clergyman but took a "flyer" in a boat sent out to harry enemy shipping. These planters and merchants around Kingston and Spanish town and the soldiers and officers in barracks and the sailors at Port Royal were the people who would make up the audiences at amusements.

Evidently the populace on occasions was given to dangerous disporting, for in 1733 the Assembly was obliged to pass a bill, obviously in the interest of fire prevention, which forbade "making, throwing or firing off of Squibs, Serpents, Rockets or other Fireworks." [15]

People in those days ran quickly to pleasure because life was so precarious. This may not have applied to all the people but it certainly did to the majority. The enjoyments of scholarship occupied the interest of only a few. There was John Wolmer, the worthy Kingston goldsmith, who on dying in 1729 left the residue of his estate to found a free school, a school that still flourishes. There was also Charles Drax, whose will, dated 1721, directed that a charity school be established in the Parish of St. Ann, but the Beckfords managed to take over for their own profit the estates that were to support it, so that the school was not finally established until 1795. In addition to these were other sums left to advance education, much of which was swallowed up by attorneys' fees and other questionable means. On the whole, the attitude among the general public was as Charles Leslie described it:

There are several Gentlemen who are well acquainted with Learning, in some of its most valuable Branches; but these are few and the Generality seem to have a greater Affection for the Moodish Vice of Gambling than the Belles Lettres, and love a Pack of Cards better than the Bible. . . . A Boy, till the age of Seven or Eight, diverts himself with the Negroes, acquires their broken way of talking, their Manner of Behaviour, and all the Vices these unthinking Creatures can teach; then perhaps he goes to School; but the young Master must not be corrected; if he learns, 'tis well; if not, it can't be helped. After a little Knowledge of reading, he goes to Dancing School, and commences Beau, learns the common Topics of Discourse, and visits and rakes with his Equals. . . . Some of the Ladies read, they all dance a great deal, coquette much, dress for Admirers; and at last, for the most parts, run away with the most insignificant of their humble Servants.[16]

That was life in 1739. The following year we find that Commodore Brown "entertain'd the Gentlemen and Ladies about Liguanea (Kingston) once a Fortnight with an Assembly." [17]

By 1741, although Spanish Town contained not more than eight hundred houses, "several wealthy Merchants and Gentlemen have Houses here and live Gayly, as much like Men of Pleasure as Business; Coaches and Chariots are perpetually plying, and a great number of Gentlemen's are seen everywhere. Here are frequent Balls and Assemblies, a Play-House and a Company of Players; the Jamaica writer assures us they are excellent Actors." [18] This report of the theatre is substantiated by Vice Admiral Edward Vernon, who commanded in the West Indies from 1739 to 1742: "They have frequent Balls and lately got a Play-House, where they retain a Set of Extraordinary Good Actors." [19]

Spanish Town had a dancing master, too, for in his will, probated in 1736, John Rose of Cottersbrook, Northampton, left £50 each to the sons of Thomas King, deceased, dancing master of Spanish Town.[20]

Another example of these loose and merry times is found in the manner of the demise of Henry Cunningham. This gentleman, Captain General and Governor (he held the post a scant period of a month and twelve days), met his end by a fall, "by an act of his own intemperance at a public entertainment" in 1736. Which, of course, was no way for a governor to act even in those days.

But we shouldn't be too hard on Governor Cunningham. The receptions that Jamaicans extended to their newly landed governors must have wearied the flesh to the point of utter exhaustion. First they were met at Passage Fort and conducted to Spanish Town, where the official and social doings took up the better part of three or four days; then they went over to Kingston, where the Kingstonians, not to be outdone, put on bigger and better and longer and more brilliant and more expensive routs and balls.

We have some of the cost accounts of the reception to Governor Major General Robert Hunter, one of Henry Cunningham's predecessors: Edward Kensall, tavern keeper, was paid £592, 13s for his part of the feasting; John Baines, another tavern keeper, £40 for feeding Hunter's servants; and five musicians—Alexander Bitti, John Michael Pachebel, Patrick Murray, Frederick Angel, and Lawrence Westenzon Linart—shared £35 "for Musick and Attendance for seven days after His Excys Arrival." [21] This quintette, incidentally, would win the distinction of being the first orchestra or band of record on the island.

Early Entertainments

We can only surmise as to the form in which these early theatricals found expression. Some were doubtless amateur productions sprung up in the army and navy circles as well as among the planters' families, although from what Admiral Vernon says, we gather that a number of those "extraordinary good actors" who were maintained must have been professionals. Besides these, there was the Army.

It was almost axiomatic of those days that where the British Army settled down, it amused itself with theatricals. Single men in barracks may not grow into plaster saints, but they manage to make enthusiastic theatregoers. Their officers and their officers' wives, accustomed to playing charades at home, fell naturally into acting for their own amusement and the entertainment of whatever audiences the barracks and surrounding appreciative populace could afford. The field was ripe for the professional theatre.

In 1735 Henry Moore, later to become Lieutenant Governor of Jamaica and Governor of New York, arrived home. A native of the island, being born at Vere, he was sent abroad to be educated. After studying at Leyden, he took the usual Grand Tour, traveling through France, Italy, and a considerable part of Germany. To Jamaica he brought with him a band of musical performers, the principal of whom were the famous Richard Charke, Colley Cibber's son-in-law, and an Italian named Creponi.[22] Charke, it seems, was a worthless man but a good violinist, "a knave with a sweet voice," and his wife, Charlotte Cibber, a wild, wayward, and rebellious girl whom he treated shamefully.[23]

Sir Henry Moore's passion for music followed him all his life and was displayed wherever he went. In New York he was known as a "show governor," because he much preferred to give weekly concerts in Government House than to work.[24]

Still another indication of the high life of these times was the fact that before the middle of the eighteenth century there was established in Jamaica the office of Master of the Revels, an institution not found in the Northern Colonies.

Master of the Revels

This office was an ancient custom, dating back to the time of Henry VIII, who so thoroughly enjoyed masques, shows, and plays at his Court that he appointed someone to look after the royal entertainment. In Elizabeth's time this control was expanded to include plays and professional actors throughout London and the kingdom at large. The Master had the right to license all plays and companies of actors. He also censored plays so that "all prophaneness, oathes, ribaldry and matter reflecting upon piety and the present government may be obliterated before there be any action in a publick theatre." [25]

The Master of the Revels in Jamaica may also have been a local echo of that effort made in the first half of the eighteenth century in England to bring under the control of the Crown, through the Lord Chamberlain's office, all theatrical amusements throughout the Kingdom. In 1735 John Barnard introduced into Parliament the Playhouse Bill, designed to give the Lord Chamberlain the direction of "all common players of interludes" within the realm. While the bill was eventually withdrawn, it was followed in 1736 by a bill proposed to establish a licenser of plays, according to whose report the Chamberlain might prohibit a play. The bill was hurried through Commons and sent to the House of Lords, where, as usual, the Lords hesitated and then passed it. So unpopular was this new move that people hissed licensed plays. [26]

Here in Jamaica the duties of the Master of the Revels included authority over theatrical performances and the direction of all balls and entertainments given by the Governor. The office ceased in 1822 on the death of its last holder, Thomas Dennis, who was Clerk of the Peace in Kingston and Major General of Militia. Before him several others held office—David Douglass in 1779; Lewis Hallam, 1781 to 1783; Henry Andrew Francken in 1784 and again from 1793 to 1795; William Smith, 1785 to 1791—and the notorious Teresa Constantia Phillips, about 1757–8. A word on this person will reflect as vividly as anything can the state of society.

The Notorious Mrs. Phillips

In her *Apology for the Conduct of Mrs. Teresa Constantia Phillips,* that vermilion lady reveals many of her escapades before coming to Jamaica. Published in 1748, the book, in three volumes, went through four editions. Hers is one of the famous blackmail books of eighteenth-century England, whereby ladies of lenient virtue, in writing their memoirs, "held up" their erstwhile paramours for considerable sums paid to escape mention in its pages.

Teresa, the daughter of an Army officer in needy circumstances, was born at West Chester about 1708 or 1709. Educated in London, she was seduced by "Thomas Grimes" (the future fourth Earl of Chesterfield) in 1721. On November 11, 1722, to avoid arrest for debt, she went through a Fleet Street form of marriage with a Mr. Francis Devall (or Delafield), whom she had never seen before and with whom she never exchanged a word. Though her love affairs were "as public as Charing Cross," she married on February 9, 1723, a Dutch merchant of good standing, Henry Muilman. Most of her *Apology* is clouded with lamentations over this marriage and Muilman's treatment of her. He did get an annulment, but he was generous enough to allow her an annuity of £200, which, by her misbehavior, she soon forfeited. Little wonder that "Con" Phillips is mentioned by Horace Walpole in his *Letters* in the same breath with Thaïs, Fredegonde, and the Czarina, and by Fielding in the same class as

Delilah, Jezebel, Messalina, and Joan of Naples!

After many and varied experiences in France and England, she came to Jamaica. The year was 1738 and she traveled under the protecting companionship of Henry Needham, member of the Assembly and later of the Council. She lived mainly in Portland and St. Thomas-in-the-Vale until 1747, when she returned to England and attempted to blackmail her friends by the aforementioned *Apology*.

This apparently did not bring in as much money as she had expected, for she again appeared in the island about 1754, this time as the wife of a Mr. Hugh Montgomery, a well-to-do land surveyor at Kingston. For a time she lived happily with him but when, through illness and, probably, worry over his wife's actions, he was reduced to a skeleton, his friends advised him to move to the country and to make his will. They suggested that he cut her off without a penny. This he did.

When the day of his departure came, "Con" said she hoped the air would do him good, but as he was so very low and weak that his recovery was uncertain, maybe he ought to make his will. If he hadn't already made it, he should do so before he went. Incidentally, as she had been an affectionate wife, he would surely provide for her. He answered that he had already executed a will, and had made ample provision for her in it. By this time the chaise was brought to the door, but "Con," not to be too easily deceived, darted into the house. She came out with fire in her eye. As he was going down the steps, she pulled him back by his collar. In her hand was his will. He had left it in another coat pocket, and there she found it. The poor fellow had to stand there while she read it to him. As there

was no legacy given her, she taxed him with it. He mut-
tered something about making another will to suit her.
"Not me," said she. "No more wills. You'd revoke 'em
when you are out of my sight. You are going to secure
everything to me by deed of gift before you leave this
house." And she forced him to submit there and then. He
died soon after, and she became possessed of all his real
and personal estate, and even collected £26 2s 6d from the
Council for road surveying her husband had done.

Montgomery had not been dead more than a year or
two before she was married to Mr. Samuel Callender, a
Scotchman, commissary for the French prisoners of war
who were brought to Jamaica. He was quite young, came
from a good family, and was well respected in Jamaica.
After his marriage he was not seen more than three times
outside his house. He died within two years. She was now
a widow again, and as Mr. Callender died intestate, she
administered his estate, which entitled her to the possession of all his effects, and to a cargo that arrived consigned
to him. This she immediately turned into money, and good
securities amounting to more than £2000 sterling. On the
strength of this fortune, she bought a chariot and horses
and lived in great style.

Before this money was all spent, there arrived in Jamaica a Monsieur Adhamar de Lantagnac, a young
Frenchman, nephew to the great Vaudrueille. Lantagnac
was among the French prisoners brought to Jamaica over
whom her recently deceased husband had control. He had
been raised among the Canadian Indians. His body, legs
and arms were marked and disfigured. Mrs. Phillips married him, on April 24, 1762, in Kingston Parish Church.
But as their dissipation of the money produced by the sale
of Callender's last cargo seriously lessened her stock, and

as it was not increased by any new consignments, she decided that Monsieur was an incumbrance, as he did nothing but dress, eat, and drink, she ordered him to decamp, and accordingly he went to Hispaniola or Martinique.[27]

Mrs. Phillips' chariot and horses were seized several times for debt, but she always found friends to get them for her again.

Finally her end came in the opening weeks of 1765. She died on January 20th, unlamented by a single person, and not one of either sex attended her corpse to the grave in Kingston Churchyard. While she was dying, she often said, "Alas! What is beauty? I, who was once the pride of England, am become an ugly object!" She had a mirror placed at the foot of her bed so that she could see her face to the last. She wished to die on a Saturday night so that her corpse might not be stopped as it was going to the grave the next day. In this particular her wish was fulfilled, and being conscious to the last, she expressed great pleasure in the thought, having reason to suspect that an apothecary would not have allowed her body to go to the grave in peace.[28]

That her body was carried to the grave unattended is extraordinary, for in Jamaica the people usually troop in great numbers to funerals.

This amazing female Bluebeard was a striking exponent of a *mot* uttered by Sir Nicholas Lawes, a Governor of the island, to the effect that the female art of getting rich in a short time in Jamaica was comprised in two significant words: "Marry and Bury." Certainly Sir Nicholas could speak with authority—he married five times, and each time a widow with a considerable fortune.

In 1757 or 1758 Mrs. Phillips was appointed Mistress

of the Revels. This exalted position gave her a degree of control over the players, and entitled her to a formal place on the stage at every performance and a benefit every season, by which she generally harvested one hundred guineas. There were two seasons a year. The Lieutenant Governor at this time was Henry Moore. We wonder how he came to appoint her to the office and how he enjoyed having her superintend his balls and entertainments.

Apart from this record of her career and her *Apology,* her existence is further marked by a poetic skit she wrote in 1758, "Jamaican Miniatures or a Collection of Impossibilities," published in the *Columbian Magazine,* Jamaica, for 1798. It is rather a dull poem full of local characters pictured in typical eighteenth-century *double entente.*

John Moody and Players Arrive

In running after "Con" Phillips we've gotten ahead of our story. If the office of the Master of the Revels was instituted, then there must have been some kind of amusements for the holder of the office to be master of. The annals of 1745 disclose an explanation. In that year there came to Jamaica the first person of whom we have record to prove his ability as a professional actor—John Moody.

Although he lived to become the subject of many biographical sketches in works on the theatre, John Moody had an obscure beginning. He was born about 1727 in Cork, son of a hairdresser named Cochran, and at first he followed his father's occupation. To hide his humble origin and because he wished to be known as an Englishman, he claimed to have been born in London, but his biographers established his Irish birth beyond a doubt.

He is also rumored to have been mixed up in the Second Jacobite Rebellion of 1745. Because of this, or after this, he set sail for Jamaica.

Here he found an amateur company playing in a ballroom. He applied for a part and made his Jamaica debut as one of Shakespeare's heroes. As Lear, Hamlet, Macbeth, and Romeo, he is said to have won a brilliant success that brought him money. It is stated that he surpassed all actors who had previously attempted these roles in that part of the world,[29] indicating that Moody was by no means the first to try Shakespeare on a Jamaican audience.

Encouraged by the patronage accorded him, Moody proposed to erect a regular theatre at Kingston and offered to go to England and recruit a company of professionals. Theatregoers of Kingston and thereabouts accepted the idea warmly, opened a subscription, and supplied the funds. The following winter, Moody, having gone to London, returned with a company. Many members of this group died, and he went to England again, to recruit a new troupe. For a time he played in Portsmouth, Norwich, and then London, where eventually Garrick offered him a flattering role, and he grew to become one of Garrick's chief supporters in comedy parts. He is said to have been the first to bring the stage Irishman into repute.[30]

When Moody finally left Jamaica in 1759, since he would no longer return to the island,[31] he transferred his managerial rights and theatrical property in Jamaica to actors in his troupe—Messrs. Douglass and Morris and their wives. Eventually Moody retired from the stage and solaced his days by market-gardening near Barnes Common, raising vegetables that he himself carted to market.

It was a pleasant ending for the uncle of the American stage. He died in 1812.

Evidently before Moody left Jamaica for that final journey to London there had already arrived quite a group of players. They may have been gathered by Moody or have come out on their own initiative; at any rate they were in Kingston in 1751. They included David Douglass, Messrs. Kenshaw, Owen Morris, Smith, William Daniell and their wives, with Miss Hamilton as leading lady.[32]

David Douglass (some say he was a Scotch gentleman by birth and fortune, some say an Englishman) was born about 1720. He was a scholar and a man of integrity. He entered the island life as a printer, although he evidently had marked dramatic talent. Later, as we shall see, the elder Lewis Hallam and most of his American Company of Comedians came to Jamaica after their first American season. Here Hallam died and Douglass married his widow and went up to the Colonies to manage the company on their second tour there. Mrs. Douglass died at Philadelphia in 1774. When the Revolutionary War brought all theatrical activities to a close, the widower Douglass returned to Jamaica with some of his troupe, where he was appointed, together with William Aikman, King's Printer for Jamaica and its dependencies. As we have seen, he also held the office of Master of the Revels. In 1779 he and Aikman began issuing the *Jamaica Mercury and Kingston Weekly Advertiser,* known from 1780 on as the *Royal Gazette.* In 1778 Douglass, now a widower four years, married Miss Mary Peters. Douglass is recorded as being lieutenant in the Apostles' Battery in 1783, member of the Council the following year, and in 1785 was appointed Master in Ordinary and Justice of the Quorum for St. Catherine's.

In a few years he is said to have acquired with an enviable reputation a fortune of £25,000. Various deeds preserved in the Record's Office at Spanish Town reveal him as an owner of lands and slaves and of a house at the capital. He died at Spanish Town, August 9, 1789, and his death certificate lists him as a "gentleman" and the cause of death, "Complaint of ye Bowels." He was buried in the churchyard at Spanish Town. His will, proved November 17th, requested that his funeral expenses not exceed £50, that his friend, the widow Eliza Calphrey, be paid an equal sum, and it provided for his wife and two children—David, Jr., who was to inherit his share of the printing business, and Mary, both minors. In June, 1795, the daughter Mary married Lieutenant Hyacinth Richard Daly of the 62nd Regiment, then stationed on the island.

Of some of the others in that first troupe—Kenshaw, Morris, Smith, Daniell, and Miss Hamilton—we shall be hearing in the next chapter.

From Harbour Street to Broadway

On Moody's trips to England he naturally circulated up and down London's Rialto the good news of his theatrical conquest of the island. This came to the ears of William Hallam, a London manager, who, at the time, was not meeting with phenomenal success, and who may have caught an inspiration from Moody. If Moody could achieve what he said he did on a little island like Jamaica, why could not a greater winning be made with the whole of the Atlantic seaboard colonies to play to?

He arranged for his brother, Lewis Hallam, to send

out a scout, one Robert Upton. Upton came, and thereby leaped to immortality as the first theatrical advance agent and business manager in America. He also had reasons for going down to infamy, for, as Lewis Hallam expressed it, "he quite neglected the business he was sent about from England" and "joined his fortunes with that sett of pretenders." This remark alludes to the fact that Upton joined the theatrical troupe of Murray and Kean, then playing in the Colonies. He returned to England early in 1752, just in time to escape meeting a Hallam face to face in this country.

The following year after Upton was sent out, William Hallam sent over his brother Lewis with a small company, some wardrobe properties and a portion of movable scenery. They arrived on the *Charming Sally* [38] and played at Williamsburg, Virginia, then an active center of culture and social life, for the first time on April 15, 1752. The bill consisted of *The Merchant of Venice*, with *The Anatomist* for afterpiece.

And thus was staked out the first part of that meandering road which will extend from Harbour Street, Kingston, to Broadway, New York.

CHAPTER II

1755–1774

Early Theatrical Troupes—Face Paint and Printer's Ink—
Thespians in Barbados—We Meet Delightful Stage Folk and
Journey Back and Forth with Them to Jamaica

OF course, it took more than John Moody's boasting of
his success in Jamaica to lure Lewis Hallam and his company across the Atlantic. The field lay ready and, as others
had discovered, receptive. When Hallam started playing
at Williamsburg, a professional troupe had already preceded him and scarred the virgin theatrical soil with an
appreciable furrow. The Company of Comedians from
Virginia, under the management of Walter Murray and
Thomas Kean had been acting for two years before Hallam arrived. It was the first organized company to play
on this side the Atlantic, Moody's Jamaica troupe being
the second and Hallam's the third.

In addition, during those first fifty years of the eighteenth century quite a few lusty and amusing beggars—
Anthony Ashton among them—attempted scenes from
currently popular plays and put on what today would be
classed as vaudeville acts. Acts such as offered the gentry
of aristocratic Williamsburg in 1738 and reported as news
in the Boston *Gazette* of May 22–29—Boston not then
being given to such frivolous entertainment—"There
lately arriv'd here a Man and his Wife and with them
two children, who perform the agility of Body, by various

sorts of Postures, Tumbling and Sword Dancing, to Greater Perfection than has been known in these Parts for many years, if ever." That was the sort of act to make the eyes of our very first families fairly pop!

The Murray and Kean company was dismissed by William Dunlap, the first historian of the American stage, as "some young men perpetrating the murder of sundry plays in the skirts of the town." [1] Considering the fact that the average early American community accounted all forms of play acting as undiluted works of the Devil, Dunlap had better have said that Murray and Kean were inviting their own murder.

Before the day that first saw John Moody arrive in Kingston, this Murray and Kean company had played at four theatres in the Northern Colonies—makeshift barns, to be sure, but still designated as theatres. The first was at Williamsburg, erected in the second decade of the eighteenth century; the next was at New York in 1732; the third at Charleston in 1736; and the fourth at Philadelphia in 1749.

Note the sort of nourishing theatrical pabulum this troupe offered the audiences of those places and times: Otway's tragedy *The Orphan,* Farquhar's *The Recruiting Officer,* George Lillo's *London Merchant or the History of George Barnwell,* Colley Cibber's ballad opera of *Flora or Hob in the Well* and Cibber's arrangement with songs of Coffey's *The Devil to Pay or the Wives Metamorphized.*

It is said that the Murray and Kean company was composed in part of players from the West Indies who had come north to try their fortunes.[2] Searches in ancient and timeworn Jamaican documents fail to throw light on Wal-

ter Murray, Thomas Kean, Nancy George, Jago,[3] Mrs.
Leigh, Mr. Marks, Mr. Moore (a William Moore will
appear in Jamaica playbills twenty years later), Master
Dicky Murray, Mrs. (Widow) Osborn, Mr. Scott, Mr.
Taylor, and John Tremaine. The most we know of Kean
is that he described himself as a writer and John Tremaine
as a cabinetmaker. When we reach the name of the final
member of that company, Charles Somerset Woodham,
light begins to dawn.

Face Paint and Printer's Ink

If you want to know what became of an actor whose
name disappears from the Jamaica bills, look either in
the graveyards or among the printers. What affinity exists
between face paint and printer's ink I cannot say, but
Jamaica seems to have bred that combination successfully.

We have already noted that David Douglass, the second manager of the Comedians, went naturally from
"make-up" to "make-ready," and here we stumble on
two more instances of the same.

Among Moody's troupers was an estimable couple, Mr.
and Mrs. William Daniell. The earliest name of a printer
authorized by the House of Assembly in Spanish Town
to print its votes occurs in the *Journals* of that august body
for 1749, and the name is William Daniell. He printed
the first book almanac issued in Jamaica, *The Merchant's
Pocket Companion or an Almanac for the year of our
Lord, 1751 . . . printed in King Street, near the Court
House, Kingston.* It consisted of thirty-two pages. Daniell's imprint is also on *An Essay on the Biliõus or Yellow
Fever of Jamaica,* 1750.

Daniell seems to have made a fair living out of his printing house. Two years running he was paid £100 for printing votes and by 1753 he is named "printer to the Assembly." He held this post until his death in 1756, when his widow's claim for payment for work done was presented to the Assembly by the administrator of his estate, Charles Somerset Woodham. He, in turn, succeeded to Daniell's place as printer to the Assembly,[4] ran a printing house in Kingston about 1755–6, and published yearly almanacs. None with his imprint is known, however.

This connection between acting and printing throws light on David Douglass' choice of work when he settled down in Jamaica in 1775.[5] Later on we will encounter another printer, William Moore.

Hallam's Troupe Goes to the West Indies

The troupe of English actors under Lewis Hallam, having opened at Williamsburg in 1752, as we read in the last chapter, and having given a short season there, went barnstorming through the southern commonwealths. They then play in New York from September, 1753, to March, 1754, after which they go on to Philadelphia, to the New Theatre in Water Street. Their season there was short, probably not more than thirty nights from April 15 to June 24. This finished, the Comedians from London, as they called themselves, travel down to Charleston, where they open Charleston's second theatre. From Charleston Hallam and his family go to the West Indies, presumably to Jamaica.

Why did they stop playing in the States and why did they choose Jamaica?

Lewis Hallam's brother, William, had come to America for a short visit, during which he sold his share in the company to Lewis. This may have drained the latter's purse. As it was, his venture had just about broken even. There was not enough patronage to support two companies. At this time the Murray and Kean Comedians from Virginia were not only competing, but were also drawing off some of Hallam's actors. Consequently, Hallam went to the West Indies to recruit new forces. He may have preceded the company, or they may all, or part of them, have gone together.

It was logical for him to choose Jamaica as a haven in which to rebuild his company, because John Moody and some of his players were presumably there. No other Caribbean island could offer the same opportunities either to play or to meet other actors. Dominica, St. Vincent, St. Lucia, and Tobago, most of them small islands, were neutral territory according to the terms of the Treaty of Aix-la-Chapelle. Dominica was not captured by the British until 1757. That left only Jamaica and Barbados as spots to which a theatrical company could have safely and profitably resorted. Barbados, the "spearhead of British colonizing in the Caribbean," was the first of the islands touched by vessels coming from the Mother Country.

Thespians in Barbados

Barbados was the first of the British Caribbean islands to enjoy an organized troupe of any kind. To be sure, it would have made Lewis Hallam raise an eyebrow of lofty contempt. A company of strolling puppeteers, come from England, set up their fairy drama at Bridgetown "where for the Novelty of the Matter, they found a good Market. From thence they went to the Leeward Islands and thence home." [6] God bless those adventurous puppeteers! May they have raked in many a penny and once in a while a piece of eight! And may they have had a safe journey back to England!

About this same time there was published in London a comedy, *Marry or Do Worse,* by a Mr. Walker, a native of Barbados. This may have been William Walker, Attorney General of the island. He may have been roused to writing a play by the poverty of amusements available in Barbados—which up to his time consisted of the above-mentioned puppeteers, a company of rope dancers from the north, and a lion brought from New England for show purposes. Indeed the urge for dramatics began stirring the genteel populace of Bridgetown and thereabout by 1729, when "some Gentlemen were pleased to act several Plays for the Diversion of themselves and their Friends, but more especially of the Ladies of this Place." [7] The bills included Crowne's *Sir Courtly Nice* and Rowe's *The Royal Convert,* with prologues and epilogues written by Dr. Richard Towne, a famous and beloved physician of the island who died in 1732.

Our next item in the meager stage history of Barbados is furnished by none other than that inveterate playgoer, George Washington, recording his first view of the stage. In 1751 he accompanied his brother Lawrence down there. Lawrence was sickly and the journey was planned to restore his health. The first week they were on the island, George writes in his diary as of November 15, "Was treated with a play ticket by Mr. Carter to see the Tragedy of George Barnwall acted; the character of Barnwall and several others was said to be well perform'd. There was music adapted and regularly conducted by Mr. ——." [8]

That sounds like a fairly competent performance. It may have been given by a few professionals aided by amateurs from the plantation and Army sets by which the Washington boys were entertained; or, again, it may have been wholly amateur. Two days later the young George was taken down with smallpox, so we hear no more from him about the theatre in Bridgetown.

Barbados was the native heath of that romantic and melancholy tale of Inkle and Yarico, which Addison related in the *Spectator* and George Coleman the Younger made into a comedy. Addison found the basis for his tale in Richard Ligon's *True and Exact History of the Island of Barbados,* 1657. Ligon describes the native maiden Yarico as "an Indian woman, a slave in the house, who was of excellent shape and colour, for it was a pure bright bay; small breasts with the nipples of a porphry colour; this woman would not be woo'd by any means to wear clothes." Nevertheless, Inkle, a figment of Addison's imagination, woos her with the promise of fine raiment after she had succored him, seduces her, and then abandons this dusky Venus for the more promising marriage with the daughter of the governor.

We have to wait until 1810 for another Barbados item. In April of that year a meeting was held at Bridgetown to raise funds for a theatre. The scheme was so well supported that by July following the foundation stone was laid. On January 1, 1812, the theatre opened with the comedy of *The West Indian* and the farce of *The Spoiled Child.*[9] Even before this building was completed Barbados was sending actors to Jamaica.[10]

As this is getting us far ahead of our dates and much too far south, we must set our course west-northwest and hope for winds to bring us across the intervening stretches of the blue Caribbean in time to be there when Lewis Hallam and his comedians from Charleston land at Kingston.

Hallam's First Visit—and Silence

Hallam's troupe that played last at Charleston in January, 1755, consisted of Lewis Hallam and his wife, Master Lewis Hallam, Miss Helen Hallam, Adam Hallam, Mr. and Mrs. Adcock, Mr. and Mrs. Rigby, Mr. and Mrs. Clarkson, Mrs. Becceley, a singing soubrette, and Messrs. Belle, Miller, Malone, and Singleton. All or only a part of the company may have come to Jamaica. With the exception of Mrs. Hallam and her two sons, Lewis, Jr., and Adam, none of the regular members of this band was seen on the American stage again.

Within a year after their arrival, Lewis Hallam, who had been ailing, died. He left a widow, a daughter, Helen, and the two sons. Adam, the younger, did not develop into an important figure; he played only small parts and, after 1759, his name disappears from the bills. Lewis, Jr., generally known as Lewis Hallam the Younger, was destined to become a famous and important actor-manager and to play in the States up into the nineteenth century. Helen Hallam, who made her first American appearance as Jessica in *The Merchant of Venice* at Williamsburg, did not appear after 1755. Later, in 1759, will appear Nancy or Ann Hallam, Mrs. Hallam's niece, to whom were assigned children's parts and of whom we shall hear.

It would naturally be expected that such a descent of

actors and actresses, fresh from an American tour, would make a stir in Kingston. They would figure in memoirs and newspapers of the day. Here, from the old Moody troupe were, presumably, David Douglass, Owen Morris, and his wife, Mary and William Daniell, Miss Hamilton, the leading lady, Mr. and Mrs. Smith, and Mr. Kenshaw. We can see them putting on their best clothes and rushing down to the wharf to greet the newcomers. A great party —heaps of native fruits and dishes, and glass after glass of rum punch and sangaree! Rapturously, they plan the plays they'll give and how they'll make Jamaicans flock to see them! Perhaps the bachelor gentlemen partook of the three universal Jamaican delicacies of that day—rum, brown girls, and mountain mullet baked in banana leaves. Alas, we can't prove any of this.

It is said that when Hallam arrived in Jamaica, David Douglass was on the point of leaving for England to recruit his corps, "death having thinned his ranks." In our day of community sanitation and universal screening, we just can't comprehend the speed with which death overtook men, women, and children in those times. If it wasn't Yellow Jack that swept them away, it was malaria or dysentery. And as soon as they were gone, they were forgotten. The purser of a British man of war lying in Kingston harbor a decade before wrote a vivid poem about sudden death in Jamaica:

> . . . death stalks forth in almost every breeze.
> Who dies this morn, ere night is in the grave;
> His friends too late implore the pow'r to save;
> His virtues with his crimes they reckon o'er
> Till the fourth day, then think of him no more.[11]

Perhaps, also, Miss Hamilton and the Smiths and Kenshaw of Moody's troupe had died or left the island. Certainly they do not appear in the company that is to return to the Northern Colonies in 1758. Of all the Moody troupers, the only ones we are certain returned were David Douglass and Mr. and Mrs. Owen Morris.

Another fact of which we are certain is that unless an unknown cache of newspapers is found, or a diary of the period, we are left completely in the dark as to what these actors did in the West Indies between 1755 and 1758. Such papers as have survived fire, earthquake, and destructive hurricane add nothing to our knowledge.[12]

The only hint we have as to the whereabouts of these actors and actresses is dropped by Mr. Singleton. He came to the West Indies in the marital state of his name and is said there to have acquired a wife. If he admired really beautiful women, she must have been a Jamaica lady. Although he will not appear on the American bills of 1758 onwards, he otherwise left his mark.

In the Hallam company of 1752 in Virginia, Singleton played only small parts. However, he did pride himself on being a poet, in fact, the poet laureate to the theatre. It was he who wrote the prologue for that opening performance of *The Merchant of Venice* at Williamsburg. In 1767 at Barbados he published a blank-verse poem, *A General Description of the West Indian Islands*. This was composed "during his excursions among those Islands." It is the usual eighteenth-century doggerel, full of classical similes and allusions, although the author does get down sufficiently to facts to descant on the luscious tropical fruit. From the subheads of the poems, we gather that Singleton's "excursions" brought him to Saba, St.

Eustatius, Nevis, St. Kitts, Antigua, Montserrat, St. Croix, Tortula, and Barbados. In spite of its spiritless versifying, the poem evidently proved popular, for it was republished in London in 1777.

Did Jamaica Have a Theatre in 1755–8?

Surely there *must* have been plays performed in Kingston or Spanish Town during the years 1755 to 1758, else why did the island have a Mistress of the Revels? Was she merely a dummy figure attending frolics at Government House to see that the Governor and his friends didn't drink too much and fall down and get killed from their own intemperance? Or attend fortnightly assemblies to keep the young blades from dancing indecorously?

Actors were coming to Jamaica in fairly noticeable numbers. If there was no theatre on the island, why did they come? Why not go straight to the Northern Colonies?

It is also a coincidence filled with possibilities that the Governor of Jamaica at this time was Henry Moore, later Governor of New York. Did this music-loving official encourage players while they were on the island? Certainly it was during his term that the scarlet-lettered hussy, "Con" Phillips, was made Mistress of the Revels. We know, too, that he used his good offices for the players when they were in New York and he Governor there in 1765, for he alienated the Presbyterians by doing so.[13]

Yes, there was a theatre in Kingston at this time. An Indenture of 1753 mentions it [14] and the tax rolls for 1754 list "the Comedians" as tenants of a piece of property on Harbour Street for which they paid the good round sum of £120 rent. It was listed as "King Store" and had probably been some government warehouse.

This playhouse on Harbour Street must have been the one John Moody arranged and at which the actors he attracted to Jamaica—Douglass, the Owen Morrises, and the rest—played. It may have been abandoned by the time Hallam came to the island.

So we can take our choice—either the Company of Comedians lately come from Charleston played at some new Kingston theatre or some long room in a tavern from 1755 to 1758; or they or some of them were barnstorming around the other British-controlled islands. I am inclined to believe that they were in Jamaica most of the time.

Those Who Return North in 1758

While we may not be able to set down chapter and verse on what the company did between its landing in the West Indies and its departure three years later, we can at least get to know some of the actors.

Daniell is dead by 1756 and what became of his wife I do not know. Miss Hamilton, the Smiths, and Mr. Kenshaw we shall have to leave in their comfortable obscurity. Let us hope they sat on wide, shady verandahs and had plenty of red snapper and mangoes and papaw to eat, and plenty—but not too much—rum to mix with their water.

Of David Douglass, erstwhile a Moody trouper, we have already learned. He was evidently a man of sterling character, enterprising, and persistent in the face of trying circumstances. "Rather a decent than a shining actor, a man of sense and discretion," [15] a contemporary calls him. He was also a most persistent builder of theatres. The theatres of that day were far from the elaborate structures we know. They were probably mere sheds, sufficient to house an audience—the one he built in Charleston was only thirty-five by seventy-five feet and run up in a month's time—and often destined to be pulled down or turned to some ordinary purpose when the company was through with them. Elaborate or plain, the playhouses David Douglass will have to his credit include the Cruger Wharf and Chapel or Beekman Street theatres in New York, the Queen Street theatre in Charleston, the Southwark in Philadelphia, a building in Annapolis, and one or two in Jamaica.

Lewis Hallam the Elder, having died, his widow, after two years of mourning (or perhaps it was two years of resisting his arduous importunities) gave her heart and hand to David Douglass who now was manager of the company and under whose leadership it went north in 1758.

Mrs. Douglass became the leading lady, equally at home in comedy and tragedy. The Queen Mother of the American Stage, she was "a respectable, matron-like dame, stately or querulous as occupation required, a very good Gertrude, a truly appropriate Lady Randolph, with her white handkerchief and her weeds." [16] She will be with the company until her death at Philadelphia in 1774.

Lewis Hallam the Younger, as we have said, will become the first great American theatrical manager. His personal life was not without its tragedy. At the time the company returned to the States he was about eighteen and already married to a West Indian girl. The marriage was not a success, for Hallam and his wife separated soon afterward. Her name does not appear in the bills after 1762. They lived apart until her death in the seventeen nineties when Lewis married Miss Tuke of his company, who made her debut as Lady Francis Touchwood at Kingston in his benefit on December 8, 1781. Lewis Hallam is described as being "of middle stature or above, thin, straight and well taught as a dancer and fencer. In learning the latter accomplishment, he had received a hurt in the corner of one of his eyes, which gave a slight cast, a scarcely perceptible but odd expression to it in some points of view; generally his face was well adapted to his profession, particularly in comedy." [17]

Owen Morris and his wife (his first wife) were old Moody troupers and will be in the company departing in 1758. Morris was especially good in drawly, old-man parts and low jest and buffoonery that appealed to the gallery gods.

The Morrises were a constant couple. December, 1767, however, sees their sad parting. The New York *Mercury* for December 14th reports the lamentable fact that "one of the Stage-Waggons, crossing the Ferry at Kill van Kull, in a scow, some of the passengers seated themselves in the Waggon; but on approaching the shore the Waggon was by some means over-turn'd into the River, by which accident two women (Mrs. Morris belonging to the Play-House and her maid) were drown'd."

After a respectable period of mourning, Owen Morris acquired a second wife, "a beautiful, stately and pretentious woman," who will play all through the Jamaica seasons and is still on the stage at the end of the century. She died at Philadelphia in 1825.

Although we have no Jamaica playbills to prove their presence on the island, it is believed that other actresses and actors came up during this period. One was Mrs. Love.

Another was Miss Hyde, who, during the Revolution, sang and acted with the British officers in Philadelphia. We may also believe that Mrs. Catherine Maria Harman was brought up from Jamaica by Douglass.

So much for those whom we know as being from a West Indian source. We may surmise that they brought some costumes with them and some good customs to boot. Lewis Hallam used to attribute his success in negro parts to having studied their dialect and manners in the South and in Jamaica.

John Paul Jones and Other Players

We should not conclude, however, that Douglass stripped the island of actors or that at his departure all interest in the theatre died. In Bryan Edward's *Poems* is a "prologue to 'Venice Preserv'd' spoken at the representation of that Tragedy by some gentlemen, friends of the Author in Jamaica, 1763." It begins:

Thro' many an age, the virtuous and the wise
Have viewed the tragic scene with fav'ring eyes.[18]

And since we are recording Jamaican contributions to the stage, we should not forget that the hero Belcour in *The West Indian,* the most popular of Cumberland's many comedies, was a native of Jamaica. Also Matthew Concanen, Attorney General of the island, 1732–44, was author of a comedy called *Wexford Wells.* It had only a brief career. A third contribution is Moncrief's *Monsieur Tonson,* which was based on a tale told by Governor Sir Henry Moore to his secretary, William Donaldson, who, in turn, versified it for recitation by Fawcett at Freemasons' Hall.[19]

Another tidy item that fits into those years when the company was not in the West Indies is the story of John Paul Jones as an actor. This gallant sailor, then known as John Paul, gained his first contact with our island when, on leaving the British Navy, he engaged as third mate on a slaver and afterward as chief mate on another, the *Two Friends* of Kingston. Two years on slavers disgusted him with the trade and in 1768 he left it while in port. He hoped there to pick up a passage back home to Scotland. While waiting for this, he accepted a job as an actor. Though his engagement lasted only a brief period, it was sufficient to have him remembered as making his debut as young Bevil in *The Conscious Lovers*.[20] Biographers of this naval hero believed that this experience "strengthened his latent histrionic gifts, taught him the use of his body and voice, enabled him to face crowds with equanimity and gave him that for which he was afterwards to become remarkable—presence." [21]

If it is true that the battles of England are won on the playing fields of Eton, then it may be equally true that John Paul Jones's naval victories and Continental successes were first begun behind the footlights of the Jamaica stage.

What with actors occasionally playing and other events, Kingston and Spanish Town were far from dull in those days. Among the other events was the change of the capital.

The people of Spanish Town had a cause for boisterous rejoicing. On October 4, 1758, news arrived that "His Majesty had been graciously pleased to disallow the bill for removing the courts and public offices to Kingston." This removal of the Capital from Spanish Town to Kingston was a pet idea of the governor, Admiral Charles Knowles. For four sessions the Assembly sat at Kingston. On receipt of the news that the king had vetoed the bill, the archives and books belonging to the different offices were removed from Kingston. On the road they were met by the inhabitants of St. Jago and others interested in the matter, in military array, and carried back to Spanish Town with much ceremony. Great rejoicing took place: an ox was roasted whole for the multitude and in the evening the town was illuminated.[22]

The Company in America

It was evident that when Douglass brought his little troupe up from Jamaica in the summer of 1758, he and they had every intention of making their home in the Northern Colonies. Moreover, they no longer called themselves the Company of Comedians from London; they were now the American Company of Comedians.

The autumn of 1758 saw Douglass and his players opening in New York at a theatre he had built on Cruger's Wharf. Thence he went to Philadelphia. To those of the troupe whom we have already watched turning their eyes —for the last time, as they believed—toward the sublime peaks of the Blue Mountains, Douglass began adding other actors and actresses. While most of them hailed direct from London, a few came up from Jamaica, among them Mrs. Harman.

Mrs. Harman (she "bore away the palm as a duenna") affords us a slim connection with our island. She was the daughter of Charlotte Charke, the abandoned wife of the Charke who came with the musicians that Henry Moore

brought back with him to Jamaica in 1735. Since she will
not be appearing in Jamaica again, let us set down the
demise of this lady. In the *New York Mercury* for June
7, 1773, we read that Mrs. Catherine Maria Harman
died on May 27th, at the age of forty-three, and was buried
in Trinity Churchyard. And it adds the touching note:
"Her little fortune she has left to Miss Cheer; and her
obsequies were attended, on Saturday night, by a very
genteel procession." She had been with the company since
1767, being next in importance to Mrs. Douglass.

Among the casts of Douglass' company that played at
Philadelphia in 1759 we find a very young lady, Miss
Nancy, or Ann, Hallam. She was so young that only the
smallest parts were given her—Fleance in *Macbeth* and
Duke of York in *Richard III*. Thereafter we hear from
her no more. But mighty oaks from little acorns grow and
no one can tell what a child actress may become. Skip the
years, and in 1775 at Kingston we shall find this young
woman, now listed officially as "spinster," marrying John
Raynard, organist of Kingston Parish Church. The joy-
ous date was May 15th. As Mrs. Raynard she will be the
leading lady of the company in Kingston.

After the Philadelphia season of 1761 Douglass reap-
peared in New York to open the Chapel or Beekman Street
Theatre. While the company was in the West Indies, the
old Nassau Street Theatre in New York, at which the
troupe of the elder Hallam played, had been pulled down.
Douglass had obtained a site and established this second
New York theatre in Beekman Street.

In 1763 Douglass and his company appeared in Charleston and remained there until the close of the season of
1766. After that first New York run—from 1759 to April,

1762—he had toured the colonies, appearing at Annapolis, Williamsburg, Charleston, Providence, and New York. In Charleston Douglass added a few new names to his bills and played there until May, 1766, when he went north to open the Southwark Theatre in Philadelphia.[23] When it was nearing completion he left for England to collect new members and to have the scenery painted for the house.

Some of these new ladies and gentlemen of the stage we might as well meet now and become fairly well acquainted with, for we shall be watching them play later in Jamaica —at Kingston, Spanish Town, and Montego Bay.

There was Miss Cheer—Margaret Cheer Cameron— who joined Douglass in Charleston. Already an English actress of established reputation, she made her American debut at the Queen Street Theatre on April 25, 1764, as Violante in the first American production of Mrs. Centlivre's comedy, *A Wonder! A Woman Keeps a Secret*.[24] She is said never to have lost her sweet accent or faltered in the clearness of her expression. Romance lingers around Miss Cheer's name the way bees buzz around a nectar-laden bush. For example, her marriage to Lord Rosehill in Maryland in 1768, which would make her almost the earliest American actress to capture a title. For a time she disappears from the stage. We next find her coming to light for a benefit in Kingston and playing in a Montego Bay season. Her last appearance on the stage in the States will be in 1794. What became of the Rosehill marriage we do not know; it may have been apochryphal after all. There is also a rumor that she eloped with her father's coachman, one Long. Certainly it was as Mrs. Long that she died in Jamaica in 1800.

The *South Carolina Gazette* of October, 1766, mentions that Mr. Douglass had recently returned to America and that he had collected some very eminent persons from both the theatres in London, "particularly in the Singing Way." While Miss Cheer was not renowned for her singing, two others were—Miss Wainwright and Mr. Stephen Woolls.

Miss Wainwright, a pupil of Dr. Arne,[25] made her debut in the "singing way" at the Queen Street Theatre on November 13, 1765, at a concert given by Peter Valton, organist of St. Philip's Church. Her career also is a bothersome puzzle to put together. Some coyly hint that in Jamaica she married a Mr. Miranda and on his death gave her heart and hand to a fellow Jamaican actor, Isaac Morales. Others state that she married a Mr. Page and retired from the theatre after two short years of acting, going to Philadelphia to live in retirement (where then and even now one can live in retirement), from which safe domestic harbor she ventured forth only a few times "out of compliment to her old manager when the company played at the Southwark Theatre for the last time before the Revolution." In the next chapter we will find Miss Wainwright on the Jamaica bills.

A pillar of strength in the singing way was Stephen Woolls. A native of Bath, England, he also studied under Dr. Arne. His American singing debut was on July 13, 1767, in a cantata and his acting debut as Mercury in *Lethe* at the John Street Theatre in New York on December 7th of the same year. He evidently had two children, a son and a daughter, as he will be giving a benefit for them at Kingston. Mrs. Woolls does not figure on any of the bills. The history of professional music in America cannot be written without giving a large measure of praise to Stephen Woolls.

In the Philadelphia season of 1767 we also begin our friendship with a most interesting group—the Storer Sisters and John Henry.

An Amorous Dynasty

When they first played in the Northern Colonies, John Henry and the Storer sisters were invariably billed as "From the Theatre in Jamaica." And whereas the various Hallam tribes might be said to constitute the first American theatrical dynasty, Henry and the Storers could well claim to be the second.

John Henry, a native of Ireland, arrived in Jamaica shortly after 1762, having just made his debut at Drury Lane under the elder Sheridan. He came up from Jamaica to New York and made his first American appearance as Publius Horatius in *The Roman Father* on October 6, 1766, in Philadelphia. He was twenty-one at the time, tall and commanding in person (although his only theatrical portrait shows him as a veritable runt); he was especially good in comedy parts. He soon became the matinee idol of his day. During the later years of the company in Jamaica, he will join with Lewis Hallam as comanager and as such give a hand in reviving the American theatre after the Revolutionary War.

The career of John Henry is so closely interwoven with the various Storer sisters that we cannot tell of one without the others.

Mrs. Storer, a singer, appeared at Covent Garden Theatre in 1761–2, billed under the name of Miss Clark. In

1763, evidently lured by the theatrical possibilities on the island, she came to Jamaica, bringing her four daughters —Helen, Ann, Fanny, and Maria.

John Henry easily wins the laurels as the first incautious amorist of the American stage, although, be it said to his credit, he restricted his activities (so far as we know and that was far enough) to the Storer girls. He first married the eldest daughter, Helen. On the way up from Jamaica to New York, she was burned to death on the boat off Fire Island. Henry and the others escaped.[26] It was a mourning Henry who made his debut that October.

> And they are gone; aye, ages long ago,
> These lovers fled away into the storm.

Time has a way of easing pain. Henry next gathered into his arms Ann Storer, and in the Philadelphia season of 1768 she is billed as Mrs. Ann Henry. There is no available evidence that Henry and Ann solemnized their passion by either parson or magistrate, so we conclude that during this interlude they lived pleasantly in sin. By Ann he is believed to have had a son who became a ship captain. Eventually, however, Ann escaped from Henry's blandishments. In 1794 she settled down and married John Hogg, an indifferent actor twenty-four years her junior, and proceeded to bear him several children. These children, once their parents were safely tucked away in the churchyard, changed their porcine name to Biddle, and for two generations Biddles figured on the American stage.

We have now disposed of—at least, John Henry, assisted by a merciful Providence, has disposed of—Helen and Ann.

The third sister, Fanny, managed to resist or evade

Henry's amorous advances by marrying a Mr. Metchler and going to England. However, she and her sister Maria did play with Henry for a season at Montego Bay. Probably Maria kept an eye on Fanny or vice versa; anyhow, in 1792 Mrs. Metchler ventured back to New York for a concert. It was a safe venture: by this time John Henry, his love affairs behind him, had answered his final curtain.

The fourth Storer sister was Maria, "dowered with beauty and magnetism" and known as the best public singer in America up to 1792 and a toast of the blades old and new both before and after the Revolution. For a time she is billed in the States as Maria Storer, and then, after 1773, as Maria Henry. She actually married Henry and, from all accounts, they were blissfully happy and eminently successful in their work together. She is said to have borne him a daughter, of whom our only information is that she eloped. We shall not sadden this merry chronicle just now with the stories of John's and Maria's demises.

More Douglass Actors

As the seasons pass and David Douglass attracts more and more promising material into his troupe, we meet other actors who will figure in the theatrical history of Jamaica. Some came directly from London, others he gathered in a quick trip to the island in 1771 while Henry went to England on the same errand. The success of the company under Douglass' management gave every reason to justify belief in a profitable future.

Meantime here are some of the actors Douglass and Henry found:—

Richard Goodman was a Philadelphia law student.

Like Tony Ashton of seventy years before, he was lured away from briefs and torts and all the rigmarole of the bar, and made his debut with the company in Philadelphia on June 1, 1770. Fame came to him for playing old men, and for both eccentric and high comedy. Once more we shall refrain from halting this chronicle with the account of his end.

Another creditable figure who pops up in this period is George Hughes, whose American debut was dated July 26, 1773. Later we shall hear from him in a number of picturesque capacities at Kingston.

The names of four other gentlemen will attract the Jamaica eye—Mr. Roberts, who was with the American Company in the colonies from 1767 to 1774 and remains with us in Jamaica till well on toward the end of the century; Mr. Johnson, who first played at Philadelphia on November 2, 1772, and to whom was assigned a great number of small parts; Mr. Dermot, who appears on the Philadelphia bills on March 10, 1773, as Solario in *The Merchant of Venice;* and Mr. Godwin. But Mr. Godwin deserves a paragraph all to himself.

Mr. Godwin, who was gifted in the dancing way, made his debut under Douglass at the Southwark Theatre in Philadelphia as Prince Edward in *Richard III* in 1766. Next we find him in Douglass' competing company—the New American—playing leads for it at Williamsburg from April to June, 1768, and at Annapolis in 1769. Godwin played with a Mr. Parker who was advertised as "From the Theatre in Jamaica," and with Mrs. Parker, a leading soubrette and singer.[27] The next winter Parker joined Douglass' company and, as we shall note, Godwin is found in its ranks at Kingston.

As the troupe grew, so did the repertoire. Douglass' company in these seasons of 1773–4 comprised twenty-seven different names, and their plays, so far as we have been able to figure them from contemporary records, totaled thirty-three, together with twenty-two afterpieces. These afterpieces were quite necessary to the programs of that time.

The stage afforded amusement or boredom in generous measure. Before the curtain parted there came a prologue. The play followed. The intermission was generally filled in with a short skit, a dance, or songs. Then came the afterpiece, usually a farce, or a short opera, with an epilogue bringing together the curtain for the last time. What more could the public ask at 7s 6d a seat?

The day was coming when they wouldn't pay even that. With the year 1774 we are approaching a calamitous date and, you may be pleased to know, the close of this un-Jamaican chapter.

The last time we shall see our friends playing together professionally is on May 16, 1774, at Charleston. On the 30th the *South Carolina Gazette* announced, "The Company have separated until the Winter when the New York Theatre will be opened; Mr. Hallam being embarked for England to engage some recruits for that service. The year after they will perform at Philadelphia and in the Winter following we may expect them here with a Theatrical Force hitherto unknown in America. Scratch me, countrymen! And I'll scratch thee."

From time to time, it appeared, troupers had been drifting up from the West Indies, nor did they last long. "The climate of the West Indies had prematurely cut the thread of life of nearly two-thirds of the original company." [28]

Hence Hallam went to London for fresher and stronger recruits. There he resided with his uncle, William Hallam, at Paddington, and played at York and other provincial theatres.

The Charleston ship sailing-lists reveal that Mr. Henry, Mrs. Henry, and Miss Storer were going to England via Philadelphia and that the Morrises, Miss Wainwright, and several others of the company were sailing for Philadelphia and New York. On June 21st, David Douglass and Mrs. Douglass sail in the schooner *Love* for New York.

By June 27th members of the American Company of Comedians have gone their separate ways. Two, at least, do not quit acting. On September 23, 1774, at the Southwark in Philadelphia Mr. Goodman and Mr. Allen "from the Theatre Royal in Edinburgh" give an Attic Evening's Entertainment—the *Lecture on Heads*. Between the first and second parts Allen recites Mr. Foote's prologue to the author and the program concluded with *Bucks Have At Ye All!* recited by Mr. Allen, "after the manner of Mr. King of the Theatre Royal, Drury Lane." There was also a concert of instrumental music.

Thus the company scattered, with many promises to meet again in the autumn. Hallam, having gone to England, sent out as his representative his cousin, Thomas Wignell. He must have been a young man at the time. Down in Jamaica there was living an actor by the name of William Wignell, evidently an elder brother, who began scribbling in a memorandum book. We shall be dipping into it when we turn the page into the next chapter. Meantime, here is Thomas Wignell and, if you please, he is about to enter a barber shop. The date is October

16, 1774. While he is being sheeted and lathered, we can turn our attention to a more serious matter.

It was all very well for Douglass and Hallam and Henry and the Owen Morrises to plan a bumper run for 1774–5; but they didn't count on the Continental Congress.

War clouds, gathering in the Colonies for some years now, grew threateningly black. On the same day that Thomas Wignell stepped into the barber shop, Congress, certain that the country was in for grim times, clamped down on all forms of frivolous entertainments. Its resolution discouraged "every Species of Extravagance and Dissipation, especially all Horse Racing and all kinds of Gaming, Cock Fighting, Exhibitions of Shews, Plays and other expensive Diversions and Entertainments."

The news was brought to Thomas Wignell as he sat in the barber's chair. It must have frightened that young man right out of his lather!

Later generations have proven how wrong the Continental Congress was in its estimate of the place of the theatre in wartime. Amusement plays a most important part in the maintenance of morale.

Douglass and his troupe may have been enough ahead of their age to realize this fact. The time, however, was not propitious for arguing the point. Besides, since coming up from the West Indies in 1758, Douglass had been careful to end his playbills with three cheers for Royalty —"Vivat Rex et Regina!" Scarcely the sort of sentiment to make the Liberty Boys pack the house!

And so, early in 1775, before any of the Revolutionary shots began reverberating around the world, Douglass and the better part of his troupe had seen Long Mountain rise like a whale out of the green sea of the Liguanea Plain and watched the Blue Mountains unfold, ridge by ridge, and had come to anchor under the reassuring guns of Port Royal.

CHAPTER III

1775-1777

Theatres at Kingston, Spanish Town, and Montego Bay—
Some of the Plays That Delighted the Genteel Populace in
These Towns

IN the last chapter we were so busy meeting members of
the American Company of Comedians who sought refuge
in Jamaica after the Congressional edict of October,
1774, that we completely overlooked an amusing character. And, since according to available newspaper reports his is the first professional diversion in this decade,
even before the Comedians parted their curtain in Kingston, he deserves the honor at the head of the chapter.

Ladies and Gentlemen, I take pleasure in presenting
Mr. Hyman Saunders.

It was the New York *Mercury* of October 25, 1770,
that first welcomed him to the Northern Colonies by an-
nouncing that "the celebrated Hyman Saunders, just arrived from Europe, would play on the 29th at the home
of Mr. Hyet on Hunter's Quay." He evidently amused
New Yorkers for several weeks, departed and returned
again, for on January 21, 1771, his advertisement ap-
prised the awaiting populace that he would continue his
performances on Tuesday, Wednesday, and Saturday.
This advertisement also reports that he had "several
new and astonishing performances, differing from what
had hitherto been attempted and such as was never seen

59

in this province." The room, he assured the public, would be illuminated and "well air'd."

But what, you ask, did Mr. Saunders do? Patience! Patience! The *Mercury* of November 11, 1771, discloses this information: Mr. Saunders "begs to acquaint the nobility and gentry that he is lately returned to this town and intends to perform in private (only) his dexterity and grand deception, to any select company; who are desired to leave a note at the printer's a day before they choose to honor him with their commands." There! The secret is out—Mr. Saunders was a conjurer, a prestidigitator, a sleight-of-hand artist!

All of this explanation prepares us for the not-too-modest notice published in the *Jamaica Gazette* on Saturday, March 25, 1775:

By Permission
This present Evening, on Monday Evening and on
Thursday Evening
The Celebrated Mr. Saunders
will exhibit his
Dexterity and Grand Deception

At the brick house, the back of Mr. Howard's, known by the name of Paplay's store. He has had the honour of performing before His Excellency the Earl of Dunmore, Governor of Virginia; his Excellency Robert Green, Esq., Governor of Maryland; the Honourable Richard Penn, Esq., Governor of Pennsylvania; and most of the Nobility and gentry in Great Britain, Ireland and America, and in particular in the capital cities.
He performs a variety of new, astonishing and entertaining performances, by dexterity of Hand, surpassing everything of the kind that has been hitherto seen or attempted, on this side the Atlantic, which will be exhibited in a

number of surprising instances, deceiving the eye of the nicest observer and appearing in a manner supernatural.

Mr. Saunders has been honoured with the greatest applause by his Majesty and all the Nobility that have seen his great performances, in Europe, America and the West Indies; and is allowed to be the most astonishing proficient in the art of clear conveyance, that ever attempted an exhibition of the kind, without descending to the low tricks of cups, balls, ribbands, etc.

Tickets, at a Mill'd Dollar each (without which no person can be admitted) may be had at the place of performance. To open at Six O'Clock and begin exactly at Seven.

N.B. Those who are desirous of having private performances, at their own houses (on the days that he does not exhibit in Public) shall be waited on, by giving a day's notice, at the place of performance.

If Mr. Saunders had played in other of the West Indies before this date, he had taken his time getting down to Jamaica. We admire his insistence on milled money—no sweated coins [1] for him! He will appear soon again, so now we can leave him and, having given him so much space, leave him with an easy conscience, and turn to the legitimate theatre.

The Comedians' Opening Performance

The American Company probably did not come all in the same boat to Jamaica. Although I have no proof for the statement, I surmised that they drifted down to the island in the same manner they left Charleston— the Hallams and Henrys came over from London and the Douglasses and Owen Morrises from New York, and then others followed. Douglass is said to have sailed for the West Indies on February 2, 1775.

Only one paper of this theatrical period affords any news of them. The troupe opened at the theatre in Kingston on July 1, 1775. This would have given them time to get their land legs and to have looked over the prospects and rehearsed. The *Jamaica Gazette* for that day announces:

By Permission of his Excellency, the Governor
By the American Company:
This Present Saturday, the 1st of July
Will be presented a Tragedy called

Romeo and Juliet

Romeo by Mr. Wignell
Mercutio by Mr. Douglass
Capulet by Mr. Henry
Friar Lawrence by Mr. Morris
Tibalt by Mr. Allen
Paris by Mr. Woolls
Mountague by Mr. Hughes
Fryar John by Mr. Dermot
Balthazar by Mr. Johnson
Apothecary by Mr. Roberts
Lady Capulet by Mrs. Douglass
Nurse by Mrs. Morris
Juliet by Mrs. Raynard

In the Masquerade Scene a Country Dance by grotesque characters, with the Funeral Procession of Juliet to the Monument of the Capulets;
And a Solemn Dirge:
The vocal parts by Mr. Woolls, Miss Wainwright, Miss Storer, etc.
To which will be added

A Wonder! An Honest Yorkshireman

Gaylove by Mr. Woolls
Sapscull by Mr. Johnson
Muckworm by Mr. Morris
Slago by Mr. Hughes
Blunder by Mr. Dermot
Combrush by Mrs. Morris
Arabella by Miss Wainwright

The Doors will be opened at *Five* and the play begin precisely at half an hour after six o'clock. No Money to be receiv'd at the doors, nor any person admitted without tickets, which are sold at the Printing Offices, and, on the evening of the performance, at the Office of the Theatre. Boxes two Spanish Milled Dollars, Pit seven shillings and six pence, gallery one Spanish Mill'd Dollar.

Places in the Boxes, and Tickets for them, may be had of Mr. Roberts in King Street, two doors above the Parade. Ladies and Gentlemen will please to send their servants to keep their places at five o'clock. No Person can, on any account whatever, be admitted at the stage Door.

Vivat Rex et Regina

N.B. Days of Performances for the future, Tuesdays, Thursdays and Saturdays.

This one item alone is extant, this and the prologue spoken on the occasion, composed by Benjamin Moseley, M.D., Surgeon General of the island, authority on tropical fevers, coffee and sugar, and, in his leisure moments, a rhymester of sorts:

When hostile strife invades the world's great stage,
And active parts are cast for ev'ry age;
When real life is filled with real woes,
And thro' the scene no ray of gladness glows;
The Muse alarm'd at the loud tempest's roar,
Seeks an asylum on this peaceful shore,
Where gen'rous worth and polish'd genius shine,
And peace and plenty all their blessings join;
Where drooping merit always finds relief,
And pity drops a tear on ev'ry grief;
Each wearied trav'ler finds a friendly host,
And ev'ry care in ev'ry comfort's lost.
This PILE a lively lasting sense imparts
Of highest gratitude to feeling hearts;
For which, exerting all our strength, we'll shew

How much we wish to pay—how much we owe!
Indulgent take the thanks your aid demands.
'Tis all you can expect at Players hands.—
Chear'd by your smiles, I feel my heart dilate,
Those smiles which give a Thespian Monarch state.
Here *Belvidera* sorrows may disclose
Where hearts like her's can sympathize her woes;
Here old distracted *Lear,* drench'd in the storm,
May shelter take;—*Cordelia* safe from harm;
The *Merry Wives* shall sport with Falstaff's flames,
And luckless *Jack* sink hissing in the Thames.
Thalia's purer stores our mirth shall yield,
While Satire's scourge drives Folly off the field;
Nor shall *Melpomene* one sentence bear,
Might wound the chastness of a Cato's ear;
Our faithful mirror shall reflect to view,
Those blooming virtues which reside in you;—
Long may they flourish—long in vigour bloom.
'Till fair JAMAICA rival *Greece* and *Rome!* [2]

In the cast we note the presence of Miss Wainwright.
Some historians of the American stage believe that she
remained behind in the States, but here she is, big as life,
in sultry Kingston, when, at this time of year, as the
negroes say, "It hot fe true"—it is intensely hot. Mr.
William Wignell is also in the cast and, in later performances, will appear Mr. Thomas Wignell, Hallam's cousin, who will go to the States after the Revolution as an
actor-manager. His son plays minor child roles. Mrs.
Anna Hallam Raynard is the leading lady.

Thus the season of 1775 was definitely launched, under the permission of Governor Sir Basil Keith, and
three performances a week are offered. Beyond this date
and all through 1776 no paper exists to furnish us with
theatrical news of Kingston.[3]

Kingston's Theatre Building

This ambitious presentation of *Romeo and Juliet* with a cast of fourteen presupposes the existence of a substantial theatre building in which they played. The old theatre on Harbour Street, as we saw in the last chapter, was no longer used for performances, apparently having been abandoned before 1753. Where was the new theatre? Lacking newspapers, we turn to diaries and histories written at the time.

First thumb over the pages of William Hickey, whose Jamaica diary covers the year 1775. Hickey and his friend Bonynge enjoy the hospitality offered at Bagg's Tavern. Bagg had kept a place in Kingston in 1760 and was so well patronized that he made a fortune of £25,-000, which he dissipated in sumptuous living in England. He turned his penniless footsteps to Jamaica again, opened his tavern, and managed to make another £8000 before he died in 1778. One of the favorite beverages at Bagg's was called "Mrs. Allen." The Allens kept the best wine store in Kingston and when Allen died his widow carried on the business. She was especially famous for her clarets. Patrons, instead of asking for Bordeaux, merely asked for "Mrs. Allen"!

But while we are off on this bibulous tack, William Hickey is left waiting. He furnishes a jolly view of how gentlemen amused themselves:

Young Bonynge told me that he kept a Phaeton, a stylish Tim Whiskey, and half a dozen blood horses, all or any of which would always be at my service. "Apropos," said he, "we must go to the town (Kingston) tomorrow, for there is a famous play performed in the evening at the theatre, being the first this season. They have a passable set of actors, besides which all the beauties we boast of will be present, to some of whom I will introduce you."

At breakfast the following morning I told Mr. Richards I was going to Kingston and the reason for so doing, to which he replied, "By all means go. I am myself a constant frequenter of the theatre when open and would accompany you had I not last night accepted an invitation to dine with Colonel Dalling, where I also promised to take you. However, I will make your apologies by fairly telling him that his burgundy, superior as it is, stood no chance when put in competition with a playhouse and a parcel of fine girls."

After a moderate proportion of claret we adjourned to the theatre, which was commodious, neatly fitted up and had a more than tolerable set of actors then recently arrived from New York in America, which city they had quitted in consequence of the popular commotion and probability of hostilities commencing with the Mother Country. The manager was Mr. Hallam, brother to Mrs. Mattocks of one of the London theatres. After being very well entertained at the play, where Bonynge had collected five as pretty girls as a man would wish to look at, we seven went to a tavern in the neighborhood of the theatre, supped and passed a jovial night. . . .

Here the journal of one day gives a calendar of a Jamaican dandy's day:

From thence, either accompanied by Bonynge or other young friends, we lounged amongst the different stores (shops or warehouses where trade is carried on) or I attended Mr. Richards in his morning visits to families of his acquaintance until towards two in the afternoon, when we went home to dress for dinner, which meal, whether at home or abroad, filled up the space until it became time to attend the theatre, assembly, concert or private party . . . retiring to sleep, in common, about midnight.[4]

The next information on the Kingston theatre is contributed by the historian Edward Long.[5] Since his book was published in 1774, and in London, it is evident that the theatre he speaks of existed before the American Company returned to Jamaica. And the existence of this theatre, in turn, leads us to believe that while, from 1758 to 1774, the American Company was playing in the Northern Colonies, there were enough professional and amateur actors in and around Kingston to justify the erection of a building devoted especially to the production of plays. Long says:

In the lower part of the town is a very pretty theatre, exceedingly well contrived and neatly finished. Dramatic performances were exhibited here during the last war [i. e., the war with Spain]; at which time there was a considerable quantity of prize money in circulation, but in time of peace, the town is not able or not disposed to support so costly an amusement."

Long also mentions taverns. One of them—Ranelagh— will figure in our history. It had a "long room for concerts, balls and public entertainments. . . . A large, loft building, commanding a fine view of the town, harbour and shipping. Here the balls and concerts are usually exhibited; and the Company are numerous and elegant in their appearance." [6]

Our third quotation places the theatre on its site: "In the north part of the town is a neat church with a low spire; and nearly adjoining is a spacious parade, with barracks for soldiers. There is also a theatre, assembly rooms and other places of public amusement." [7]

There can be no doubt, then, that at this time Kingston had its definite structure devoted to theatrical purposes. It was probably built in the middle of the eighteenth century and was located at the northeast corner of the Parade or present Victoria Park. A drawing of it appeared in the Almanac for 1831 and a glimpse of it can be seen in the view of the Parade in Kidd's "Views of Jamaica."

While the picture of Kingston's theatre at this time shows it as a substantial enough building, it followed many customs that would appear crude to us. It, and all theatres of this period, for instance, were lighted throughout with candles. Sconces holding candles were along the walls and projecting from balconies and boxes, where they could be easily trimmed by an usher or an individual seated near by. Candles were also used for footlights. A Jamaica audience thought it not at all unusual if, during a tender love scene or a dramatic passage, a stage hand came down and snuffed the smoldering wicks. In the flimsy wooden buildings that served for theatres, these candles were always a fire menace. Later, oil lamps without chimneys were used. Although they were thought to be an improvement, they were no less dangerous: they once did cause a near-tragedy in the Kingston theatre.

Kingston in those days—1775—was a thriving port. Its populace included 5000 whites, 1200 free negroes, and 5000 slaves. It had thirty-five major streets and sixteen lanes, on which stood 1565 houses and innumerable uncounted negro shacks and warehouses, bringing the total number of buildings to between 2000 and 3000. A few miles off was Half-Way Tree, a small town of villas.[8] Altogether it was a much more prosperous place than when the comedians were here twenty years before.

The Spanish Town Theatre

With the theatre in Kingston established, we can now take the long, hot, dusty coach ride to Spanish Town. Our way will go through the Parade, past the slums of Smith's Village (surely they existed then as they exist today) and along the rutted road between fences of cactus and "grow-stick" [9] hedging in sugar and grazing lands and "ruinate" fields, stop for a drink at old Ferry Inn, and finally cross the stone bridge over the Rio Cobre into the capital.

On second thought, it is unfair to dismiss that Spanish Town road in even a long sentence. This Via Appia of Jamaica has figured in so much legislation and in so many novels and diaries and has been so much traveled that we should, out of respect for it, halt our chattering about the theatre and give it a measure of praise.

As early as 1681 the legislating fathers were arguing about its width—that it should be 60 feet wide when it passed a woods and 24 in open ground, and so they went on wrangling until by 1777 they finally agreed that it should be between 30 and 40 feet. Halfway between Kingston and Spanish Town was a toll ferry and beside it the famous Ferry Inn. This building has survived earthquakes and hurricanes and still offers refreshments of sorts. *Tom Cringle's Log* [10] gives a description of this historic road and the torture it was to travelers; Lady Nugent's [11] diary mentions it again and again, and even so relatively recent a novelist as Colonel William G. Hamley, writing of life in the eighteen thirties, explains its social ratings:

Then all men had to whip along the highway and the style in which they travelled this much-frequented road was a criterion of the traveller's wealth or acumen or of their horses' value. . . . They were eternally patching and mending it and incredible sums were reported to be spent on its repairs, yet, except for the first mile out of Spanish Town, it was always in scandalous condition. One half its breadth was villainously paved . . . the other half was by courtesy said to be macadamized; in wet weather it was a mire and in dry a sample of the great Sahara.[12]

Tourists by the thousands travel over that road today so that it requires no great stretch of the imagination to see the American Company of Comedians trundling back and forth along it between the port and the capital.

And now that we have arrived finally at Spanish Town, we must explain that even in this busy era of 1775–6 it offered chances for public entertainment only at certain seasons—during the meetings of the Assembly and the sittings of the courts. Once more we shall turn the page over to Edward Long:

As this is an inland town, it derives its chief support from the residence of the governor and publick officers; the gentlemen of the law; the assembly and council; and the conflux of people who resort hither from the country parts on business, particularly during the sittings of the supreme or grand court of law near four months in the year; and the session of the assembly, which generally lasts from the beginning of October till the Christmas holidays. At these times universal gaiety prevails; balls, concerts and routs, alternately hold their reign. The governor, according to antient custom, gives a ball and entertainment once a year at the king's house in honour of his majesty's birth-day. The appearance of company on this occasion is

generally brilliant, the ladies vying with one another in
the richness of their dresses; every one makes a point of
exhibiting a new suit or finery; and this regulation is so
lavishly indulged, that such a ball is seldom attended with
less than three or four thousand pounds expence to the
guests.[13]

Still, Long does not mention a theatre building in Spanish Town. However, since his book was published in
1774 and probably written a year or so before that date,
we couldn't expect him to speak of a theatre. This building, as we shall see by the next (and roundabout) approach, was not built until 1776.

In November, 1793, as the *Journal of the Assembly* reveals, that august body began to be pestered with petitions.

Certain persons, proprietors of the Spanish Town theatre and their heirs [stated that in the year 1776, they] and
others entered into a subscription for building a theatre
at their own private expense, for the use and accommodation of the said town, the cost thereof amounted to £2471,
16s, 1¼ pence,[14] part of which said sum is still unpaid.
That on the expected arrival of the 20th regiment of light
dragoons (there being no barracks provided for them),
the petitioners permitted the said building to be altered
and fitted up for their reception. That by such appropria-
tion the petitioners have not only deprived the inhabitants
of the said town of their only public place of amusement,
but have in some measure injured the absent proprietors
whose permission could not be obtained.

This 20th Regiment of Light Dragoons was a Jamaica
outfit, established in 1792.

By the end of the century the surviving proprietors
or heirs of this theatre were John Stone of Kingston, the

Honorable John Rodon, the Honorable James Jones, Sarah Baldwin Harrison, widow of an original subscriber, and Hyacinth R. Daly, widower of Mary Douglass, daughter of the manager, David Douglass. Mr. Stone was allowed £25 for his losses, Mrs. Harrison £70, but the hopeful son-in-law of the late David Douglass nary a cent.[15]

These petitions reveal that the theatre was occupied as a barracks for the seven years from 1792 to 1799, which leaves the building a stretch of fifteen or sixteen years during which it was used as a theatre.

The Theatre at Montego Bay

Since all tourists land at Kingston and many of them visit Spanish Town, the locations we have been mentioning will be familiar to them. In these places we have managed to establish the existence of two theatres by the third quarter of the eighteenth century. The next theatre was also located in a town that today—during the winter months especially—is a thriving tourist center: Montego Bay.

It would probably surprise the sybaritic sun worshipers who throng the streets of this little harbor town in shorts and slacks and disport their (nominally) virginal white bare legs and backs (until they turn beet red or chocolate) on the white sands of Doctor's Cave Beach—it would probably surprise them that Montego Bay was once called Lard Bay. Under the Spaniards it was a sort of prehistoric Chicago. They called the place Mantica Bahia, which means hog's butter or lard. Hillsides and lush gullies of this part of the north shore abounded with wild hogs—"Wild Hoggs, Fat and Large, that cannot but thrive well upon so bountiful commons as falls from the trees in a very liberal Contribution." [16] These the Spaniards hunted down in droves (the annual slaughter of wild hogs by the Spaniards in Jamaica has been estimated at eighty thousand) and brought them to Mantica where they rendered the fat into lard and salted down the pork and bacon. Ships put into Mantica for their meat supplies.

After a hundred years or so of this porcine existence, Mantica saw the British arrive. They followed the old Spanish coast road from the capital to the north side and took up patents of land. In their usual way of Anglicizing place names, they changed Mantica to Montego. By 1670 Captain Sam Jenks, one of the early British soldiers, had staked out his claim to Miranda Hill and the adjacent stretch of foreshore where the bathing beach and smart hotels are today. Under the stimulation of British settlement, the town grew, trade increased, the harbor filled with ships coming and going, big houses sprang up on the hillside in the midst of cultivated plantations, a church was built, taverns came into being, and "in a brief period a once lonely savannah, deep in wild grass and bush, took on the aspect of an English landscape, with smiling fields and pleasant homesteads." [17]

The first church went the way of hurricanes and a new one was built—the present lovely old structure. A slave market began and throve under the shade of a huge cotton tree still standing on a spot halfway up what is now Union Street. In one year alone, during the last decade of the eighteenth century, close to ten thousand slaves were landed at Montego Bay. As sugar estates began to multiply in the western parishes, Montego Bay became, next to Kingston, the chief port of disembarkation of slaves. One merchant there, in 1771, sent home to England £50,000, his profit on slaves he had sold in this thriving seaport.

The British Government under Cromwell had hoped to populate Jamaica with quantities of small landholders. This effort failed. With the change of regime at home, the land in huge parcels was soon gathered into the hands of a few wealthy planters who, raising sugar cane and numerous families of all tints and tones of complexion, laid the basis of the island aristocracy. In 1739 there were only five large sugar plantations in the neighborhood of Montego Bay. Forty years saw their numbers increase and their owners prosper to such an extent (the average return on capital invested in sugar plantations was ten per cent) that they could afford to take a part in the governing and legislating of the island—men such as the Halls of Tryall, the Lawrences of Running Gut, the Irvings of Ironshore, the Barretts of Cinnamon Hill, the Sterlings of Content and the Sills of Providence Plantation. Each of these estates employed large numbers of overseers and bookkeepers, many of them young men come out from the old country. The town grew—shops and warehouses increased, and offices were staffed and a court set up. Indentured servants and workers were landed here in quantity.[18] By 1774 the town could count 400 houses, most of them brick, a good harbor in which 140 ships cleared a year and barracks for 1000 men, making it unquestionably "the emporium of the western part of the island."

It was to such a populace that the theatre in this striv-
ing provincial town might look for patronage. As the
town grew and the planters and merchants waxed richer,
the district could well support the stage and such other
amenities of luxuriant and cultural life as concerts and
assemblies.

Imagine the joy, then, when the young ladies in the
big plantation houses, lounging over "second breakfast,"
which is our luncheon, crackled out the *Cornwall Chronicle* of December 21, 1776, and read:

On Saturday, December 28, 1776, will be exhibited at
Mr. Lugg's [19] Great Room, a new Exhibition, called, A
Dish of Mr. Foot's Tea. In which the principal scenes of
the following characters will be played in their proper
dress: King Lear, with thunder and lightning . . .
Ranger . . . Fribble . . . Old Man in Lethe . . .
Barnwell . . . My Lord Duke . . . Lothario . . .
Mercutio in Romeo. The Prologue, spoken in honour of
St. Andrews' Day at Westmoreland, will be given. To
which will be added, Bucks have at ye all, or the Inside
of a Play-house. To conclude with the Tent Scene and
Death of King Richard III.

Tickets to be had at all the taverns, at 6s. 8d. each.

This was obviously a "feeler." Actors had come to
town! Who were they? The notice doesn't say. With this
olio they were testing popular sentiment. Perhaps already
some of them, in their best clothes, had ridden out to
the big estates to talk over the venture with the rich
planters. Or they had buttonholed merchants in town.
Something was in the wind.

Sure enough, on February 15, and on the 22nd, 1777,
the paper carried this announcement:

To the Inhabitants of the County of Cornwall:

A well regulated theatre has ever been held, by the wisest and most learned men of the present age, a matter of the highest utility; not only, as the most rational entertainment human nature is capable of enjoying, but, in being highly conducive to enlarge the mind, polish the manners, and, while it entertains and improves, is as it were, to use the words of that great judge of nature, Shakespeare, to "shew virtue her own image, vice her own feature, and the very age and body of the times, his form and pressure." While it is productive of such desirable purposes; and that it is so, Experience evinces: It lays an undoubted claim to attention and patronage. In Kingston and Spanish Town, it has received both with a warmth that reflects honour on its patrons, and does particular credit to the talents of the American Company of Comedians. An exertion of the talents of the major part of that company are now humbly offered to the Ladies and Gentlemen of the county of Cornwall. A theatre is fitting up on Montego Bay, neat, commodious and rendered, in every respect, as convenient as possible, for the accommodation of the Public. An entertainment will be provided; which, it is presumed, will not be unworthy attention. Constant application and unwearied diligence will be an unerring rule; their success, they wish to depend on their merit, with this respectful assurance, that they flatter themselves, while they deserve, they will meet encouragement; and no longer do they either expect or desire it.

From this we learn that the company has been playing successfully in Kingston and Spanish Town. While the notice is unsigned it brings news of old friends—"a major part of the American Company of Comedians." Will Hallam or Douglass appear or the sprightly John Henry? We find a hint as to this company in a modest advertisement in the issue of March 8:

Coats of Arms, Crests, Cyphers, etc.
Engraved on Stone Seals
By T. Wignell

This same edition of the *Chronicle* and that of the 15th carries the joyful news:

By Permission of his Excellency, By the American Company. At the New Theatre on Montego Bay. On Monday, March the 17th, 1777. Will be presented a Tragedy, called *Jane Shore*.

Hastings ....Mr. T. Wignell
Gloster ....Mr. Allen
Ratcliff ....Mr. Hughes
Catesby ....Mr. Dermot
Bellmour ....Mr. Wignell
Derby ....Mr. Morris
Dumont ....Mr. Henry
Alicia ....Miss M. Storer
Jane Shore ....Mrs. Morris

To which will be added the *Irish Widow*, Garrick,

Sir Patrick O'Neal ....Mr. Henry
Whittle ....Mr. Morris
Kecksey ....Mr. Hughes
Nephew ....Mr. T. Wignell
Bates ....Mr. Johnson
Thomas ....Mr. Dermot
The Widow Brady (with the Epilogue Song) by
Mrs. Morris

Places in the boxes, and tickets, to be had of Mr. Roberts, at the theatre. No money will be received at the door, nor any person admitted without their tickets, which are to be had of Mr. Henry at Mr. Nathan's store, and the Printing Office . . . Boxes 10s, Pit 6s 8d

Hallam and Douglass are missing from these first casts and so are Miss Wainwright and Mrs. Raynard. Lewis Hallam we know played in London for a brief period. John Henry is evidently in charge and Mr. Roberts serves as business manager. Mr. T. Wignell appears, the first time we have met him on a playbill.

This event in Montego Bay history is commented on at length in the *Chronicle* of March 22nd:

Monday evening the theatre in this town opened with the tragedy of Jane Shore and the farce of the Irish Widow, to a polite and crowded audience, who testified their approbation of the entertainment they received by loud and repeated bursts of applause.

The commodious and neat construction of the house (which for its size is equal to any on the island) at once surprised and manifested the Company's endeavours to claim the good opinion of their audiences. On Wednesday and Thursday the plays of She Stoops to Conquer and Hamlet, with the farces of the Padlock and Cross Purposes, were performed; the characters, particularly in Hamlet, were well sustained, and justly merited the applause bestowed each night.

From the general satisfaction they have given this week, under the disadvantages of a theatre newly fitted up, we may venture to say, they promise to afford the Public an agreeable entertainment in their future performances; therefore, it is but barely doing justice to say, that as they have expended a large sum in endeavouring to amuse the inhabitant of this county, they ought to be rewarded for their labour and expence.

From this point on we can make a little playbook of the Montego Bay theatre, giving the casts where available. The company is all here except Hallam and Douglass.

March 17th—*Jane Shore,* Rowe
    Irish Widow, Garrick

March 19th—*She Stoops to Conquer,* Goldsmith
    Padlock, Bickerstaff

March 20th—*Hamlet,* Shakespeare
    Cross Purposes, O'Brien

March 22nd—*A Bold Stroke for a Wife,* Mrs. Centlivre

Col. Feignwell .... Mr. Allen
Obadiah Prim .... Mr. Henry
Sir Philip Morelove .... Mr. Hughes
Periwinkle .... Mr. Morris
Freeman .... Mr. T. Wignell
Sackbut .... Mr. Johnson
Tradelove .... Mr. Wignell
Simon Pure .... Mr. Dermot
Mrs. Prim .... Mrs. Morris
Betty .... Miss Wainwright
Masked Lady .... Mrs. Allen
Ann Lovely .... Miss M. Storer

Citizen, Murphy

The Citizen .... Mr. T. Wignell
Old Philpot .... Mr. Morris
Young Wilding .... Mr. Allen
Beaufort .... Mr. Wignell
Sir Jasper .... Mr. Johnson
Dapper .... Mr. Dermot
Quilldrive .... Mr. Roberts
Corinna .... Mrs. Allen
Maria .... Miss Wainwright

On account of the shortness of the Company's stay, they being obliged to be in Spanish Town at the May Court, there will be four plays every week, viz.: Monday, Wednesday, Thursday and Saturday.

Miss Wainwright has arrived in Montego Bay. Note also that this is to be a short run. The court will open in May and thither they must go to amuse the judiciary, the litigants, the solicitors, the clerks, the hangers-on, the dusky paramours of various and sundry gentlemen of affairs and the populace of the capital. But Montego Bay will not be permitted to suffer—four plays are to be given each week. A crowded program indeed.

What, I wonder, would Montego Bay think of such a rush of amusements today? I very much doubt if, with its hotels packed to the eaves with visitors from all parts of the world, Montego Bay could support a legitimate theatre today even in the height of the February and March season. At present a cinema and a small boxing stadium in an open lot have to struggle for patronage. How times and tastes in amusements have changed!

But let us continue with our playbook.

March 29th—*Beggar's Opera,* Gay

Capt. M'Heath	Mr. Henry
Peachum	Mr. Allen
Lockit	Mr. Morris
Filch	Mr. T. Wignell
Mat o' the Mint	Mr. Dermot
Crook-Finger'd Jack	Mr. Johnson
Wat Dreary	Mr. Wignell
Ben Budge	Mr. Hughes
Lucy	Miss M. Storer
Mrs. Peachum	Mrs. Morris
Mrs. Coaxer	Mrs. Allen
Moll Brazen	Mr. Roberts
Polly	Miss Wainwright

The company must have presented an abbreviated form of *The Beggar's Opera.* Our cast totals only thirteen actors, whereas the original cast as given in London provides for fourteen male and twelve female parts.

King and Miller of Mansfield, Dodsley

The King .... Mr. Henry
The Miller .... Mr. Morris
Dick .... Mr. Hughes
Lord Lurewell .... Mr. Allen
Joe .... Mr. Dermot
Courtiers .... Messrs. Wignells
Keepers .... Messrs. Johnson
                   and Roberts
Peggy .... Mrs. Allen
Kate .... Miss M. Storer
Margery .... Miss Wainwright

April 12th—*West Indian,* Cumberland

Belcour .... Mr. T. Wignell
Stockwell .... Mr. Allen
Capt. Dudley .... Mr. Morris
Young Dudley .... Mr. Hughes
Fulmer .... Mr. Dermot
Varland .... Mr. Johnson
Stukely .... Mr. Wignell
Servant .... Mr. Roberts
Major O'Flaherty .... Mr. Henry
Louisa Dudley .... Miss M. Storer
Mrs. Fulmer .... Miss Wainwright
Lady Rusport .... Mrs. Allen
Charlotte Rusport .... Mrs. Morris,

An English Burletta, called *Midas,* O'Hara

Fabulous Deities:

Apollo .... Mr. Henry
Jupiter ....Mr. Morris   Juno ......Mrs. Allen

Mars . . . . Mr. Allen   Neptune . Mr. Wignell
Pan . . . . . Mr. Roberts   Pluto . . . . . Mr. Hughes

Mortals:

Midas . . . . Mr. Dermot
Sileno . . . . Mr. Johnson   Daphne . . . Mrs. Morris
Damaetas . . T. Wignell   Mysis Miss Wainwright
Nysa . . . . Miss M. Storer

We can sense that the season is coming to its end by one infallible sign—the benefits commence. We read today of the fabulous salaries paid cinema stars, but in this period of the theatre, especially in such a far-off spot as Jamaica, the earnings of Thespians were meager indeed. They added to their slim wages by taking benefits. On April 19th Owen Morris, respected for having amused Jamaicans ever since Moody's time, takes his benefit.

April 19th—*Gamester,* Mrs. Centlivre

Beverly . . . . Mr. Henry
Stukely . . . . Mr. Hughes
Lewson . . . . Mr. T. Wignell
Jarvis . . . . Mr. Morris
Bates . . . . Mr. Allen
Dawson . . . . Mr. Wignell
Waiter . . . . Mr. Roberts
Charlotte . . . . Miss M. Storer
Lucy . . . . Miss Wainwright
Mrs. Beverly . . . . Mrs. Morris

Catherine and Petruchio—a comedy of three acts altered from Shakespeare's *Taming of the Shrew*

Petruchio . . . . Mr. T. Wignell
Grumio . . . . Mr. Morris

Baptista ....Mr. Johnson
Hortensio ....Mr. Wignell
Music Master ....Mr. Henry
Pedro ....Mr. Dermot
Taylor ....Mr. Roberts
Peter ....Mr. Wignell
Biondello ....Mr. Hughes
Curtis ....Miss Wainwright
Bianca ....Mrs. Allen
Catherine ....Mrs. Morris

N.B. Mr. Morris begs leave to acquaint the Public that the ceremony of waiting on Ladies and Gentlemen, at the time of Benefits, has been for many years laid aside in this Company. As instead of a mark of respect, which it was originally intended, it has often, and not without reason, been looked upon in the light of a troublesome solicitation.

That last paragraph is courteous. No more badgering local worthies to buy tickets, no more importuning busy merchants and housewives. Mr. Morris and his fellow Thespians were gentlemen and ladies of the theatre.

Benefits can be traced back to the time of King James. Managers were reduced to paying their actors half in good words and half in ready money. So they compounded what was owed them and made up the profits by a benefit performance. In a few years the benefit became the chief article in every actor's agreement. The American Company had adopted the policy of not soliciting attendance at benefits as far back as 1767. In the Pennsylvania *Journal and Weekly Advertiser* of May 7th that year, Miss Cheer and the other members of the company called attention to the fact that the custom had been abolished. After all, it was undignified for an actor or actress to go from house to house presenting benefit bills and soliciting patronage.

The next benefit, on May 3rd, is for Mr. Roberts, the business manager.

May 3rd—*Fair Penitent,* Rowe

Lothario ....Mr. Allen
Sciolto ....Mr. Morris
Horatio ....Mr. Henry
Altamont ....Mr. T. Wignell
Rossano ....Mr. Johnson
Lavinia ....Miss M. Storer
Lucilla ....Mrs. Allen
Calista ....Mrs. Morris

In Act II, singing by Miss Wainwright. End of Act IV, *The Cries of London,* by Mr. Roberts.

A Picture of a Play-House or *Bucks Have at Ye All,* by Mr. Henry.

Midas, O'Hara

Same cast as on April 12th

May 10th—*Mourning Bride,* Congreve

Osmyn ....Mr. Allen
King ....Mr. Henry
Gonsatez ....Mr. Morris
Garcia ....Mr. T. Wignell
Heli ....Mr. Dermot
Perez ....Mr. Hughes
Sekim ....Mr. Wignell
Alonzo ....Mr. Johnson
Zara ....Mrs. Morris
Leonora ....Mrs. Allen
Almeria ....Miss M. Storer

An occasional prologue by Mr. T. Wignell—for this is his benefit. Preceding the farce, a prologue in the character of a drunken Sailor (written by D. Garrick, Esq.) by Mr. T. Wignell. End of the farce, "an Epilogue by Somebody, in the character of Nobody, being a Satire on Everybody, without offence to Anybody."

Contrivances or the Captain in Petticoats, Carey

Rovewell . . . . Mr. Dermot
Argus . . . . Mr. Morris
Hearty . . . . Mr. Johnson
Robin . . . . Mr. Wignell
Boy . . . . Mr. Roberts
Betty . . . . Mrs. Allen
Arethusa . . . . Miss Wainwright

And so the first Montego Bay season ends. The players are packing up. Soon they will be loading their wardrobe and scant scenery and themselves into a boat and go around to Kingston and thence to Spanish Town for that May Court run. It is unbelievable that they took the tortuous and dangerous road via Falmouth and St. Ann's Bay and Mount Diabolo, which even today challenges the skill of a good automobile driver. With them gone, Montego Bay lolls back in its shady corners and wide verandahs. The air is humid. Yet the town will indulge itself to one more amusement. We delight in quoting the announcement of it because it displays the honor maintained by all gentlemen troupers. *The Chronicle* for May 10th states:

The Subscribers to E. Allen's Concert will please to take notice that the performance is deferred 'till Thursday the 15th Instant, that it may not prejudice the benefits of the Players.
Mr. Kelly having refused to comply with his agreement in letting his room, the Concert and Ball will be at the

house of John Lugg, who has fitted up a room for that purpose.

Well, the town couldn't be expected to support two rival entertainments on the same evening. It was gracious of Mr. Allen; it was a friendly act of Mr. Lugg to re-arrange his tavern; as for Mr. Kelly—may ten black cats have crossed his trail!

We have spent considerable time at Montego Bay, nor do I think the time ill-spent. Historians of the American stage have completely overlooked this theatrical episode. Historians of St. James's Parish, of which Montego Bay is the court center and largest town, are also silent on it. Mr. James Roby, who first wrote the history of the parish and was collector of customs at the Bay and an antiquarian of the first flight, halted his history at 1740. The others may be forgiven because in 1795 fire practically destroyed the town, and subsequent other excitements, such as bloody slave revolts and lurid romances, crowd the historian's canvas. Digging into the files of the *Cornwall Chronicle* preserved in the Public Library at Bristol, England, brought up this treasure trove of the 1777 season at Montego Bay and subsequent seasons and amusements there. In the heyday of the sugar and slave trade, Bristol was a thriving port for Jamaica.

The Spanish Town Court Season

Your servant, the researcher, is not a dog, my masters, but he must have the nose of a dog and follow the slightest scent however far afield it may lead him. Yet it is somewhat baffling to him, once the scent is hot, not to find it leading to his quarry.

Here, for example, we have the scent of a season at
Spanish Town in May, 1777, during the court term. We
know the building in which the court sat—the one on
the east side of the Square. It still stands. We know that
the judges, in their robes and wigs, were received then,
as they are today, by a bodyguard lined up in front of
the building. We know, from accounts of the time, that
the town was looking forward to its amusements, since
the Assembly had ceased sitting at Christmas and even
Spanish Towners could stand only a few months of som-
nolence. But—but where are the papers that will tell us
of this May run? Gone into the ultimate limbo of trash.
Hurricanes, earthquakes, fires, floods, devouring bookworms, and ants have wiped out this page in Spanish
Town theatrical history.

All we know—from that petition of the owners of the
Spanish Town theatre—is that a theatre building did exist in May, 1777, and that it was available for plays from
1776 to 1792. It may have been the responsibility of this
theatre together with that at Kingston which prevented
Lewis Hallam and David Douglass from coming to Montego Bay. Besides, Douglass was going into the printing
business—a much less precarious means of making a livelihood than acting—with William Aikman and planning
the establishment of a good newspaper—the *Jamaica
Mercury*.

Then, too, things were popping both in and around the
Island, affairs of the sort not calculated to help the stage.
Martial law, for instance, was declared in the fall of
1777. Since the theatre's existence is closely interwoven
with contemporary events, we shall start a new chapter
by considering them.

CHAPTER IV

1779–1780

The Backdrop of History—A Rush of Plays—Mr. Hughes
Departs and So Does a Valuable Wardrobe—Military
Thespians

THE decade from 1774 to 1784, during which the American Company flourished on the island, was one of the
most vivid in Jamaica's long and checkered history.

By the opening of that period the populace stood in
round numbers at 210,000; of which 13,000 were whites,
4000 free colored, and 193,000 slaves. Sir Basil Keith was
governor. During his administration bills passed by the
Legislative Assembly to restrict the slave trade were dis-
allowed by the Crown. There was too much money in this
slave business and in the profits from slave labor to permit
any interference of mawkish sentiment. In June, 1777,
Governor Keith died and Colonel Darling took over his
post. Within six months martial law was declared. This
grim circumstance was brought around both by troubles
without and troubles within.

America had challenged the Crown with its Declaration
of Independence and the island colonies began to tremble.
The year before, in 1775, Commodore Hopkins of the
American Navy had captured Nassau and carried off the
Governor. The French lined up with the Americans and
the repercussions of that alliance were soon felt in the
Caribbean. D'Estaing, with a fleet of twenty-six ships of

the line, boasted that within a year he would capture every British island in the West Indies. He made good his boast by snatching St. Vincent, Grenada, and Dominica. But the English put an end to D'Estaing's success and the French fleet sailed for the coast of Georgia. Jamaicans breathed easier again.

Nelson came to Jamaica in 1779 and was made governor of the forts, arsenals, and shipyard at Port Royal: the year before he had taken part in Governor Dalling's expedition against San Juan de Nicaragua and, stricken by malaria, barely escaped with his life. England sent over a powerful fleet under Rodney who in April engaged the French. His bad luck was further increased by a hurricane that cost him thirteen ships and all aboard. Soon afterward the Spaniards joined the French, and Rodney, being outnumbered, made a strategic retreat. Sickness appeared on his side: so many of the enemy's sailors came down with fever that they were obliged to return to Martinique. There the French and Spanish commanders quarreled, so the French fleet sailed home, convoying a number of sugar-laden boats. Again Jamaicans had cause for rejoicing.

As if there weren't trouble enough, fire destroyed Savanna-la-Mar, an important town on the southwest shore of the island. Against its enemies Jamaica rallied itself for defense, raising by lottery £23,750—a big sum in those days—for the subsistence of its troops. Corps of slaves and free mulattos were formed.

The year 1781 saw a new governor on the island— Major General Archibald Campbell. The previous December England had declared war against Holland. Her ring of enemies was now complete. Rodney opened the year with victories—in February he took St. Eustatius and £3,000,000 worth of war materials; in March he captured Essequibo and Demerara. Prizes began to fill Port Royal harbor. Meantime the French were taking Tobago, Turk's Island, and St. Kitts. Islands large and islands small shuffled their owners back and forth with dizzy speed. By the end of 1781 Britain sat behind a largely depleted pile of chips: the only islands left to her in the West Indies were Antigua, Barbados, and Jamaica.

Besides all this, in October, came a great hurricane that devastated Westmoreland, with damages estimated at £700,000. England, though hard pressed, dug down into her treasury for a grant of £40,000 relief.

But England's luck was eventually bound to turn. In April, 1782, off Dominica, Rodney signally defeated the French fleet under De Grasse, thereby saving the British West Indian islands to the English Crown. Jamaica went delirious. For many a year afterward, toasts were drunk to Rodney on April 12th. Today the Rodney Memorial at Spanish Town—the most ambitious structure of its kind in the West Indies—reminds Jamaicans of the man who kept the British flag flying over their island.

With the peace of Versailles in 1783, bringing the American Revolution to a close, England recovered from France, Grenada, St. Vincent, Dominica, St. Kitts, Nevis, and Montserrat and ceded St. Lucia and Tobago. Demerara and Essequibo were handed back to the Dutch.

July of 1784 found the island smitten with a destructive hurricane. The next year in August came an equally destructive storm and Kingston was visited with fire. The population of the island had now reached 30,000 whites. 10,000 free colored, and 250,000 slaves.

That roughly is the backdrop of activities without and within the island against which the American Company of Comedians in Jamaica played during its fullest years there. It also accounts for some of the blank spots we encounter in its activities.

The Stage in Doldrums

In his *History of the American Stage Before the Revolution,* Seilhamer states "that part of the company gave performances at intervals between 1775 and 1778 is certain, but I have been able to ascertain nothing in regard to them." This blank spot is now partially filled in by that opening in Kingston on July 1, 1775, and the first Montego Bay season. Seilhamer continues:

"It is clear, however, from a letter dated at Kingston, January 9th, 1779, and printed in the *Pennsylvania Packet* in April, that there were no performances during the latter part of 1778, for it is said that the theatre had been "for some time shut up." It was announced, however, that it was to be speedily opened under the management of Mr. Hallam "for whose theatrical qualifications, it was said, the public may expect their usual agreeable entertainment."

Unfortunately, the date of the opening has not been preserved, the first of this series of performances on record being that of May 1, 1779. Seilhamer further states that the theatre seems to have remained closed from November 27, 1779, to February, 1780.[1]

We have a contemporary record of these days in the diary of the Reverend William Jones, who came to the island on April 10, 1778, as tutor to the children of

Thomas Harrison, Attorney General of Jamaica, and left for England January 24, 1780.[2] In addition to implying that Jamaica was a suburb of Hell, Mr. Jones sets down a vivid picture of the excursions and alarms of those days. He tells of the regiment made up of negroes and mulattos and how their white officers were perpetually sounding alarms. Martial law brought a whole train of troubles: "What distress has it not occasioned! How many through this have been hurried to their graves!" Many of the planters were verging on bankruptcy—they could not ship their crops, so closely did the enemy watch the ships leaving Kingston harbor. On Wednesday, August 25th, "an alarm was spread in Kingston that many ships were seen off shore; the militia consequently were kept all night under arms and the troopers galloping their horses to and from . . . I was rouzed from sleep about 3 o'clock, by a loud general beat, and soon after got up. A great muster was made." Finally the martial law proclaimed in August was lifted and the corps of officers in which Jones was a private was disbanded.

What chance did the theatre have in such circumstances? Little wonder we hear nothing from it. And even after it has started again, it is only a patchy playbook that we can make of its performances as recorded in the *Mercury* for the last six months of 1779. Nevertheless, by 1780 the theatre is going full blast and that year and the year 1781 afford us views of a busy program. The populace seem to have gotten a second wind and acquired a new valor. Kingston was full of soldiers and sailors coming and going. Unlike the Continental Congress of seven years before, the Jamaican Assembly saw no need for clamping down on plays. It was safer for public morale to keep the theatre playing and the boxes, pit, and gallery packed.

The Kingston Playbook

So the Kingston playbook will start with:

1779—May 1st—*Douglas*, Home
     Citizen, Murphy

Between the play and the farce came a comic dance, called *The Drunken Peasant*, performed by Mr. Godwin, who is now a part of the company; he has been in the States, playing with a troupe that called itself the "New American Company of Comedians." In the play, Norval Douglas was played by Lewis Hallam and Natilda (Lady Randolph) by an unnamed lady, "being her first appearance." In those days the stage had a distinct aversion against naming the ladies and gentlemen who performed "for their own amusement." It was customary not to publish an amateur's name on the bills until such a person had decided to become a professional and follow the stage as a career. In these first four performances of 1779 no casts are available.

May 15th—*Percy*, Hannah Moore
    High Life Below Stairs, Townley

Mr. Godwin lightens the intermission with a hornpipe and in Act II of the farce comes a mock minuet by Sir Harry and Miss Kitty.

June 1st —*Choleric Man*, Cumberland
    Catherine and Petruchio, Shakespeare

June 22nd—*Choleric Man*, Cumberland
         High Life Below Stairs, Townley

With the mock minuet repeated.

June 26th—*Percy*, Moore

Earl Douglass ....Mr. Hallam
Earl Raby ....Mr. Goodman
Sir Hubert ....Mr. Morris
Edric ....Mr. Wignell
Earl Parcy ....Mr. T. Wignell
Harcourt ....Mr. Woolls
Bertha ....Miss Wainwright
Elvina ....Mrs. Morris

Lying Valet, Garrick

Sharp ....Mr. Hallam
Gayless ....Mr. T. Wignell
Justice Guttle ....Mr. Goodman
Dick ....Mr. Woolls
Trippet ....Mr. Wignell
Melissa ....Mrs. Hamilton
Mrs. Gadabout ....Mrs. Morris
Kitty Pry ....Miss Wainwright

In the bills *The Lying Valet* is attributed to "the late
Mr. Garrick," that eminent playright having died on
January 20th of this year. The announcement also reads:
"To prevent any future Complaints about Late Hours,
the Curtain will be drawn up precisely at 7 o'clock." After
all, some of the audience had to get back to barracks
within a reasonable hour, and the planters had to drive inland to their cattle pens along the savannah.

Moreover, it was the custom to go to bed early. Now
and then young blades and some of the fancy girls might

roister in a tavern until dawn, but the general populace both in Kingston and Spanish Town, and even more so in the deep country, kept early hours for both rising and retiring, as is sensible in the tropics. William Long, writing of Kingston life in 1774, says that "at eleven o'clock at night it is very rare to see a light in any house, except the taverns, and even these are now very seldom infested with riots and drunken quarrels, which formerly were so common." [3]

July 7, 10, 24—Mr. Saunders.

We should probably apologize for interrupting a serious playbook of the legitimate stage by letting this mountebank appear, but he does keep popping up and his announcements prove that his show is getting "Bigger and Better." What's more, we are attempting not alone a tale of the Jamaica stage, but making a record of all sorts of high times. So in goes Mr. Saunders.

Mr. Saunders does not venture into the theatre, for reasons which we shall see later, choosing to exhibit his "Dexterity and Grand Deception" at the "house where Mrs. Riz lately resided in Orange Street." Kingston, even in those days of wars and rumors of wars, was still a small enough town for its inhabitants to have remembered where Mrs. Riz recently lived. His tickets are sold at Mr. Lyon's in King Street and at the New Printing Office on Harbour Street where Douglass or Aikman may have had to wipe the ink off their hands before passing out tickets or making change.

If you think we are giving too much space to Hyman Saunders, regard the fact that he is throwing in a hornpipe "by a Gentleman," and offers to teach his tricks to

any of the curious at a reasonable rate. Besides, consider
the generous bill he gives:

Mr. Saunders will, among sundry of his astonishing performances, take any gentleman's hat in the room and fry
German pan-cakes in it.

He will exhibit some very astonishing performances
with walnuts. Will also pull off his shirt without taking off
his coat or waistcoat, and the shirt may be examined by
any gentleman in the company.

He will take any lady or gentleman's ring and introduce
it on the blade of a sword, it being held by two indifferent
persons at both ends. The ring shall receive no damage by
its being put on or taken off.

Mr. Saunders will let any piece of money fly from one
hand into the other, his arms being extended at full length.

August 21. On this date the supplement to the *Mercury*
relates a lamentable affair that gives us an insight both into
Kingston doings and the state of the theatre:

Thursday morning, one of the Maroons quartered at
the theatre shot himself whilst the others were on Parade.
. . . Their commander, Old Grey, on being Interrogated
by the superintendent-general about the matter, told him
that the deceased was a worthless scoundrel who, he supposed, was afraid to do his duty in the service of his king
and country . . . that he should order his body to be
kicked into some ditch, and would have cut it into pieces for
the dogs, had he not left a deserving brother and other
trusty friends.

So that is the sort of fellows Maroons were! Descended
from the slaves held by the Spaniards and other runaway
negroes, the Maroons fled into the fastnesses of the
interior and for a century and a half were a constant irri-
tation to the government and a danger to the island

planters. Not until 1795 were they finally subdued. Now and then, by heavy bribes, the government managed to induce them to become mercenaries. They were so used as late as the "rebellion" at Morant Bay in 1865.

Here was Mr. Hallam's theatre on the Parade, all cluttered up with filthy Maroons—probably the only place the government could find to house them during this period of martial law—and consequently the theatre, as the *Pennsylvania Packet* informs us, was shut up. Evidently the Maroons made pretty havoc of the place—"pulled to pieces and destroyed many parts of the said house; also the machinery and necessary furniture belonging thereto." So states Lewis Hallam in his petition to the Assembly in December.[4] He claimed £186 10s damages, but the Assembly allowed only £124 18s 9d, which is fairly generous for an Assembly, although for the life of me I can't see why they tacked on that nine pence.

Nevertheless, by September, Hallam seems to have made the necessary repairs "and is now fitting up in a genteel stile"[5] so that our playbook can go on.

September 29th—*School for Fathers,* Bickerstaff

October 2nd   —*She Stoops to Conquer,* Goldsmith
          Thomas and Sally, Bickerstaff

Mr. Godwin dances his *Drunken Peasant* and adds a hornpipe.

October 9th   —*Love in a Village,* Bickerstaff

October 22nd   —*Merry Wives of Windsor,* Shakespeare

Falstaff .... Mr. Goodman
Slender .... Mr. Hughes
Parson Evans .... Mr. Morris

Doctor Caius	Mr. T. Wignell
Host of the Garter	Mr. Godwin
Shallow	Mr. Morales
Page	Mr. Wignell
Pistol	Mr. Woolls
Robin	Master Woolls
Ford	Mr. Hallam
Mrs. Page	Miss Wainwright
Ann Page	Mrs. Raynard
Mrs. Quickly	Mrs. Hamilton
Mrs. Ford	Mrs. Raynard

Lying Valet, Garrick

Again Mr. Godwin favors the audience with his *Drunken Peasant* dance at the end of Act I of the *Lying Valet* and also dances between the play and the farce. Master Woolls makes his debut.

October 30th—*Devil upon Two Stick*, Foote

Asmodeus	Mr. Hallam
Dr. Squib	Mr. Hallam
Sir Thomas Maxwell	Mr. Goodman
Jalap	Mr. Hughes
Apoxem	Mr. Morris
McPherson	Mr. Godwin
Invoice	Mr. Wignell
Fingersee	Mr. Woolls
Diachylon	Mr. Morales
Dr. Last	Mr. T. Wignell
Margaret	Miss Wainwright
Harriet	Mrs. Raynard

Devil to Pay, Coffey

The intermission was filled by an interlude of dancing called *The Handsome Lady*. Miss Storer for the first time plays Nell in *The Devil to Pay*.

November 13th—*Maid of the Mill*, Bickerstaff

Apprentice, Murphy

November 27th—*Duenna*, Sheridan

Carlos .... A Gentleman
Ferdinand .... Mr. Hallam
Don Jerome .... Mr. Goodman
Antonio .... Mr. Woolls
Lopez .... Mr. Morris
Fr. Paul .... Mr. Hughes
Fr. Dominick .... Mr. Godwin
Meagre Porter .... Mr. Wignell
Diego .... Mr. Morales
Isaac Mendoza .... Mr. T. Wignell
Louisa .... Miss Storer
Margaret .... Mrs. Hamilton
Clara .... Mrs. Raynard

Carlos, we are informed, is "by a Gentleman for the Night Only, for his Amusement." At the end of the opera came dancing by the hard-worked Mr. Godwin.

Evidently the *Duenna* caught on and the girls around town were humming its tunes. William Aikman made a venture; in the *Mercury* for November 27th he announces:

This Day, at three o'clock, will be published and sold at the New Printing Office in Harbour-Street and at the shop of W. Aikman in King-Street
(Price 3s. 9d.)
The
New Comic Opera
of the
Duenna
As it is to be acted this Evening at the Theatre.

The very extraordinary merit of this Opera (which was acted 74 nights successively the first season, and repeated every winter since oftener than any piece that ever appeared on the stage) induced the proprietors to decline printing it, in order to increase the avidity of the Public for its frequent representation; and the copy now offered for sale is the only edition in print, except a very incorrect one that crept into the world in Dublin, under the title of "The Governess," mangled, hackt and alter'd, in order to avoid the penalty of the acts of parliament for securing literary property.

This book was evidently delayed, for it finally appeared December 4th.

Mysterious Report

At this point a mystery crops up. John Henry, so active at Montego Bay last year, is not appearing on these Kingston bills. Miss Storer, on the other hand, is constantly in these autumn-of-1779 casts. While I was puzzled over a garbled bit of news from England reprinted in the *Mercury* of January 22–29, 1780, Kingstonians may not have been. Had the town not known the characters, there would have been no point in printing it:

Camp at Warley-Common, Oct. 16th.
Oct. 19th. Saturday night last the play of Othello was performed at Drury-Lane Theatre for the purpose of bringing forward a young gentleman in the character of the Moor: we heard that his name is Henry, brother to the young lady who made her appearance on the same evening at Covent-Garden, and son to an unfortunate pair of the Thespian tribe, who were drowned in their passage to the Indies.

Several passages in the part of Othello proved that he was more capable of giving dignity and ease to the temperate, than to the violent style of declamation. He has a good deal of that weakness which affects most spouters and country-players, tearing passion to fritters: There is, however, no part which is more difficult, nor more ineligible for a first appearance, than Othello; and he must indeed possess very capital ability who comes off with success. We shall therefore wish to see Mr. Henry again, before we ultimately decide on his merits.

The comic opera of the Maid of the Mill was, on Saturday night last, represented at Covent-Garden Theatre, in order to introduce a young lady in the character of Patty, being her first appearance on any stage. . . .

This young lady's name is said to be Storer, the daughter of an actress some twenty years ago equally celebrated for her vocal abilities, as for the propriety of her private character, but who had the misfortune, along with her husband, and others of her family, to be burnt on shipboard, going from one of the West India Islands to another.

In point of person she is rather below the middle size, neatly made, but not handsome. She seems to possess a good ear, some taste, and a knowledge of music; but her voice is thin, and without much compass, which seems to arise from the delicacy of her constitution. She spoke the part of Patty with propriety, but the thinness of her voice was equally conspicuous in speaking as in singing.

The Actors Seek Other Work

Of one thing we are sure at this point—the Company found no easy path to its pot of gold. Some of the players were forced to seek other employment. In the *Mercury* of September 4, 1779, Isaac Morales of the company began advertising:

The Spanish Language
To be Taught
On very reasonable Terms
by
Isaac Morales
In Princess-Street

Who will attend any Gentleman, either at his house, or at his own, two hours every day; and will engage, in three months (if they are any way intelligent) that they shall make great progress.

Translations from Spanish or French will be received and executed with greatest dispatch.

Isaac Morales evidently made enough by his teaching and translating to find a permanent post in the government, for the Assembly in December, 1799, paid him the sum of £100 "in full" "for his trouble as interpreter of the Spanish and French languages in the Kingston courts, for several years past." [6] He had worked regularly at this post since 1793.

Another member of the company to find outside work was George Hughes. The *Mercury* for October 23–30, 1779, carries his advertisement of the sale by auction of a valuable collection of books—a three-day sale of a library in Jamaica, accompanied by a printed catalogue—which will be conducted "by George Hughes, Auctioneer, Being his First Appearance in that Character." In later issues he offers his services in the accepted theatrical parlance:

George Hughes

Having been flattered by his friends that he possesses, in some degree, those requisites that are necessary to point out the value, explain the uses, and illustrate the merits of many articles that are commonly put up at Public Sale, respectfully offers his Services to the town as an

Auctioneer

Those Gentlemen who have Books, Plate, Furniture, or goods of any kind to dispose of, will do him a singular favour, by giving him an opportunity of serving them.

Mr. Godwin of the nimble legs is likewise forced to fatten his anaemic purse. In the *Gazette* of November 27th, he proposes opening a dancing school, and from the edition of December 18th we gather that the school is ready.

A Dancing-School

In the Long Room at the House of Mr. Harris, Limner, adjoining Mrs. Hatton's in the Savannah:

Mr. Godwin

Proposes to improve and perfect young Ladies and Gentlemen in Dancing—The Minuet and proper steps to be used in Country Dances, will be taught in a complete manner—Juvenile Gentlemen may attain the Italian Hornpipe, which will conduce to perfection in Country Dances, etc.

Mr. Godwin will open school on Monday the 3rd of January, and continue to teach on Mondays and Fridays, from 9 to 12 and from 3 to 6 o'clock— In the evenings of the same days the Italian Hornpipe will be taught. The terms are a Mill'd Pistole to be paid at entrance and a Guinea per month. For the Hornpipe a Mill'd Pistole for entrance and two Guineas when completed.

Particular instructions will be given to the young Ladies and Gentlemen whom Mr. Godwin may have the honour to attend in regard to their behaviour to parents and strangers at home and abroad. Juvenile Gentlemen not

choosing to be taught the Minuet and Country Dance steps
on school days, will be waited on in private any hours convenient to them.

Hallam's Subscription Scheme

Though prospects were looking very dark for members
of the company, Lewis Hallam never lost faith in the
stage. In the *Mercury* of January 24, 1780, he proposes
the following subscription scheme:

Kingston, 24th January, 1780

Several Gentlemen having expressed their wishes that a
plan could be fallen upon for the future Support of the
Theatre, calculated to render the Expence of frequenting
Plays easier to the Public, and at the same time, the Sum
received of a sufficient Value to the Manager and Actors,
to enable them to carry on their Profession: the following
Scheme is humbly submitted to the Friends and Patrons of
the Liberal Arts, for their consideration.

A Subscription is proposed for Three Months, to commence some time in February and end in May, in which
time twenty-four Plays may be acted, at the rate of two in
a week.

It is supposed that £74 per a night would be a Sum equal
to the incidental Expence, and a moderate Support to the
Performers.

    24 Plays at £75 each £1,800
    200 Subscribers, at £8 each (which is
        only rating a Ticket for admission
        for each Play at 6s 8d will produce
        .... £1,600

But there will be a Deficiency of £200

This Deficiency, it is apprehended, may be supplied from
the Pit Audience, and the Non-Subscribers to the Boxes,

who are to pay the customary prices.

When a competent number of Subscribers are obtained, to give a prospect of the Plan's succeeding, the Tickets will be delivered, upon the Payment of the Money.

The Manager, on his part, promises and obliges himself, to do everything in his power that can conduce to the Entertainment of the Public: to get up as many New Plays as possible; to revive the most approved old ones; in short, he will make it his Study, as it is undoubtedly his Interest, to superintend and conduct the Amusements of the Public in such a manner, as to recommend his Labours to the future Countenance of his Patrons.

The Season of 1780

Evidently Hallam found patronage, for the season of 1780 started in with a rush. Between February and December, we shall be able to add twenty-one performances to our book of amusements.

1780—February 16th—*Lyar*, Foote

Young Wilding ....Mr. Hallam
Old Wilding ....Mr. Goodman
Sir James Elliot ....Mr. Woolls
Papillion ....Mr. T. Wignell
Miss Godfrey ....Miss Wainwright
Lucy ....Miss Storer
Miss Grantham................Mrs. Raynard

Theatrical Candidates

Mercury ....Mr. Hallam
Harlequin ....Mr. T. Wignell
Punch ....Mr. Dermot
Pierrot ....Mr. Morris
Comic Muse ....Miss Wainwright
Tragic Muse ....Mrs. Raynard

The farce on this occasion was a homemade production revealing the troubles and merry experiences of the company on the opening and alteration of the theatre.

February 23rd—*Lyar*, Foote
             Theatrical Candidates
             Old Maid, Murphy

February 26th—*Love in a Village*, Bickerstaff
             King and Miller of Mansfield, Dodsley

March 4th   —*Shipwreck*, Cumberland
             Miss Storer played Violetta

             Harlequin Collector

March 11th   —*Duenna*, Sheridan
             Reprisal, Smollett

March 18th   —*Countess of Salisbury*, Hartson

Alwin . . . . Mr. Hallam
Gray . . . . Mr. Goodman
Moreton . . . . Mr. Morris
Lerocher . . . . Mr. Woolls
Lord Randolph . . . . Mr. Dermot
Lord William . . . . Master Woolls
Raymond . . . . Mr. Wignell
Eleanor . . . . Miss Storer
Ella . . . . Mrs. Morris

             Genii, Woodward

April 1st   —*Shipwreck*, Cumberland
             Genii, Woodward

The advertisement of this performance states that "the very pleasing Pantomime of *The Genii*, which has already been performed three nights successively, will be presented for the fourth time, by particular desire, after that excellent comedy of Mr. Cumberland's, *The Broth-*

ers, or *The Shipwreck;* for the entertainment of the
Volunteers that are engaged in the expedition against the
Spanish Main." This was the expedition against Nicaragua. The notice also reveals two more performances of
The Genii than we find recorded in the fragmentary newspapers.

April 8th—*Roman Father*, Whitehead

Horatius ....Mr. Hallam
Valerius ....Mr. T. Wignell
Tullus Hostilius ....Mr. Morris
Soldier ....Mr. Dermot
1st Citizen ....Mr. Woolls
2nd Citizen ....Mr. Godwin
Volscinius ....Mr. Morales
Publius Horatius ....Mr. Goodman
Valeria ....Miss Storer
Horatia ....Mrs. Morris

Man and Wife, Colman

Marcourt ....Mr. Hallam
Kitchen ....Mr. Goodman
Col. Frankly ....Mr. Woolls
Landlord ....Mr. Godwin
Luke ....Mr. T. Wignell
Snarl ....Mr. Dermot
Fleece ....Mr. Morales
Cross ....Mr. Morris
Mrs. Cross ....Mrs. Hamilton
Charlotte ....Miss Storer
Lettice ....Mrs. Morris
Landlady ....Miss Wainwright
Sally ....Mrs. Raynard

In addition to playing Sally, Mrs. Raynard sang
"Sweet Willy-O" and the performance concluded "with a

Grand Pagent, exhibiting the Characters of Shakespeare, with songs and choruses as performed at the Theatres-Royal."

April 18th—*The Tempest,* Shakespeare
　　　　Who's the Dupe? Mrs. Cowley

May 1st. Concert for the benefit of Mr. Patch. I suspect that Mr. Patch was the musical director of the Comedians and he was in bad financial straits. His benefit was "a concert of Vocal and Instrumental Music at Ranelagh House, followed by a Ball for the Ladies." On August 25th, David Duncomb, his assignee, announces: "The creditors of Samuel Patch prior to 1st May, 1778, are requested to send an Account of their several Demands against him, properly attested, to the Subscriber, that he may ascertain the Proportion coming to each, from the sale of the said Mr. Patch's Effects and divide the same accordingly."

May 6th—*English Merchant,* Colman, Jr.

Lord Fallbridge	Mr. Hallam
Freeport	Mr. Morris
Spatter	Mr. Wignell
Owen	Mr. Woolls
La France	Mr. Godwin
Messenger	Mr. Dermot
Sir W. Douglas	Mr. Goodman
Lady Alton	Mrs. Morris
Molly	Miss Wainwright
Mrs. Goodman	Mrs. Hamilton
Amelia	Mrs. Raynard

Who's the Dupe?—Mrs. Cowley

Granger	Mr. Hallam
Doiley	Mr. Morris

Sandford ....Mr. Wignell
Gradus ....Mr. Godwin
Charlotte ....Miss Wainwright
1st Nosegay Girl ....Mrs. Hamilton
2nd Nosegay Girl ....Miss Storer
Miss Doiley ....Mrs. Raynard

May 13th—*Hamlet,* Shakespeare

Hamlet ....Mr. Hallam
Ghost ....Mr. Goodman
King ....Mr. Wignell
Polonius ....Mr. Morris
Horatio ....Mr. Godwin
Guildenstern ....Mr. Dermot
Rosencrantz ....Mr. Woolls
Francisco ....Mr. Bacon
Laertes ....Mr. Goodman
Queen ....Mrs. Morris
Player Queen ....Miss Wainwright
Ophelia ....Mrs. Raynard

Genii, Woodward

Mr. Bacon's is a new name to us; otherwise the company consists of old friends.

This is the first time Hamlet is played in Jamaica. It is Garrick's version. *The Genii* is followed by "a new scene, representing the storming of Fort Omoa, with a view of the Fort, etc., painted from a drawing taken on the spot." Fort Omoa was in Nicaragua where the expedition had been fighting, so that this diversion might be dubbed Kingston's first newsreel.

June 3rd—*Rivals,* Sheridan

Sir Anthony Absolute ....Mr. Goodman
Captain Absolute ....Mr. Hallam

Acres	Mr. Morris
Sir Lucius O'Trigger	Mr. Godwin
Fag	Mr. Woolls
Coachman	Mr. Dermot
Servant	Mr. Bacon
Lydia	Mrs. Morris
Mrs. Malaprop	Miss Wainwright
Lucy	Miss Storer
Julia	Mrs. Raynard

Genii, Woodward

By now *The Genii* must have been worn threadbare, for at this performance Hallam assures the public that it will have "New Scenery, Machinery, Choruses and Dances."

July 1st—*Law of Lombardy,* Jephson

Paladore	Mr. Hallam
King	Mr. Goodman
Rinaldo	Mr. Woolls
Liscio	Mr. Morris
Ascanio	Mr. Dermot
Forrester	" "
Alberto	A Gentleman
Officer	Mr. Bacon
Bireno	Mr. Wignell
Alinda	Mrs. Raynard
Laura	Miss Storer
Maria	Miss Wainwright
Sophia	Mrs. Morris

Ghost, Mrs. Centlivre

Roger	Mr. Hallam
Capt. Constant	Mr. Wignell
Trusty	Mr. Goodman
Sir Jeffery Constant	Mr. Dermot
Clinch	Mr. Morris

Belinda .... Miss Storer
Dorothy .... Miss Wainwright

This is the first performance of *The Ghost* in Jamaica. Originally advertised for June 21st, it had to be postponed to the 28th and then to July 1st with Hallam's apology:

The Indisposition of Performers, and the Badness of the Weather, having been for Some Time past the Occasion of postponing plays very frequently, Mr. Hallam respectfully hopes The Public will not censure the Company for their unavoidable Accidents, which no Means in their Power could have provided against, and which, though certainly Disappointments to the Friends of the Theatre, have been real misfortunes to the Performers.

I suspect that the spring rains had continued on into late June and some of the company had been down with fever.

July 8th —*Busybody*, Mrs. Centlivre

Marplot .... Mr. Hallam
Sir Geo. Airy .... Mr. Wignell
Charles .... Mr. Goodman
Sir Francis Gripe .... Mr. Morris
Sir Jealous Traffick .... Mr. Dermot
Whisper .... Mr. Woolls
Isabinda .... Miss Storer
Patch .... Miss Wainwright
Miranda .... Mrs. Morris

High Life Below Stairs, Townley

July 15th—*Stratagem*, Farquhar

Archer .... Mr. Hallam
Aimwell .... Mr. Wignell
Foigard .... Mr. Goodman
Boniface .... Mr. Dermot

Bagshot .... Mr. Bacon
Gibbett .... Mr. Woolls
Sullen .... Mr. Worn
Scrub .... Mr. Morris
Dorinda .... Mrs. Raynard
Cherry .... Miss Wainwright
Gipsey .... Miss Storer
Mrs. Sullen .... Mrs. Morris

Ghost, Mrs. Centlivre

In this cast of *The Stratagem* we meet Mr. Worn's name for the first and last time.

This is the first of several Masonic benefit performances in Jamaica. It is advertised as "By particular Desire of the Ancient and Honorable Society of Free and Accepted Masons, who propose to attend in their proper cloathing." Mr. Hallam recited a prologue in the character of a Master Mason and at the end of the play Mr. Woolls sang a Mason's song.[7]

July 22nd   —*Orphan,* Otway

Chamont .... Mr. Hallam
Castalio .... Mr. Wignell
Acasto .... Mr. Morris
Ernesto .... Mr. Woolls
Chaplain .... Mr. Dermot
Page .... Master Woolls
Polydore .... Mr. Goodman
Serina .... Miss Storer
Florella .... Miss Wainwright
Monimia .... Mrs. Morris

Devil Upon Two Sticks, Foote

August 5th   —*Orphan,* Otway
              Devil Upon Two Sticks, Foote

August 15th—*Countess of Salisbury,* Harrison
        Mock Doctor, Fielding

September 2—*Merchant of Venice,* Shakespeare

Shylock ....Mr. Hallam
Antonio ....Mr. Goodman
Gratiano ....Mr. Morris
Lorenzo ....Mr. Woolls
Launcelot ....Mr. Dermot
Solanio ....Mr. Madden
Officer ....Mr. Bacon
Bassanio ....Mr. Wignell
Jessica ....Mrs. Raynard
Nerissa ....Miss Storer
Portia ....Mrs. Morris

The Padlock, Bickerstaff

September 9—*Law of Lombardy,* Jephson

Virgin Unmasked, Fielding

At this point we lay aside our book of Jamaica amusements to record a sad event.

Kingston, September 23rd, 1780: On Thursday night last, after a painful illness of twenty-one days, departed this life Mr. L. D. Hallam, Jr. in the 19th year of his age. The loss of this amiable and worthy young man is deeply regretted by every person that was connected with him in friendship or business: in friendship he was steady, disinterested and honorable; in his medical capacity, ingenious, faithful and industrious. With most heart-felt concern, one who well knew him, feels the influence of his virtues, in deploring that they exist no more.

Well spoken, Lewis Hallam! . . . So this son did not follow his father's footsteps, preferring to become a physician. He was evidently a child from the early marriage of Lewis Hallam the Younger and the wife from whom he separated and lived apart for so many years. However, another son, Mirvan, did become an actor and, after the Revolution, appeared quite regularly on the American stage.

Army Players

October 7th—*Venice Preserved,* Otway
Lethe, Garrick

Lethe, or Aesop in the Shades, on this occasion, was performed by "Gentlemen of the Army" for the benefit of the American Company of Comedians. Also we note that the company was playing to full houses: the playbill assures the public that "no more Tickets will be issued than the House can conveniently contain, therefore, to prevent Disappointments, no Money on any Account will be received at the Door." To this was added the information, indicating prosperity, that "part of the Pit to be laid into Boxes." The price of box seats was 13s, 4d and for the Pit, 10s.

This first appearance of military Thespians brought forth a review in the *Gazette:*

The principal characters in both pieces were supported with a degree of spirit and propriety that would have reflected honour on approved veteran actors; but as any eulogium we could make on a performance so much beyond our most sanguine conceptions, would fall infinitely short of its real merit, we shall content ourselves with observing that, high as the expectations of the public were raised, we do injustice to the theatrical abilities of the gentlemen who gave this rich repast, when we barely say that those expectations were amply gratified.

The following prologue, written for the occasion, was spoken by the Gentleman who performed *Pierre*:

In vain we've begg'd th' unwilling Wits to write
A smart new Prologue for this strange new sight;
Nor Wit they'd give your Plaudits to engage,
Nor tuneful verse to sooth the Critic's Rage;
Instead of Prologue, then, dry, droll and terse,
Cloathed in the pleasing Dress of polished Verse,
If an unvarnished Tale may claim your ear,
I'll tell you who we are and why we're here:
   In Days of Yore, when first this fruitful land
Disclosed its Wealth to Cultivation's Hand,
And, like a Statue from the rugged Stone,
At each new Labour with new Beauties shone,
Two Sisters from Parnassus wished to try
Their fortunes in the growing Colony:—
Thalia and Melpomene their Names,
And this enchanted Spot received the Dames;
Long here they flourished, but of late they found
Their Crops less ample, tho' still rich the Ground
Anxious Melpomene first took th' Alarm,
"I'll call new labourers to the failing Farm,"
She cry'd. "Soldiers I claim, the Sons of Rage,
Decked in my Terrors when fell war they wage,
With my sublimest sentiments still fraught,
They will assist me, for they know they ought,"
Thalia smiling said, "They too are mine.
Vot'ries of Love, of Friendship, Mirth and Wine,
When social Pleasures elevate the Soul,
Bacchus and I replenish every bowl,
Together let us call them to our Aid."—
The Sisters summoned us, and we obey'd:
Now let me see—where shall our Work begin?
Sure that fine Mountain * can't be Rock within;
All round th' Enclosures † sweet straight canes I view,

---

* Upper Boxes   † Side Boxes

A fine Savannah ‡ that, well watered too—
May still such Harvests drooping Merit prop,
And each Night's Labour bring as fine a crop [*Going*]
[*Returns*]
But hold—one word, as we're New Negroes here,
King overseers, be not too severe.

Such a fine spirit of cooperation and such a promise of
properity was encouraging at a time when the island had
every reason for being discouraged. Its enemies lurked
without. The elements were always potential foes. And
such they proved in October. The Great Hurricane in
Westmoreland Parish, in the southwest corner of the island, was one of the most destructive that Jamaica has
ever known, piling up damage estimated at $3,500,000.
William Beckford, who lived through it, wrote a vivid
report in his *Descriptive Account of the Island of Jamaica.*

October 21st—*Zara,* Hill
Duke and No Duke, Cokaine

Again the farce is played by Gentlemen of the Army
for the benefit of the American Company. Apart from the
fact that the Army wished to show its appreciation of the
company's persistent efforts to amuse them in the face of
great odds, it may also have been moved by a loss that the
company sustained. The *Gazette* for October 6th reports:

Stolen

Out of the Men's Wardrobe in the Theatre, a great
Number of valuable dresses, amongst which are
the following, viz:

‡ Pit

A Scarlet Coat and Waistcoat with blue Cuffs and
Collar, richly laced with Silver, with soil stone
Buttons.

A Pompadour Suit with a broad Gold net Lace.

A Suit of Scarlet Cloth with a broad Gold Lace.

A white Cloth Coat and Waistcoat with a Silver Lace

A brown Cloth Coat and Waistcoat trimmed with a
broad Gold Lace

A brown Cloth ditto with a broad Silver Lace

A purple Cloth Suit trimmed with a narrow Silver
Lace

A Pompadour Coat and Waistcoat trimmed with
narrow Gold Lace

A blue Coat, waistcoat and Breeches, faced with red
and trimmed with a broad Silver Lace

A blue Coat and white Waistcoat trimmed with gold,
resembling the uniform of a Captain in the
Navy

A Pompadour Coat and Waistcoat laced with Silver

A scarlet Coat trimmed with Gold Lace

A scarlet Coat lappelled with blue and a blue Waistcoat richly laced with Silver

A blue Coat and Waistcoat trimmed with Silver
Lace, that on the Waistcoat rather broader
than the Lace on the Coat

A scarlet Waistcoat with a broad Silver Lace

A buff Waistcoat with a plain regimental Silver Lace

An old fashioned white Silk Waistcoat richly embroidered with Gold, Etc.

As the Wardrobe has not been examined for some time
past, and as no marks of violence appear, it is impossible
to ascertain the time when these cloaths were carried off;
but it is imagined the business was done in the course of a
month past, as some of the articles were seen in the wardrobe within that period.

Whoever will discover the perpetrators of this villainy,
so that the goods may be recovered, and the offenders

brought to justice, shall receive a reward of Fifty Pounds, or a proportion of that Sum for any part.

L. Hallam, M.R.

I suspect this was an "inside" job, done by a gentleman of color who sold these gaudy coats to an Obeah man up in the bush. An Obeah man in a blue coat with silver lace trimmings could strike terror to any heart and command the awe of an entire township of natives. But what about the pants? With one exception, no breeches are mentioned in this theft. Did the actors go on in their ordinary breeches and change costume by merely changing coats? It is recorded of John Henry that when he played *Othello* he wore "the uniform of a British General, his face black and hair woolly." [8]

And while we are off the playbook, we might set down here a cultural note. Mr. Morgan, we gather from this and a later notice, was now musical director and ballet master of the company. He advertises in the *Gazette* of October 13:

Music, Fencing & Dancing

Mr. Morgan respectfully begs leave to acquaint the Ladies and Gentlemen of the town of Kingston, that he purposes opening an Academy for teaching Music, Fencing and Dancing, particularly the Harpsichord and Violin, and Cotillions and Alleman'es in the present taste. Those Ladies and Gentlemen who are desirous of attaining Music will be duly attended at their own houses.

As the strictest attention will be paid to the elegant deportment and polite behaviour of the Pupils committed to his care, Mr. Morgan hopes for the favour and indulgence of the Public, to merit which he will assiduously exert his utmost endeavours.

N.B. Mr. Morgan is to be spoke with either at the Theatre, At Mr. Dancers's, the King's Arms in Harbour-Street, or Mrs. Nicholsons's Lodging-house in King-Street.

Now we must take up the playbook again, since five more performances will be given before the year 178c comes to a close:

October 31st—*Suspicious Husband,* Hoadley
Lethe, Garrick

Once again the roles in *Lethe* are supplied by Army officers, and the performance this time is for the benefit of the distressed widows and orphans of the army. A gentle hint is dropped in the advertisements: "Those Ladies and Gentlemen who choose to take this opportunity of subscribing to so useful a charity by lodging *more* than the regulated prices of the Tickets, will be pleased to enter their names in the books provided for that purpose . . . specifying the sums they subscribe." From a later report we find that this performance attracted a crowded audience and "the characters were supported with ease, spirit and judgment." The prologue was gallantly spoken:

With doubt, joy, apprehension! almost dumb,
Once more to face this awful court I come,
Lest Frankly suffer by my anxious fear,
Before he enters, I myself appear.
I'm told (what flatt'ry to my heart) that you
Have wished to see me, nay, have prest it too.
Alas! 'Twill prove another much ado—
I like a boy who long has truant played,
No lessons got, no exercises made,
On bloody Monday take my fearful stand,

And often eye the birchen-septer'd hand;—
'Twis twice three years since last the flags I trod
Sans Friendship smile, or e'en the Critic's nod,
A very ninepin, I this Int"im thro',
Knock'd down by sickness, now set up by you,
In six such tedious years the spirits cool,
And yet again, I feign would play the fool,
'Tis my heart's first wish; because I know,
Oft from example virtuous actions flow,
Worn in the service you my faults will spare,
And make allowances for wear and tear?
A Chelsea pensioner, rich in fears,
Fights o'er in prattle all his former wars,
Those past the service may the young ones teach
To march, present, to fire, and mount the breach.
Should the drum beat to arms, at first he'd grieve
For wooden leg, lost eye, or armless sleeve,
Then cock his hat, look fierce and swell his chest,
The widow! orphan! calls and, zounds, I'll do my best.

November 14th—*Macbeth*, Shakespeare
          Thomas and Sally, Bickerstaff

The Gentlemen of the Army (what ambition!) assume
the characters for *Macbeth* and the Comedians do
Thomas and Sally or The Sailor's Return. The performance was for the benefit of the company. We gather that
it needed aid and probably none of the troupe had been
paid for some time. On November 17th, Mr. Godwin, as
Mr. Morgan had done, opens a school for dancing—this
time an evening school. Evidently Godwin had little
chance to play. . . . The town had changed. Flooded
with soldiers and sailors, it had a false gaiety. Even William Aikman felt it. Aikman, Douglass' printing partner,
conducted a stationery store on King-Street. He advertised the fact that he was discontinuing his circulating

library, since it didn't even pay to import new books. Like our own South, Jamaica at this time was not much given to literature.

November 25th—*Duenna,* Sheridan
                  Ghost, Mrs. Centlivre
December 9th   —*Rule a Wife,* Fletcher
                  Midas, O'Hara

Still the Army supplies the characters in the opening comedy. Their loyalty to the stage is impressive. And yet, as we know, this loyalty to the theatre was not peculiar to the troops in Jamaica. While the officers stationed at Kingston, Port Royal, and Spanish Town were playing *Lethe* and *Macbeth* and *Rule a Wife and Have a Wife,* officers in other Colonies were making a reputation for themselves as Thespians—Burgoyne's in Boston, Howe's Thespians in Philadelphia, and in New York Clinton's soldier-actors.

It was gracious of these gallant gentlemen of the army and their ladies to lend the company a hand; yet we regret to say that there were times when they probably proved a nuisance. Old John Durang, writing of Howe's Thespians at Philadelphia, did not rate officers' wives any too highly. "Many of the soldiers' wives," he said, "helped the officers on the stage. They were generally of no character. They and the officers were about the theatre all day. When any piece was to be rehearsed, they would flock about the back door on the side lot." Doubtless those in Kingston did about the same.

Durang's remark was not merely the scorn of the professional for the amateur. I am quite certain it was the character of these Army wives that annoyed the troupers.

Apparently many of them were just light ladies who followed the drum.

It must be remembered that, apart from the John Henry-Storer Sisters episodes, the American Company of Comedians was composed of men and women who strictly observed the proprieties. In many instances people of highly commendable character, they realized that public and private virtue and the good regard of the community were essential to their being accepted in American towns both before and after the Revolution. While Kingston could scarcely have been called a pinnacle of virtue in those days, nevertheless public respect was necessary for public support.

CHAPTER V

Morals and the Lack of Them—Houses and the Manner of
Living and Entertaining—The Pace of Life—The Coming
of Art

SINCE, in the last chapter, we presumed to press a faint
halo upon the heads of the American Company of Comedians, you will naturally wonder how many of the audience
this distinguishing mark might also fit. At the period we
are considering—the last quarter of the eighteenth century—doubtless many men and women on the island could
deservedly wear a halo with distinction and grace. The
profligate whites among the aristocracy were found mainly
in the ranks of recent settlers. By this era, many descendants of the early proprietors had recaptured some of the
old Puritan code of morality and were proving that a
capacity for gallant and righteous living had not entirely
died out.

Morals and the Lack of Them

Up to this point we have jogtrotted along comfortably
with good actors, yet our excursions into Jamaican social
life will not be complete unless, for a short time and at the
safe distance of many decades, we associate with some of
the bad 'uns.

The morals of the buccaneers of Port Royal in their
balmiest days, before the earthquake of 1692, probably
set the world's record for depravity, and established a

standard under which Jamaica labored—to its disadvantage—for well-nigh two centuries. Once on shore after a successful raid, the buccaneers spent their money just as drunken sailors are supposed to. Although the town had a church and could count two thousand buildings, not a few of them were grogshops and bawdy houses. There were an appalling number of tavern signs creaking in the Trade Winds that swept up Port Royal's lanes and streets. One ribald and bibulous pirate squandered his pieces of eight for a barrel of wine, which he broached in the public highway and demanded at pistol point that every passer-by drink with him.[1] A halo would have sat very uneasily on Henry Morgan's head, even though, toward the end of his days, he did reform enough to make an efficient Lieutenant Governor and to oblige his erstwhile partners in crime and vice solemnly to attend church.

Among the lassies at Port Royal, one especially piques our curiosity—Mary Carleton, "the German Princess." Born in 1639, she was well started on her career of imposture in London by the age of nineteen. In 1663 she married John Carleton and was promptly arrested for bigamy—this "plump and succulent girl" had three other husbands alive at the time and was "as common as a Barber's Chair"— but so great was her following that the court acquitted her "by publique proclamation." Turning actress, she gathered considerable repute on the boards. A play, *The German Princess,* was written in her honor. Her old habits would keep cropping up, and in 1671 she was caught stealing, for which she was sentenced and transported to Jamaica. She wrote "News from Jamaica in a letter from Port Royal to her fellow collegiates and friends in Newgate." Like "Con" Phillips, she also penned her memoirs,[2] which were published in London in 1673. Having served a two-year sentence on the island, during which time she brought to ruin three substantial persons, destroying both them and their families, she returned to London, went blithely along her evil ways, and finally wound up at Tyburn. What stories *she* could have told about Port Royal!

Now it may have been that the buccaneers and their Doxies did not set the style for early island morals—that profligate living was just the normal eighteenth-century way of social diversion. Or again, we might blame it on the climate.[3] In any event, life was all too often rich and racy. Drinking and gambling were the common amusements of the aristocracy and gentry. On more than one occasion, some gambling buck, his money gone, would wager even his horse and carriage waiting for him at the door. And if he lost it, he'd walk home! Drinking, dancing, and gambling parties were among the amusements of race week, an occasion that brought together a mixed concourse of local folk and people from neighboring parishes. Dueling, too, was prevalent. But even more universal was the practice of concubinage.

Of the ordinary run of males, those who were bachelors found their pleasure in the arms of some negro or mulatto slave, usually a "housekeeper" or a likely wench about the plantation. Every estate employed a number of book-keepers who were also supervisors of the field and sugarhouse work. Each man had a dwelling of sorts to himself and it was customary for him to select a girl for housekeeper. This sable Venus did his domestic work and was on hand for such other services as were required of her. Once accustomed to this sort of living, the young Englishman or Scotchman felt that he could drink, wench, and blaspheme without a sigh or blush. He made no bones about displaying his darky mistress, and he showed his wit and smartness by ridiculing the clergy and by drinking "corkers," as strong rum punch was called. Few even of the lusty youths could stand such a pace; they soon found an early grave.

Higher up in the social scale of desirable ladies came the comely, sleek-skinned brown girls, with blue-black hair. Desirous of the finery and advancement in social status that such connection brought them, they were only too happy to serve as mistresses of men of affairs. They considered it more genteel to be the paramour of a white man than to marry; in fact, they viewed marriage with their own kind as an unnecessary restraint, agreeing with the native proverb: "Marriage hab teet' an' bite hot."

The mulattos and the brown girls comprised a distinct social set. These comely quadroons and handsome mestees gave parties that were just as expensive and gay as the whites. At their dances, sometimes men of their own complexion were invited and at others mulatto men were excluded and only the white were welcomed. Since these girls were beautiful, infectious, and tireless dancers, the young white blades didn't hesitate to accept. Nor was there any social stigma attached to this Terpsichorean mixture.

Some men continued in the illicit state of concubinage all their lives. Others, having had their taste of mistresses, either returned to England or settled down to marry white girls of the island. The colored offspring of the more respectable classes were generally well cared for, as many a bill for their inheritance offered in the Assembly eloquently attests. A white parent could not bequeath to his colored children more than £2000 currency unless the Assembly set the ruling aside. Some of these children were sent to England to be educated. By no means were they neglected.

Robert Graham of Gartmore, who lived on the island for several years and then returned home to rise to great respectability, provides an example of the better-class young man in the toils of the Jamaican social vice. His dusky mistress presented him with a boy and girl. Before leaving the island, he provided for their education. They were taught trades that would make them self-support-ing.[4]

It was not unusual to see the white children of a man by his white wife being brought up together with his mulatto children by his dusky companion.

At one time this concubinage was almost universal, embracing nine-tenths of the male inhabitants. Nearly every man, from the planter down to the lowliest indentured servant, had his female companion. In the upper ranks, she was his friend, often his adviser; she managed his household affairs and displayed herself in his carriage. Although protesting her affection, yet she was not above being untrue to him and without a qualm she would drain the contents of his purse. She was often a tyrant, so much so that, when occasion offered, he was likely to escape from her jealous watchfulness and "find consolation in the arms of some other dingy nymph."[5]

Here and there exceptions could be found—some outstanding professional man or a leading merchant or an attorney who held himself above these temptations. The Jews, who controlled much of the shop trade of the day, also seemed free of the concubine habit: they married their own kind. The situation on the island in our period is epitomized by the historian Edward Long in the statement that the name of family man was held in the greatest derision. "He who should presume to shew any displeasure against such a thing as simple fornication, would for his pains be accounted a simple blockhead; since not one in twenty can be persuaded that there is either sin or shame in cohabiting with his slave." [6]

Marriageable English girls were comparatively few in the eighteenth century. The available Creole white ladies who, by the way, bore off the Caribbean palm for their fine figures, were also limited. In towns these native girls kept up appearances—rivalry with others would naturally produce care in dress and an attempt at charm in demeanor. In the country they were inclined to grow languid, slatternly, and lazy except at dances, when their liveliness and endurance was beyond belief.

If a bachelor decided to marry, he would choose from either the town or country set. His housekeeper would stay on until within a few days of the nuptials and doubtless conveniently hover near by afterward. "Outside families," as broods of illegitimate children were called, proved to be more the rule than the exception. In fact, this condition of domestic affairs was so prevalent that everyone—often even the poor wife—accepted it. And it lasted well up through the first quarter of the nineteenth century, after which it grew less common, until today it appears only sporadically.

These mixed relations gave rise, in time, to three distinct classes. On top were the whites, natives of Great Britain and the Creole whites and their descendants, together with those whose colored blood could be measured only by a small fraction. Next came the freedmen, some of them descended from white or partly white parents, or slaves who had been manumitted by their masters. Finally at the bottom of the ladder lay the bulk of the population, the black slaves.

By the middle of the eighteenth century, the Scotch comprised one-third of those of European birth on the island. This is surprising when we discover that the whites displayed a marked weakness for luxuriant living and improvident habits that involved many of them in difficulties. A man would burn to be accounted a large landed proprietor, and would borrow money at extortionate rates merely to acquire and cultivate several estates.[7]

Once they managed to make any considerable money, these ambitious planters almost invariably succumbed to the temptation for putting on great style. They would dress their servants in liveries and fill their coach houses with excellent carriages. A well-to-do family would keep a coach, one or two gigs, and a stable with fifteen or twenty horses and mules with their proper attendants. It was considered not unduly extravagant for a prosperous planter to spend £2000 sterling on his horses and carriages.

While they may not strictly come under the head of morals, the rowdiness of the Assembly on occasions and the belligerency of some public personages on others, must have added to both the wrath and the amusement of the populace. The former occasions are almost too numerous to mention; rows between the Governor and his legislature appear to have been the normal state in eighteenth-century Jamaica. The latter type of conflict is best represented by the assault made on Governor Trelawny at Spanish Town by Admiral Sir Chaloner Ogle, which gave rise to quite a wagging of tongues and pens.

Town and Country Houses

By the middle of the eighteenth century the island began to take an interest in the amenities. It showed an active desire, for instance, to do something about its domestic architecture. For the first hundred years after the island's occupation, British planters paid very little attention to the design, appearance, or furnishing of their homes. The plantation might have elaborate and expensive sugar and rum works, while the owner was content to live in a makeshift, thatched hovel of wattle and daub. However, there must have been some gentlemen who took pride in their homes, else why did the *Weekly Jamaica Courant* for April 15, 1719, advertise "Painted Papers for Hangings"?

In Kingston fine residences began to spring up. Between some of the Kingstonians there flourished a rivalry that would have done credit to the newest of our *nouveau riche*. Four of the local merchant princes entered a race to see which one could erect the most magnificent and expensive house. "Constantine House," built by Jasper Hall, Receiver General and Speaker of the Assembly, ran neck and neck with "Hibbert's House," built by Thomas Hibbert, one of Kingston's wealthiest merchants.

In the country, after the hovel type of home had disappeared, came a kind that is still seen today—a comfortable two-story structure with an open verandah in front. They were usually of stone. The window openings were filled with jalousies.

Besides these, were built some really admirable great houses on plantations and pens. "Teak Pen," in Clarendon, where lived Chief Justice Thomas Fearon, had, in addition to a fine residence, a separate building connected with it by a colonnade, where was kept the justice's extensive library. He, by the way, was Jamaican born and had never been off the island. "Decoy" in St. Mary's, seat of Sir Charles Price, was famous not alone for its excellent furnishings and superb garden, but also for its collection of birds and wild animals gathered from foreign lands. "Rose Hall," near Montego Bay, cost its owner £30,000. The glory of its fine woodwork now gone, the ruins of the house still stand. Today "Rose Hall" is remembered by most visitors as being the scene of the sultry and murderous romances of Mrs. Ann Palmer.[8]

Many of the great houses deep in the country were built and equipped so that they could withstand siege in case of negro insurrection. "Good Hope," on the fringe of the Cockpit Maroon country, one of the best extant examples of eighteenth-century Jamaican architecture, was originally so fortified. "Stokes Hall," in St. Thomas, was loopholed against attack. "Colbeck Castle," near Old Harbour, of which the ruins still stand, could well have withstood siege and Sir James de Castillo's house, to the east of Kingston, was equipped with swivel guns to ward off enemy pirates.

Living in many of these plantation great houses was pursued with carefree luxury and abundance. As taverns were practically unknown outside of towns, the duties of hospitality devolved upon the planters. Open house was the order of the day and it was offered equally to friends and strangers. Consequently each big house supported a sizable retinue of servants.

Where there were children in the family, twenty to forty servants were not unusual. None of them, of course, did more work than they had to and they delegated it to others whenever others appeared. Each child would have a nurse and the nurse had an assistant. Each lady in the house had her own maid. Besides these, the in-servants included butlers, footmen, cooks, laundresses, and half a dozen housemaids, many of the house girls being expert with their needles. Outside were yard boys, grooms, and stablemen. Often the servants were the mulatto offspring of bookkeepers and their dusky mistresses.

In these Jamaican houses, carpets were practically unknown. Instead, the floors were laid in mahogany, wild orange, or some other hard wood that six to a dozen maids kept polished into darkly tinted mirrors by hours of scrubbing with wax and brushes made, as today, of cocoanut husks.

The lighting throughout was by candles. Many a drawing-room ceiling supported glistening crystal chandeliers, and the walls expensive silver sconces.

The cooking was invariably done in a separate cookhouse and the dishes brought into the dining room across a stretch of the near-by yard. The most primitive sort of open fireplace hung with pots did service in the cookhouse. One wonders how, with such inadequate equipment, even half a dozen cooks could have prepared the elaborate meals that were set on some planters' tables.

While most residences were scantily furnished, in the better type of both town and country houses the furniture was often distinguished. Much of it came from England.

Also much of it was fashioned out of mahogany and other native woods by local cabinetmakers. Quite often a big estate would have a cabinetmaker among its indentured servants, who soon became adept in copying English pieces or modifying them to local conditions. Sideboards and four-poster beds were especially well made. The four-poster, with the headboard carved in a device like a setting sun and its surrounding rays, became a favorite style. These beds were all large and high, the tall posts carrying the mosquito net under which everyone slept. Indeed most of the native furniture was made large in scale. Since the rooms these pieces occupied were also large and the ceilings either finished in the lofty tray form or left open to the roof, such noble furniture was suitably proportioned.

Those who owned plate or fine china and glass always displayed them. Sideboards were piled high with silver and cupboard shelves with china. It was frankly an age of display.

As massive as the furniture were the stairs in great houses. Fashioned out of mahogany planks and with carefully turned balusters, they attained a high degree of the builder's art. Some rooms were paneled, at least part way up, richly carved mahoe wood being used for the purpose.

Despite all this magnificence and display, sanitary arrangements in Jamaica, as in most of the world at that time, scarcely rose above the lowest ebb. Plumbing was simply nonexistent. There is still to be seen in Falmouth a house where washing water from the upstairs bedrooms is disposed of by the simple method of pouring it into an open hopper beneath the window. One of the daily early-morning sights of Kingston used to be the negro slaves, walking toward the water front, bearing on their heads open tubs of slops that they dumped into the sea. In the deep country the sanitation must have been even worse than in towns.

The Pace of Life

Life in a great house aroused at daybreak, at about five or six o'clock. Hot morning coffee was brought up to the bedside, a sure reviver after a night of intense heat and mosquitoes buzzing around one's bed. Breakfast was served from eight to nine, second breakfast—equivalent to our luncheon—came at noon, and dinner between six and seven. Country people in those days sometimes took afternoon tea but rarely indulged in supper before bed. Ordinarily the house quieted down a few hours after sunset. By nine everyone was asleep.

In town the European-born kept later hours, whereas Creoles followed the wise custom of early to bed, early to rise.

Both in town and country, dinner became a major sport, nor were the provisions for it difficult to obtain. The rivers and the sea furnished June-fish, calipever, red snapper, mullet, and kingfish. Pigeon was shot in the woods and there also wild boar was hunted down. Turtle, a favorite dish, came offshore or was brought in by fishermen from the Cayman Islands. Native oysters were gathered from branches of swamp-mangrove trees. The black crab then, as today, was the island's greatest delicacy. Next in popularity came pepper pot, a gorgeous mélange compounded by native cooks out of fresh fish, shrimps, and vegetables, all stewed together and highly seasoned. The Creoles still have a weakness for poignant sauces, about the last possible indulgence anyone living in the tropics should give way to; yet they seem to survive it.

While the ordinary fare might consist of vegetables and "bread kind"—yams, plantains, etc.—and fruit, with an occasional bit of fish or meat from the estate cattle, the presence of a guest immediately raised the cuisine to lofty proportions. The table would be loaded down with dishes of flesh, fish, fowl, and game. After this would follow the dessert of tarts, cakes, puddings, sweetmeats, and fruit.

Accompanying these courses, the men would drink ale, porter, rum punch, claret, or Madeira. In those days the master of the house would be considered lacking in hospitality if, ere his guests quitted the table (the ladies having withdrawn long before to their music and gossip, and sipping an innocuous cup made from the granadilla), they were not deprived of their wits or the use of their legs. "This constant manuring the stomach with such a heterogeneous compost," as Edward Long agriculturally expressed it, soon raised a plentiful crop of ailments.

Gormandizing and excessive drinking seem to have been the way with the English from the very beginning. When Sir Hans Sloane was on the island in 1687 he listed the ailments and symptoms of his patients. "The Patients I had to do with," he put it, "happened for the most part to have been Jolly Companions and hard Drinkers."

There was Mrs. L., aged forty, "who on drinking too much wine, fell into a Cholera Morbus." And one R., a tavern keeper's wife, about forty years of age, "fat and phlegmatic, was, upon excessive drinking of Brandy, taken with a Lethargy." Another patient, Dr. Cooper, "of a yellowish swarthy complexion, was a great drinker of Rum Punch and told me that he had had twenty-five violent fits of the Belly-ache with drinking that sort of Liquor." The descent to Avernus was often swift and logical. "Major Thomas Ballard, Plethoric, of a Sanguine Complexion, aged about thirty-five, much given to extravagant drinking and sitting up late, sometimes for several nights together without sleep, was, after a Debaugh in Brandy for some days and nights without rest, taken extremely ill."

The really Gargantuan drinker among Sloane's patients was Mr. J.

About twenty-four, extremely Corpulent and Fat, used to eat very heartilly and drink very hard without any great prejudice. One evening he made a challenge to another, who thought himself able to bear more drink than he, desiring him before the present company to come to a fair tryal in that matter. They had drunk by Computation about a Quart and a half before Supper, and at Supper in about three-quarters of an hour's time, drank to and pledged each other in six Draughts of Madeira Wine, drunk out of six Calabashes or cups, holding each a quart by measure. The drinking so hard and in so short a time, seiz'd this Gentleman all of an instant, so that his Eyes turn'd in his Head, stood fix'd and he began to sink down in his chair. . . . Both of these Gentlemen died since in England.

Well that they might!

One more Sloane story, for I've never been able to figure whether it should come under the head of the result of excessive drinking or just plain idosyncrasy. In Sixteen-Mile Walk there lived a Dr. Foster, who "had Tamed a great Snake or Serpent, and kept it about him within his Shirt; it would wind itself fast around his arm and drink out of his Mouth and leap at a Call on the Table, to eat crums of Cassada Bread." [9]

These cases, of course, were violent exceptions. Still, it must be confessed that even in our last quarter of the eighteenth century, what Yellow Jack didn't carry off, drink most certainly did. Kingston in 1771, for example, recorded 988 births and 2085 deaths. I marvel that porter and ale, heavy malt drinks usually associated with cold climates, should have been so popular on this tropical island, and that Madeira, a strongly fortified wine, so conducive to gout, should have been chosen above the lighter and less dangerous claret.

For more temperate tipplers there were sangaree—Madeira or rum with water and sugar—and a mild drink called Honey Dram, brewed from honey, water, chew-stick (*Gouania domingensis*), and rum. The chew-stick is bitter and took the place of hops.

Festive Occasions

Christmas and New Year's were especially festive occasions and marked by elaborate eating and drinking both in towns and on plantations. Sunday dinner was usually a prodigious gastronomic effort. Sundays, too, were the favorite days for the meeting of overseers and bookkeepers. They would ride in from the various parts of the parish to meet and dine alternately at one another's houses and spend the evening smoking, drinking, dancing, and playing cards. At this time the Sabbath was kept unholy both by the whites and, as we shall see in a later chapter, by the blacks as well.

In addition to the private parties were the semipublic tavern dinners given on stated occasions—military dinners, vestry dinners, king's-birthday dinners, governor's dinners, grand jury dinners, victory dinners, club dinners, Freemasons' dinners, when a man "was considered as a disaffected person who did not get most loyally drunk." [10] Imagine what lip-smacking went on among members of the European Club, for instance, when they read of the dinner to be given at Francis Allwood's tavern in Kingston, as set forth in the *Daily Advertiser* of April 12, 1790: they were to dine together at three o'clock and the bills were to be called for and settled at eight in the evening; those "desirous of joining in the hilarity and conviviality of the said intended meeting may depend upon receiving a cheerful and hearty welcome." The legislators, too, saw that they never lacked official food: once a year a committee of the Assembly, for instance, junketed over to Port Royal to inspect the fortifications, and were allowed £60 to pay for their dinners!

Just why did Jamaicans in those days snatch so hard and with such abandon at the fleshpots? Perhaps it was the ever-present grave.

You were never quite certain whether your sugar (or your daughter) might not be seized on the high seas by the French frigates or a pirate brig, when you bade them farewell in a West Indian man of war, bound for England and comparative safety. After a prolonged and hectic dinner party, from which you had to be supported by trusty bondsmen to your four-poster bed, you could not be sure of not awakening to the nausea and dreadful weakness of Yellow Jack scourging your body and brains. [11]

But there were pleasant customs, and so to one of them. For a long time the Jamaica country set followed a local equivalent of the Italian *villegetura*. Families went visiting. Entire households with personal attendants would journey to the house of a relative or friend on some other plantation, there to stay a month, six weeks, or even two months. The migration was preceded by a party of twenty or thirty female slaves loaded with trunks, beds, chairs, and band boxes. Next followed the family, some in carriages, some on mules and horseback, with their maids, waiting men, grooms, footmen, postilions, and sometimes even the family's pet fiddler. The ladies wore handkerchief masks over their faces to protect them from dust. They stayed until their welcome wore out, which point was determined by the number of fowls, turkeys, pigs, and ducks that remained and the amount of vegetables left in the provision ground. The visit, in due time, was returned. To accommodate another entire family and its personal servants required large quarters. Even today on some of the estates, both the big house and its various appendages attest to the elaborateness of the hospitality offered at the end of the eighteenth century.

These elaborate houses and the sumptuous hospitality were predicated on unpaid slave labor. After Emancipation, of course, the number of domestic servants was greatly reduced, and with it, life toned down to a quiet humdrum. On the other hand, however, the standard of morals rose perceptibly.

The Coming of Art

As we have seen, music, dances, the theatre, fine eating, and elaborate drinking were already established phases of the genteel life. Painting and etching, too, began to be recognized as handmaids of culture and aristocratic living.

Between 1766 and 1770 a series of six plates showing

Jamaican scenes were produced by an unknown artist. Six others appeared in 1778, after paintings made by George Robertson for William Beckford, cousin of the author of *Vathek*. Beckford had met Robertson while traveling in Italy and, like Henry Moore of a previous generation bringing home his own band of musicians, Beckford induced Robertson to come along home with him for the express purpose of painting scenes on some of his properties. He also brought with him a portrait painter, Philip Wickstead, a pupil of Zoffany. Wickstead later took to planting, then to drink, and finally died in 1790.

In March, 1780, Kingstonians crowded in to see an exhibition of portraits in oil by J. and H. Stevenson, limners. It was held at their house in Duke Street. They also executed miniatures and family "conversational pieces," and did coach painting and "high varnishing." Their prices were so attractive that even a comfortable middle-class family might have had itself pictured for future generations:

A Bust the size of Life £5.5
A Ditto of a Lady or a Child £6

Payments must be made in Mill'd Money before Delivery of any Work. Miniatures and Family Pieces at their usual prices. As they keep a Carver and Gilder, they provide Frames of any kind at the easiest rates.

The Stevensons had a Kingston competitor in James Claypole, who painted portraits not only in oils but also in crayon, and did miniatures and was equally adept at painting and varnishing coaches.

CHAPTER VI

1781

Our Servants Precede Us to the Playhouse—We Enjoy an
Uninterrupted Run—Montego Bay Has a Lecture—Some
Portentous Doings in the States

ABOUT six o'clock on any day that the actors were playing,
the sandy streets and lanes of Kingston or Spanish Town
or Montego Bay would see a drift of people all going the
same direction. Negro servants of various shades, shapes,
and sizes and in all kinds of liveries and lack of them,
would be moving toward the theatre. Straight-back, velvet-
skinned, sleek young negresses with crisp bandannas
folded around their kinky heads step along barefooted,
their provocative round hips swinging sassily. Grooms in
slouchy Osnaburg pants and blue jean coats saunter by. A
chocolate-colored barracks batman in his officer's castoff
tunic. Faithful old Nanas, released for an hour from the
care of their mistress's brood, still erect for all their years,
gold bangles in their ears and bandanna-crowned, shuffle
past. Ebony errand boys in rags and tatters. A footman
from King's House, distant and proud in his livery, but as
barefooted as the others.

There was no such accommodation as the reserved seat
in those days. Hallam and Henry didn't make this convenient innovation until some time after their return to
the States and the theatre there was a going concern again.
Hence the motley throng of servants sent by their masters

and mistresses to hold their seats for the evening's performance. And there the servants sat until their owners appeared.

What a clatter and chatter they make in the theatre! What rude pushing to get the front chairs in the boxes! What a cackle of backchat from those who come in late and have to hold less favorable seats! And once they are seated in the barnlike gloom of the building, what a social affair they make of it, these darkies bowing to their friends in the opposite boxes, calling to acquaintances in the pit, putting on airs to those whose mistresses are beneath their own, joking, passing the time of day, exchanging the gossip and reports of little intrigues in the barracks and the great houses on the near-by cattle pens, in the homes and shops in town and in the villas on the fringe of it. Some are slouched moodily in the chairs and some fidget. Some munch sugar cane.

They sing, too, for whenever two or three Jamaican negroes are gathered together, once they have exchanged gossip and complained of their miseries, someone is sure to start a song. Not anything loud or disorderly, just a hum of an old air sung over and over. Often they sing hymns.

And so the hour passes until their masters and mistresses start coming in. One by one, as the seats are taken, the negroes trickle out. Ushers light the box candles and turn to bow obsequiously to aristocratic box holders. And if the servants made a gay and exotic motley, even more so does the audience that begins to appear. Officers from the barracks, gallant in gold lace, with pretty ladies on their arms. Government officials in the current Jamaican interpretation of what the well-dressed man should wear at the theatre. Planters and their pale-faced wives; some of them have driven up in chaises, some in curricles and gigs, and not a few rode into town on horseback. Kingston could boast five hundred carriages at that time, a full third of the number on the island. Here are shopkeepers of affluence and planting attorneys grown rich on managing estates for absentee landlords and on gobbling up land from others. The Governor and his lady are lighted to their box by the manager. English faces, Scotch faces, Irish faces, and with them mingled all the tints and tones of complexional distinctions of this mixed society.

The Creole, the native-born Jamaican, was given to thoughtless extravagance and expensive pomp, come the supplies whence they may. What more desirable place to display them than the theatre? So here are the Creole ladies in brocaded silks and satins just as you would find them at a London theatre, their hair piled high and daintily powdered; their menfolk in gold-laced coats. There's many an olive-tinted mestee among them, for even in those days, all above the color degree of quinteron—offspring of a white and a Quateron—were classed as English and enjoyed the privileges of the pure whites.[1] Polished by a genteel education, little distinction could be made between the upper classes of such a mingled society.

There may even have been some comely Jewesses in the boxes. Hebrew shopkeepers were beginning to prosper. In a sense, after the Spaniards, the Jews are the aristocrats of the island—if aristocracy is based merely on who got there first—for the Jews had been thriving ever since they were the money-changers and bankers for the buccaneers of Port Royal. Then, too, it was no little distinction to be able to pay 13s 4d for a seat at the play.

In the pit were those who paid ten shillings—less prosperous shopkeepers, clerks, overseers, and bookkeepers come from the plantations to town for a frolic, soldiers and sailors on leave. Among them, too, there's many a yellow Quasheba in her finery. Toward the rear, crowded ordinary people and all the rest of the town that could afford the price of a seat.

Here they are in their places a little before seven o'clock. The ushers come down and touch a taper to the footlight lamps—by now the candles have been supplanted by oil lamps without chimneys. Rustling and chatter cease. The violins of the orchestra begin to squeak. The curtains move. It is the evening of February 6, 1781 —and the play is on!

February 6th —*Wonder*, Mrs. Centlivre
     Duce Is in Him, Colman
     Vintner Tricked, Yarrow

Not all the casts are available, so we are obliged merely to name the attractions.

February 10th—*Love in a Village*, Bickerstaff
     Harlequin Collector

February 17th—*Hamlet*, Shakespeare

Hamlet . . . . Mr. Hallam
King . . . . Mr. Wignell
Ghost . . . .
Laertes . . . . Mr. Goodman
Horatio . . . . Mr. Godwin
Polonius . . . . Mr. Morris
Rosencranz . . . . Mr. Woolls
Guildenstern . . . . Mr. Sale
Player King . . . . Mr. Morgan
Francisco . . . . Mr. Bacon

Gravediggers ....Mr. Morris
Mr. Morgan
Queen ....Mrs. Morris
Player Queen ....Miss Wainwright
Ophelia ....Mrs. Raynard

Messrs. Morgan, Sale, and Bacon are new to the company. Sale was probably a Jamaican aspirant. Bacon will be insignificant.

Harlequin Collector

March 31st—*Distressed Mother*, Philips
Old Maid, Murphy

April 7th   —*Distressed Mother*, Philips
Spanish Fryar, Dryden

April 14th —*Lionel and Clarissa*, Bickerstaff
Irish Widow, Garrick

This is Mrs. Hamilton's benefit.

April 21st—*Virginia*, Crisp

Virginius ....Mr. Hallam
Lucius Scilius ....Mr. Wignell
Claudius ....Mr. Morris
Rufus ....Mr. Woolls
Caius ....Mr. Morales
Appius ....Mr. Goodman
Marcia ....Mrs. Morris
Plautia ....Miss Wainwright
Virginia ....Mrs. Raynard

This is Mr. Hallam's benefit.

Love à la Mode, Macklin

April 28th —*All for Love*, Dryden
Tony Lumpkin in Town, O'Keeffe

Tony Lumpkin ....Mr. Hallam
Mr. Jonquil ....Mr. Goodman
Tim Tickle ....Mr. Wignell
Belville ....Mr. Morales
Frank ....Mr. Woolls
Tailor ....Mr. Sale
Painter ....Mr. Goodman
Diggory ....Mr. Morris
Lavender ....Miss Wainwright
Mrs. Jonquil ....Mrs. Raynard

May 12th—*She Wou'd and She Wou'dn't*, Cibber

Trapanti ....Mr. Hallam
Octavio ....Mr. Goodman
Don Philip ....Mr. Wignell
Don Louis ....Mr. Woolls
Diego ....Mr. Godwin
Vasquez ....Mr. Morales
Corrigidore ....Mr. Sale
Don Manuel ....Mr. Morris
Rosana ....Mrs. Raynard
Villetta ....Miss Wainwright
Flora ....Mrs. Hamilton
Hypolita ....Mrs. Morris

Triumph of Genius, Cawdell

Harlequin ....Mr. Godwin
Witch ....
Mercury ....Mr. Wignell
Van Dunder ....Mr. Morales
Cross Stitch ....Mr. Sale
French Valet ....Mr. Woolls
Dutch Boor ....Mr. Morris
Columbine ....Mrs. Morris

Mrs. Morris took her benefit this evening.

May 26th—*School for Scandal*, Sheridan

Sir Peter Teazle	Mr. Goodman
Charles Surface	Mr. Hallam
Joseph Surface	Mr. Wignell
Sir Oliver Surface	Mr. Morris
Sir Benjamin Backbite	Mr. Godwin
Crabtree	Mr. Morales
Moses	" "
Rowley	Mr. Woolls
Trip	Mr. Roberts
Snake	Mr. Sale
Lady Sneerwell	Mrs. Morris
Mrs. Candour	Miss Wainwright
Maria	Miss Storer
Lady Teazle	Mrs. Raynard

Padlock, Bickerstaff

June 2nd—*The Gamester*, Moore
       Shadows of Shakespeare, Pratt
       Comus, Milton

Mr. Goodman has his benefit.

June 30th—*Chapter of Accidents*, Miss Lee

Woodville	Mr. Hallam
Governor Harcourt	Mr. Goodman
Captain Harcourt	Mr. Wignell
Lord Glenmore	Mr. Morris
Vane	Mr. Godwin
Grey	Mr. Woolls
Jacob Gawkey	Mr. Morales
Cecilia	Miss Storer
Miss Mortimer	Mrs. Morris
Mrs. Warner	Mrs. Hamilton
Bridget	Miss Wainwright

Anatomist, Ravenscroft

The afterpiece is an old friend of the company. This farce Lewis Hallam the Elder played at Williamsburg in 1752, in his first American performance. Miss Wainwright took her benefit tonight.

So far, this has been a reasonably uninterrupted run. Occasionally a performance has to be postponed because of the indisposition of one or other of the actors [2]—an occasion to be expected in this island which, as we have seen, bore not too good a reputation for health. John Henry especially appears to have succumbed quite often. Nevertheless, Mr. Henry recovers and on June 30, 1781, he announces in the *Gazette* a business arrangement that will definitely affect American stage history for several years to come: "Mr. Henry respectfully acquaints the Public that he has jointly with Mr. Hallam undertaken the superintendence of the American Company of Comedians and flatters himself, by attention and perseverance, to merit (the summit of his wishes) their Approbation."

In this announcement we also read the inference that David Douglass has gotten so engrossed in his printing venture with Aikman and has become so much a part of the island life that his connection with the American stage is definitely severed. In fact, we have no Jamaica playbill in which Mr. Douglass is named.

John Henry, the new comanager, gets down to business. The *Gazette* for August 18th advertises for

A Taylor

Who can be well recommended for sobriety, honesty and industry, is wanted as Wardrobe-keeper at the Theatre. Wages will be paid annually, monthly or weekly at his option. A person answering this description may meet with

liberal terms and a desirable situation by applying to
John Henry

It was just as well that Henry required honesty of his
wardrobe keeper, for, as we saw in the previous chapter,
honesty is an essential rule and guide for anyone who holds
that post.

Let us end this chitchat and glance at the playbook
again.

July 18th   —*Measure for Measure,* Shakespeare
                Linco's Travels, Garrick
                Daphne and Amintor, Bickerstaff

Amintor ....Mr. Woolls
Mindora ....Miss Storer
Daphne ....Mrs. Morris
Scaramouch ....Mr. Wignell
Harlequin ....Mr. Godwin
Pantaloon ....Mr. Morales
Columbine ....Mrs. Hamilton

August 4th—*Orphan of China,* Murphy

Timurkan ....Mr. Morris
Octar ....Mr. Godwin
Zamti ....Mr. Moore
Etan ....Mr. Sale
Hamet ....Mr. Wignell
Merat ....Mr. Woolls
Orasmin ....Mr. Dermot
Zimventi ....Mr. Morales
Mirvan ....Mr. Goodman
Mandane ....Mrs. Morris
Zapheniri ....Mr. Hallam
Arsace ....Miss Storer

   Maid of the Oaks, Burgoyne

Perhaps this presentation of General Burgoyne's *Maid of the Oaks* was a patriotic gesture. At the time this gallant and playful soldier was in Boston amusing the Tory and not too Puritan inhabitants with his military Thespians. We also note the addition of Mr. Moore, who will become quite a figure.

August 8th—*Romeo and Juliet*, Shakespeare

Romeo	Mr. Henry
Mercutio	Mr. Hallam
Friar Laurence	Mr. Goodman
Capulet	Mr. Morris
Benvolio	Mr. Wignell
Tibalt	Mr. Godwin
Paris	Mr. Woolls
Montague	Mr. Dermot
Friar John	Mr. Sale
Apothecary	Mr. Morales
Page	Master Woolls
Lady Capulet	Mrs. Hamilton
Juliet	Miss Cheer

Author, Foote

Cadwallader	Mr. Hallam
Young Cape	Mr. Wignell
Vamp	Mr. Goodman
Governor	Mr. Dermot
Sprightly	Mr. Godwin
Printer's Devil	Mr. Morris
Poet	Mr. Woolls
Robin	Mr. Morales
Arabella	Miss Storer
Mrs. Cadwallader	Mrs. Gardner

Here is news indeed. First, this is Miss Storer's benefit and second, here is Miss Cheer again! Third, we meet

Mrs. Gardner for the first time, and she is playing "by particular desire for that night only." She was from the Theatre Royal, Covent Garden, and had long been a favorite in comic parts.

August 25th—*School for Soldiers,* Henry
Quakers, Mrs. Centlivre

This is John Henry's benefit and we shall print the comanager's bill:

Theatre

(Not Yet Performed)

For the Benefit of

Mr. Henry

This present evening Augst 25th will be presented a Dramatic Piece (in four Acts) written by a Gentleman on this island, called A

School for Soldiers

or

The Deserter

The Principal Characters

Mr. Henry

Mr. Wignell	Mr. Dermot
Mr. Goodman	Mr. Woolls
Mr. Morris	and

Mr. Hallam

Mrs. Morris	Miss Storer

and (for this night) Miss Cheer

In Act IV A military Procession to the
Execution of

The Deserter

By particular Desire at the End of the Play
Mr. Henry will recite a Monody called
The Shadows of Shakespeare or

Shakespeare's Character paying Homage to
Garrick
To which will be added a Farce, altered from
Mrs. Centlivre called
The Quakers, or
The Guardians Outwitted

I suspect that Henry had an eye on his military audience when he wrote his *School for Soldiers*. However, since Charles Dibdin had written a musical drama with the same subtitle as Henry's play, the editor of the *Royal Gazette* explained that he had

been informed by some friends of the author, who had been favored with a perusal of it, that it possesses a very considerable share of dramatic merit and that it is written with an elegance of diction and purity of sentiment which would do credit to a more experienced son of Apollo; that the language is peculiarly adapted to the plot, which is of the pathetic kind, and totally different in every respect from a piece of the same name, for which it has been mistaken.

Henry's play was printed in Kingston in 1783, in his absence, and some changes were made in it by the printer, of which he afterward disapproved.

September 1st—*Richard III,* Shakespeare

Richard ....Mr. Godwin
Richmond ....Mr. Moore

King Henry .... Mr. Henry
Buckingham .... Mr. Morris
Catesby .... Mr. Wignell
Lord Mayor .... Mr. Goodman
Duke of York .... Master Woolls
Stanley .... Mr. Dermot
Ratcliffe .... Mr. Woolls
Norfolk .... Mr. Morales
Tressel .... Mr. Hallam
Queen Elizabeth .... Mrs. Morris
Duchess of York .... Miss Storer
Lady Ann .... Mrs. Godwin

Lilliputian Camp, Anonymous

This is Mr. Godwin's benefit and we see that he has acquired a wife. She will share his sorrows and joys for many years to come.

It must have sounded odd, amid all the alarms and excursion of war, to have heard Gloucester read the lines—

Our bruis'd arms hung up for monuments;
Our stern alarums changed to merry meetings,
Our dreadful marches to delightful measures,
Grim-visaged war hath smooth'd his wrinkled front.

September 15th —*Rivals,* Sheridan
Reprisal, Dr. Smollett

September 22nd—*Constant Couple,* Farquhar
Genii, Garrick

This is Master Woolls's benefit and he also shall have his casts printed in full.

Constant Couple, Farquhar

Sir Harry Wildair .... Mr. Hallam
Col. Standard .... Mr. Wignell

Alderman Smuggler .... Mr. Morris
Vizard .... Mr. Dermot
Young Clincher .... Mr. Godwin
Dicky .... Mr. Woolls
Tom Errand .... Mr. Morales
Servant .... Master Woolls
Beau Clincher .... Mr. Goodman
Angelica .... Miss Storer
Parly .... Miss Wainwright
Lady Darling .... Mrs. Hamilton
Lady Lurewell .... Mrs. Morris

Genii, Garrick

The Characters by

Mr. Goodman   Mr. Morris
Mr. Wignell   Mr. Woolls
Mr. Morales   Miss Storer
Mrs. Morris   Mrs. Hamilton

At the end of the third act of the *Constant Couple*,
Master Woolls recited Shakespeare's "Seven Ages,"
and between the play and the pantomime, "The Buck's
Ramble."

Then on September 29, 1781, readers of the *Royal
Gazette* encountered this "card":

Miss Cheer presents her respects to the public and at the
same time that she takes this method of informing them
that a Play will be performed for her benefit, on Saturday the 6th of October, she wishes to obviate some objec-
tions which she hears are made to a farce which is to be
presented the same night, and to declare, that nothing is
so foreign from her intentions, as any idea of offending a
public from whom she has received the greatest obligations:

She hears it has been objected, that the Heroine of the Farce, whom she intended for as finished a character as her humble abilities would enable her to draw, should even for a short time assume the dialect peculiar to a few in this Island; but when she recollects the success the Irish Widow met with in Dublin, who assumes the *Brogue* in order to disgust a disagreeable lover, and the success that Maria, in her assumed character in the Citizen, meets with in London; as she is persuaded that the public of Jamaica yield to none in candour and discernment, so she has no doubt but they will, without disapprobation, see the West Indian Lady for a time lay aside the elegance of her character and assume an awkwardness by which she is to get rid of three *English Sharpers,* and reward the passion of a countryman of her own with a large fortune.

October 6th—*Jealous Wife,* Colman

Oakly . . . . Mr. Hallam
Charles . . . . Mr. Wignell
Lord Trinket . . . . Mr. Hughes
Sir Harry Beagle . . . . Mr. Morris
Capt. O'Cutter . . . . Mr. Goodman
Russet . . . . Mr. Dermot
Paris . . . . Mr. Woolls
John . . . . Mr. Morales
Major Oakly . . . . Mr. Henry
Lady Freelove . . . . Mrs. Morris
Harriet . . . . Miss Storer
Toilet . . . . Miss Wainwright
Maid . . . . Mrs. Hamilton
Mrs. Oakly . . . . Miss Cheer

West Indian Lady's Arrival in London,
Miss Cheer

Harvey Lewis . . . . Mr. Hallam
Lord Snap . . . . Mr. Godwin

Sir James Frisk . . . . Mr. Woolls
Mr. Wimble . . . . Mr. Goodman
Charlotte Loftus . . . . Miss Cheer
Belle Hastings . . . . Miss Storer
Sally, Maid to Miss Loftus . . . . Mrs. Hamilton
Four Blacks, Etc.

Final Curtain for Mr. Hughes

Although October will be a busy month, we should divert our attention for a moment to Mr. Hughes of the theatre. He had been with the company since 1773. We see him last in the cast of *The Jealous Wife* on the 6th. His appearances have been rather few and far between. A card in the *Gazette* of July 27 shows that he is leaving the stage: "Ranelagh House will be opened on Thursday next, the 22nd of August by Mr. Hughes, who humbly solicits the Countenance and Patronage of his Friends and the Public."

On the 9th we read what sort of fare Publican Hughes offers.

The undermentioned Ranelagh House Entertainments, with the most assiduous attention, are respectfully offered to the public, by their obliged and
    Very obedient humble servant

    George Hughes

Cold collations from 9 till 11 o'clock

Rich soup, beef steaks or mutton chops from 11 o'clock till one

Elegant dinners provided at the shortest possible notice

The run of the Larder for transient diners

Hot and cold suppers and the very best liquors of all sorts

While occasionally he picks up an outside job of auctioneering, Mr. Hughes, ably supported by Mrs. Hughes, soon gains a reputation for Ranelagh House—Hughes welcoming the guests and keeping an eye on the bar, while his good wife, Katherine, superintends the kitchen and dining room. Ranelagh House had a splendid reputation. The gentry, officers of the barracks and from the ships patronize it. The far-off *Chronicle* of Montego Bay even reported one of its dinners—when Hercules Ross, Esq., of Kingston gave a dinner there for the Governor, General Campbell, General Garth, Lord Charles Greville Montague, and other officers and principal inhabitants.

It would be pleasant to picture Mr. and Mrs. Hughes down the years—he seeing that the wine was wrapped in wet cotton towels to keep it cool; she insisting that the steak be cooked exactly as each guest wished it:—the two waxing comfortably cushioned with this world's goods and living to a ripe old age.

The theatre proposes a send-off for him. It advertises a benefit for Mr. Hughes for October 20th at which *Much Ado About Nothing* will be played, with Hughes as Don Pedro, followed by Garrick's *Irish Widow,* in which he will assume the character of Kecksey. There were to be Country Dances by Godwin and an Epilogue Song by Mrs. Morris. . . . But death came swiftly and unheralded. On the 16th, Mr. Hughes "formerly of the American Company of Comedians" died. What would have been his benefit was turned into a performance for his widow. The bill is changed and Mr. Hallam suggests that, on this date—October 22nd—"the benevolent and humane will, by their appearance at the Theatre, have an opportunity of contributing, in some degree, to the relief of the distressed Widow."

October 22nd—*Beaux' Stratagem*, Farquhar

Archer	Mr. Hallam
Aimwell	Mr. Wignell
Sullen	Mr. Henry
Foigard	Mr. Goodman
Boniface	Mr. Dermot
Gibbet	Mr. Godwin
Sir Ch. Freeman	Mr. Woolls
Hounslow	Mr. Morales
Scrub	Mr. Morris
Dorinda	Mrs. Hamilton
Cherry	Miss Wainwright
Gipsy	Miss Storer
Lady Bountiful	Mrs. Godwin
Mrs. Sullen	Mrs. Morris

Irish Widow, Garrick

Kicksey	Mr. Godwin
Whittle	Mr. Morris
Nephew	Mr. Wignell
Bates	Mr. Dermot
Sir Patrick O'Neal	Mr. Goodman

October 27th —*Recruiting Officer*, Farquhar

Captain Plume	Mr. Hallam
Captain Brayers	Mr. Wignell
Justice Balance	Mr. Morris
Worthy	Mr. Woolls
Bullock	Mr. Goodman
Costar Permain	Mr. Godwin
Tummas Appletree	Mr. Dermot
Sergeant Kite	Mr. Henry
Rose	Miss Wainwright

Melinda .... Mrs. Hamilton
Lucy .... Miss Storer
Sylvia .... Mrs. Morris

Reprisal, Dr. Smollett

Ben Block .... Mr. Hallam
Lieut. O'Clabber .... Mr. Goodman
Ensign M'Claymore .... Mr. Godwin
Heartly .... Mr. Dermot
Brush .... Mr. Morris
Lieut. Lyon .... Mr. Woolls
Mons. Champignon .... Mr. Wignell
Harriet .... Mrs. Hamilton

This is the first time *The Recruiting Officer* has been performed in six years. At the end of the play Mr. Wignell spoke *Joe Haines's Epilogue* riding an Ass, an old diversion the elder Hallam had used at Philadelphia and it always "brought down the house." Between the play and the farce, John Henry recited *Shadows of Shakespeare.* The *Reprisal* concluded with "Rule, Britannia." We also note that Henry and Wignell relinquish a certain sum from this night's box-office receipts to other members of the company.

November 3rd—*Love in a Village,* Bickerstaff
              Devil upon Two Sticks, Foote

This performance, it seems, was for the benefit of Master Woolls and the Company who relinquished the earnings on a benefit previously advertised for them.

December 8th—*Belle's Stratagem,* Mrs. Cowley

Doricourt .... Mr. Hallam
Hardy .... Mr. Morris

Saville ....Mr. Goodman
Sir Geo. Touchwood ....Mr. Wignell
Courtall ....Mr. Godwin
Villers ....Mr. Woolls
Gibson ....Mr. Dermot
Monsieur ....Mr. Morales
Flutter ....Mr. Moore
Mrs. Racket ....Miss Cheer
Lady Frances Touchwood ....A Young Lady
Miss Ogle ....Miss Storer
Kitty Willis ....Mrs. Hamilton
Letitia Hardy ....Mrs. Morris

Kingston Privateer, Pillon

Debenture ....Mr. Morris
Young Belford ....Mr. Hallam
Bronze ....Mr. Wignell
Old Belford ....Mr. Dermot
Wilmot ....Mr. Woolls
Mons. Martinique ....Mr. Godwin
Midships ....Mr. Morales
Capt. Teneriffe ....Mr. Goodman
Fanny ....Miss Wainwright
Adelaide ....Miss Storer
Harriet ....Mrs. Hamilton

This bill, originally advertised for November 24th, was postponed until December 8th. It was the benefit of the Master of the Revels, Lewis Hallam. Who the "Young Lady" was, we have no way of learning, although we suspect she was Miss Tuke. She is given a puff, however, on the occasion of this, "her first appearance on any stage," in the special notice printed in the *Royal Gazette* of December 8th:

We are this evening to be entertained with that first-rate Comedy, the Belle's Stratagem, written by Mrs. Cowley; and as it has never been published, though it ran equal with the School for Scandal, and is as replete with sentiment, and incidents peculiar to high life, as well as the first appearance of a young lady from New York, whose person and figure seem to point her out as an addition to our stage, tho' the character of Lady Frances Touchwood does not seem calculated to show a new actress to the greatest advantage, being of a singular cast, and one that she cannot have been a copy of.

The entertainment of the Kingston Privateer, is an alteration from that much-admired piece of Mr. Pillon's the *Liverpool Prize,* which cannot fail of pleasing: These added to its being for the benefit of Mr. Hallam (as Master of the Revels), whose readiness on all occasions to oblige this community, cannot fail of procuring a full and splendid house.

Mr. Moore at Montego Bay

In this cast of December 8th we are glad to see Mr. Moore's name again. He has been missing from the Kingston bills and we hear of him in a roundabout way. The *Cornwall Chronicle* prints in its issue of October 13th a news item, doubtless inspired, to this effect:

We hear Mr. Moore, who has been delivering the Lecture on Heads and other entertainments, with universal applause, in Kingston and Spanish Town, is on his passage for this quarter, where he intends repeating the same; and, from the general approbation he has met with, we may expect both pleasure and amusement.

He was coming to Montego Bay by boat. The roads across the island in those days were execrable. Boat travel in a little island trawler that stopped at every port was safer and much more comfortable than the road.

So Mr. Moore lands in the Bay and on November 6th,

"by Particular Desire," delivers the *Lecture on Heads* at Mr. Booth's Long Room and follows it with other entertainments. It had been two years now since the ladies and gentlemen of the town and the plantations about Montego Bay had enjoyed theatrical entertainments. They came in sufficient numbers to encourage Moore, for on the 10th he pays his respects to them and "begs leave to assure them language is too weak to express his Gratitude for the generous support and universal approbation he has met with; and at the same time begs leave to acquaint them, after he has visited Martha-Brae, etc., he intends returning to Montego Bay again." He comes back after his little tour, thanks to ladies and gentlemen of Montego Bay and Martha-Brae for "their brilliant and frequent appearance at his repeated performances," and on the 17th reports that he is obliged to go to Town, as Kingston was universally called, but will attend the Savanna-la-Mar court, then proceed to Lucea and back to Montego Bay, Martha-Brae, and St. Ann's—in fact, a tour of the west-and north-shore sugar ports.

These names are all well known to visitors trooping down to Jamaica—Savanna-la-Mar, with its one wide street running down to the sea front; Lucea, with its old church and fort on the headland overlooking a magnificent harbor; St. Ann's, the thriving town of a parish of the same name and once a Spanish settlement. But Martha-Brae may prove a puzzle. Today it is nothing more than a cluster of houses a mile or so inland behind Falmouth; yet in the days of which we read it was an important place, with a courthouse, and was quite a swirling little center of social and commercial life. The few scattered buildings on the bay that subsequently grew into the present town of Falmouth were referred to as "the Point."

Meantime, while Mr. Moore is making his Thespian way around the north shore, let us cast an eye on the Northern Colonies.

Revolutionary Events

A succession of dates catches our attention—September 30th to October 19th. During this period the company had played *The Jealous Wife* and Miss Cheer's *West Indian Lady's Arrival in London*. Moore leaves Kingston for Montego Bay to deliver the *Lecture on Heads*. One would think, from the placid way these Thespians go about their business, that world events were not happening. Nevertheless, between September 30th and October 19, 1781, Lord Cornwallis was besieged at Yorktown and on the latter date he surrendered to Washington, seven thousand British soldiers grounding their arms. This defeat was greatly assisted by the French fleet under De Grasse who had bottled up the British by closing Chesapeake Bay. His presence no longer required, De Grasse turned his vessels southward to harry British islands and shipping in the Caribbean. The year closed with Britain having lost Pensacola, Tobago, St. Eustatius, Demerara, Essequibo in British Guiana, St. Kitts, Nevis, and Montserrat. The prospect for Britain on this side the Atlantic was very dark.

These matters of world war and world politics were not bothering Mr. Moore or the American Company of Comedians. They kept on playing right up through December, although by that time news of Cornwallis' defeat and De Grasse's sailing had reached the island. Mr. Moore was especially anxious.

He was due a benefit. Hallam, Henry, Miss Cheer, the Woolls' children—all had had their benefits. It was his turn next. His benefit is slated for December 19th—*Belle's Stratagem, Florizel and Perdita,* a musical interlude called *Linco's Travels,* and a Masonic Oration by Moore to his fellow Masons—it was to be a full program. But the performance had to be postponed because Mrs. Hamilton fell sick. It is billed for the 22nd, and again illness in the company prevents the play. He makes a third try, however—the benefit will surely be given on January 5, 1782, and this time may Dame Fortune smile on him.

CHAPTER VII

1782

A Busy Year for the Comedians—Jamaica Is Saved by Rodney—Feelers for American Theatrical Support—Three-Fingered Jack

THE New Year did shine on Mr. Moore. We hope the audience was large enough to make that patient and oft-postponed actor feel Dame Fortune on his side once more. For his benefit on January 5th, the company gave a full measure of entertainment. It was also a promising indication of what they would offer theatregoers of Kingston in the busy year of 1782.

So we pick up the playbook to record Mr. Moore's benefit and the performances that follow:

January 5th—*King Henry IV*, Shakespeare
with the Humours of Sir John Falstaff

Hotspur ....Mr. Hallam
Prince of Wales ....Mr. Wignell
King ....Mr. Morris
Sir Walter Blunt ....Mr. Goodman
Poins ....Mr. Godwin
Bardolph ....Mr. Dermot
Northumberland ....Mr. Woolls
Westmoreland ....Mr. Morales
Prince John of Lancaster ....Master Woolls
1st Carrier ....Mr. Goodman
2nd Carrier ....Mr. Morales
Sir John Falstaff ....Mr. Moore

Hostess ....Miss Wainwright
Lady Percy ....Mrs. Morris

Linco's Travels, a musical Interlude by Garrick, came after the play. In this is given a Description of France, Germany, Italy, and England. The cast was:

Linco (the merry Shepherd) ....Mr. Moore
Clown ....Mr. Wignell
Old Woman ....Mr. Morales

Florizel and Perdita, or the *Sheep-Shearing*
from Shakespeare's *Winter's Tale*

Florizel ....Mr. Wignell
Alson ....Mr. Goodman
Autolicus ....Mr. Moore
Camillo ....Mr. Dermot
Clown ....Mr. Morris
The King ....Mr. Hallam
Perdita ....Mrs. Morris

January 19th—*Grecian Daughter,* Murphy

Evander ....Mr. Hallam
Philotas ....Mr. Wignell
Phocion ....Mr. Goodman
Melanthon ....Mr. Dermot
Arcas ....Mr. Morris
Calippus ....Mr. Woolls
Dionysus ....Mr. Moore
Erixene ....Mrs. Godwin
Euphrasia ....Mrs. Morris

After the play, Mr. Godwin recited an epilogue, "in the character of *Somebody,* with a *malicious* Design against *Nobody*"; a pantomime interlude called "A New Year's Gift"; the first scene from *Harlequin Collector,*

including a comic dance, the *Drunken Peasant,* and a hornpipe by Godwin. This *Drunken Peasant* was one of Godwin's favorite and oldest divertissements; he had given
it when he was playing with the Virginia Company of
Comedians.

Harlequin Collector

Harlequin .... Mr. Godwin
Magic (with a song) .... Mr. Woolls
Masquerade Pye Woman .... Master Woolls
Dutchman .... Mr. Dermot
Clown .... Mr. Moore

After the interlude came a favorite Scotch song,
"Thro' the Wood, Laddie," sung by Miss Wainwright,
and a new song, "The Kingston Grenadiers," by Godwin;
and then the farce (never performed here)—

A Trip to Dover, or The Cheats of Scapin

Old Gripe .... Mr. Godwin
Leander .... Mr. Hallam
Octavian .... Mr. Wignell
Shist .... Mr. Dermot
Thrifty .... Mr. Morales
Scapin .... Mr. Morris
Clara .... Mrs. Godwin
Lucia .... Miss Wainwright

This performance of January 19th was a benefit for
Mr. and Mrs. Godwin. He, poor fellow, had suffered a
long and painful illness, but promised to exert "every
Ability in his Power to render the Entertainments for the
night worthy Attention." We hope the audience re-
sponded generously.

At the end of the notice we find that this performance,

slated for January 16th, had to be postponed till the 19th on account of the General Muster. . . . The ominous thud of drums on the horizon! Mr. Godwin's new song about the Kingston Grenadiers may well have been a timely concession to current military stirrings.

February 7th—*Scandal Club, or Virtue in Danger,* by a West Indian Lady

Mr. Tindar	Mr. Hallam
True Love	Mr. Wignell
Hickabout Bareface	Mr. Moore
Trelooby Babble	Mr. Dermot
Timothy Lucher	Mr. Godwin
Richard Tatter	Mr. Woolls
Sneak	Mr. Morales
Brush	A Young Gentleman
Counsellor Clearpoint	Mr. Morris
Counsellor Puzzle	Mr. Goodman
Fidget	Mrs. Hamilton
Harriet Clever	A Young Lady (her second appearance on any stage)
Mrs. Tinder	Mrs. Morris

A prologue, written by a Lady, was spoken by Mr. Goodman. Mr. Moore delivered a Masonic Oration "in which the Lessons of that Order are poetically pictured and add a lustre to Masonry." Next came the pantomime interlude, *A New Year's Gift.*

Catherine and Petruchio, Shakespeare

Petruchio	Mr. Goodman
Baptista	Mr. Morales
Pedro	Mr. Woolls
Biondello	Mr. Wignell
Hortensio	Mr. Dermot

Taylor ....Mr. Godwin
Grumio ....Mr. Morris
Bianca ....Mrs. Hamilton
Curtis .... Miss Wainwright
Catherine ....Mrs. Morris

To top off Shakespeare, the management displayed "A Grand Set of Chinese and Italian Fire-Works." This item carries us back to the Douglass Company in Philadelphia, where he tried the same attraction for the first time on December 9, 1768—"An Elegant Sett of Fireworks" displayed by two Italian brothers, and he had the ceiling "opened to carry off the Smoak." [1] Maybe the same was done at Kingston. We marvel at Hallam's attempting such a dangerous display in a flimsy wooden building. From the advertisement, we gather that Mr. Goodman had charge of the fireworks, which was natural for one of a scientific mind.

Mr. Goodman apparently resided at Spanish Town for a time and there his interest in scientific affairs of the day attracted attention and brought him the friendship of men of like mind. In this period of the eighteenth century, it will be remembered, an interest in science was considered among the requisites for a cultured gentleman. Jamaica was not lacking in men of this type; both Dr. Benjamin Moseley, who wrote learnedly on fevers and on coffee, and Dr. Dancer, the island botanist, were members of the American Philosophical Society.

War Stirrings on the Island

Either the theatre was interrupted by internal troubles or else play advertisements are lacking, for March passes without record of a performance. Yes, there were wars and rumors of wars all around. On the 10th of March, by virtue of a billet from the deputy Quartermaster General, the St. Mary's and St. George's regiments of foot militia —some two hundred men—took possession of Ranelagh House, where Mrs. Hughes, since her husband's death the previous October, had struggled to keep the place going. The rent was £200 a year and the Hugheses had laid out a considerable sum on furniture, fixtures, papering, and painting. Here the militia stayed till May 3rd. Then in April, when Rodney's fleet returned to Kingston, her house was taken again for prisoners—and what these Frenchies did to her furniture and wallpaper was beyond description. The following year, December 18, 1783, the Assembly awarded Katherine Hughes £83 5s 7½d damages.[2]

These early days of April, 1782, saw the darkest clouds of apprehension settle over Jamaica. The previous fall the French fleet, commanded by De Grasse, had been released from service in the Northern Colonies after the surrender of Cornwallis at Yorktown. It had headed toward the Caribbean, and by the end of the year had captured St. Kitts, Nevis, and Montserrat. Jamaica, the largest and most important of the British West Indian islands, would inevitably be the next.

To stem the tide of his success, Britain called Rodney back into action. Rodney knew the Caribbean well. For three and a half years he had been on the Jamaica station. A strict disciplinarian and a man of great ability, Rodney had brought Port Royal up to a point of splendid efficiency—laid down a new water supply, built docks and arsenals, and practiced his fleet constantly. If anyone could meet the situation, Rodney was the man.

He took command of the West Indian station in January, 1782. At sea he joined with the forces of Admiral Sir Samuel Hood, and the combined fleets made a presentable armada. Presentable, but not efficient. Rodney put in at St. Lucia, and began a hectic and thorough overhauling and drilling of his fleet. Meantime, Count de Grasse had been doing the same at Martinique, and took on board six thousand troops designed to invade Jamaica. His plan was to join forces with the Spanish at Cape François, St. Domingo, which would increase his fleet to sixty ships of the line. Together they would wipe out the British fleet, and go on to Jamaica. The Spaniards had agreed on Jamaica as their share of the booty. Their old possession would be once more back in their hands.

On the island itself defensive preparations were going on at top speed under the direction of Colonel Edward Marcus Depard. Kingston had suffered a destructive fire, and half the town was in ashes: the damage had amounted to £300,000 sterling. The militia was called up. Jamaica sent a company of marines to join Rodney. Extra taxation was imposed to meet the cost of the defense. Roads were rendered impassable by felling trees across them. Every man did his bit. Down at the Apostle's Battery in the harbor, David Douglass was serving. All that could be done was done.

The fate of Jamaica hung on Rodney.

Probably on the principle that the populace had better be amused in its darkest hours, the Lieutenant Governor gave his permission for the Comedians to act. And so, "by particular desire"—

April 6th—*Richard III*, Shakespeare

King Richard .... Mr. Hallam
King Henry .... Mr. Moore
Buckingham .... Mr. Morris
Tressel .... Mr. Wignell
Stanley .... Mr. Dermot
Ratcliff .... Mr. Woolls
Richmond .... Mr. Goodman
Lady Anne .... Mrs. Hamilton
Duchess of York .... Miss Wainwright

Apprentice, Murphy

Dick .... Mr. Moore
Charlotte .... Miss Wainwright

A week passes. A great event has been happening off Martinique. But news traveled slowly in those days. The company gives another performance to a tense audience.

April 15th—*Countess of Salisbury*, Hartson

Alwin .... Mr. Hallam
Gray .... Mr. Goodman
Moreton .... Mr. Morris
Lord William .... Master Woolls
Lerocher .... Mr. Woolls
Peasant .... Mr. Godwin
Oswald .... Mr. Morales
Raymond .... Mr. Wignell
Eleanor .... Miss Storer
Countess of Salisbury .... Mrs. Morris

Mock Doctor, Fielding

Gregory .... Mr. Morris
Sir Jasper .... Mr. Dermot

Harry .... Mr. Wignell
James .... Mr. Goodman
Squire Robert .... Mr. Morales
Leander .... Mr. Woolls
Charlotte .... Miss Storer
Dorcas .... Miss Wainwright

Still no news from Rodney. Trees lie across the roads. Militia hurry in and out of Ranelagh House. Officers and messengers gallop back and forth the long way from Kingston to Spanish Town. Depard goes from battery to battery to see that all is ready should enemy ships appear on the horizon off Port Royal. His lookouts are stationed at Salt Pond Hill and Green Bay opposite Port Royal— Rodney's old observation posts. Still another week, and no word from Rodney. The company plays on:

April 20th—*Grecian Daughter*, Murphy

With the same cast as on January 19th, except that Miss Storer replaces Mrs. Godwin in the role of Erixine

King and Miller of Mansfield, Dodsley

King .... Mr. Moore
Richard .... Mr. Wignell
Joe (with a song) .... Mr. Woolls
Lord Lurewell .... Mr. Dermot
The Miller .... Mr. Morris
Margery .... Miss Wainwright
Kate .... Mrs. Hamilton
Peggy .... Miss Storer

April 25th dawns. A fast boat slips by the fortress of Port Royal. A letter from Rodney. It was written on the 14th and has been all this time coming: Rodney dated it "between Guadaloupe and Montserrat" and announced his victory over De Grasse. Four days later, just before sunset, the long line of Rodney's tall ship is sighted and nine prizes, including the famous *Ville de Paris,* swing under the cover of the Port Royal guns. Three thousand of De Grasse's six thousand men designed to invade Jamaica had been killed; the rest were brought to Jamaica as prisoners. The island goes into a frenzy of rejoicing.

Evidently planned before this good news arrived, the Free Masons conduct a charity benefit performance. The notice in the *Royal Gazette* reads:

By Order of the Right Worshipful Grand Master of Free and Accepted Masons, under the Constitution of England. On Saturday evening, the 27th of April, will be performed a Comedy called The School for Scandal
(Written by R. B. Sheridan, Esq.)
With a Masonic Prelude and Epilogue. To which will be added an Entertainment called High Life Below Stairs.
The Brethren are desired to meet at half past 6 o'clock precisely, at the House of Brother Davidson, in Church Street, in their proper Cloathing; from thence to accompany the Right Worshipful Grand Master to the Theatre.
W. Walker, G. Sec.

The Grand Master of English Masons in Jamaica at this time was Rear Admiral, Sir Peter Parker, patron and lifelong friend of Nelson and at the time commander of Port Royal. The "proper cloathing" referred to in the notice doubtless meant that the Brethren wore their aprons and the officers their jewels and the Craft evidently marched in procession to the theatre, as was the custom in those days.

The cast and program for this evening were:

April 27th—*School for Scandal,* Sheridan

Peter Teazle	Mr. Goodman
Sir Oliver Surface	Mr. Morris
Joseph Surface	Mr. Wignell
Sir Benjamin Backbite	Mr. Moore
Crabtree	Mr. Dermot
Rowley	Mr. Woolls
Moses	Mr. Morales
Charles Surface	Mr. Hallam
Lady Sneerwell	Mrs. Hamilton
Mrs. Candour	Miss Wainwright
Maria	Miss Storer
Lady Teazle	Mrs. Morris

Before the play was recited a Masonic prelude in which Mr. Wignell played Sir Timothy Tattle, a fop, and Mr. Moore a Master Mason. After the play Mrs. Morris recited a Masonic epilogue and Mr. Woolls sang a Masonic song. This song, which began,

> When the Deity's word
> Thro' all Chaos was heard

appeared in *The Elements of Free-Masonry Delineated,* which Mr. Moore printed at Douglass & Aikman's in Kingston in July, 1782. From the subscribers to this book and from later evidence, it is safe to say that David Douglass, Lewis Hallam, Jr., Mr. Owen, Mr. Morris, Mr. Dermot, Isaac Morales, Stephen Woolls, Richard Goodman, and Thomas Wignell were Masons.

High Life Below Stairs, Townley

Lovel	Mr. Hallam
Sir Harry	Mr. Godwin
Lord Duke	Mr. Wignell

Philip ....Mr. Morris
Freeman ....Mr. Goodman
Coachman ....Mr. Woolls
Kingston ....Mr. Dermot
Lady Charlotte ....Miss Wainwright
Lady Bab ....Mrs. Hamilton
Chloe ....Mr. Morales
Kitty (with a song) ....Mrs. Morris

The Play Goes On

May 4th—*Countess of Salisbury*, Hartson

The same cast as April 15th performance

Reprisal or The Tars of Old England, Smollett

Mons. Champignon ....Mr. Wignell
Lieut. O'Clabber ....Mr. Goodman
Ensign McClaymore ....Mr. Godwin
Heartly ....Mr. Dermot
Brush ....Mr. Morris
Ben Block ....Mr. Hallam
Harriet ....Miss Kirk

The bill ended with a hornpipe and the singing of "Rule, Britannia," which must have brought the audience to its feet.

We note a new name here—Miss Kirk's. Alas, she will not be with us for long.

May 11th—*School for Scandal*, Sheridan

The cast is as before except that Mr. Godwin plays Sir Benjamin Backbite in place of Mr. Moore. Sheridan's plays were all the rage in England. Hallam produced them in Jamaica as fast as he was able to procure them.

Mock Doctor, Fielding

Here, too, the cast is changed slightly from that of April 15th. These comedians could jump into each other's parts with little effort.

May 18th—*Cymbeline*, Shakespeare

Posthumous Leonatus . . . . Mr. Hallam
Cymbeline . . . . Mr. Morris
Cloten . . . . Mr. Moore
Belarius . . . . Mr. Goodman
Guiderius . . . . A Gentleman (being his
                                          first appearance)
Arviragus . . . . Mr. Woolls
Caius Lucius . . . . Mr. Godwin
Pisanio . . . . Mr. Dermot
Cornelius . . . . Mr. Morales
Iachimo . . . . Mr. Wignell
Queen . . . . Miss Kirk
Helena . . . . Miss Storer
Imogen . . . . Mrs. Morris

Invasion or A Trip to Brighthelmstone, Pilon

Sir John Evergreen . . . . Mr. Moore
Charles Evergreen . . . . Mr. Hallam
Beaufort . . . . Mr. Woolls
Roger . . . . Mr. Morris
Sergeant Drill . . . . Mr. Goodman
Tattoo . . . . Mr. Godwin
Chameleon . . . . Mr. Wignell
Emily . . . . Miss Kirk
Brussels . . . . Mrs. Hamilton
Sally . . . . Miss Storer
Cook . . . . Mr. Dermot
Lady Catherine Rouge . . . . Miss Wainwright

The advertisement in the *Gazette* states that *Cym-*

beline had not been acted in Jamaica "these four years" and *The Invasion* had never been performed here.

June 1st—*Constant Couple, or A Trip to the Jubilee,*
        Farquhar

Sir Harry Wildair ....Mr. Hallam
Col. Standard ....Mr. Wignell
Alderman Smuggler ....Mr. Morris
Young Clincher ....Mr. Moore
Vizard ....Mr. Dermot
Dicky ....Mr. Woolls
Beau Clincher ....Mr. Goodman
Angelica ....Miss Storer
Lady Darling ....Mrs. Hamilton
Parly ....Miss Wainwright
Lady Lurewell ....Mrs. Morris

Invasion

Cast as before, except that Mr. Morales supplanted Mr. Godwin as Tattoo

June 15th—*Belle's Stratagem,* Mrs. Cowley

Doricourt ....Mr. Hallam
Hardy ....Mr. Morris
Sir George Touchwood ....Mr. Wignell
Courtall ....Mr. Dermot
Saville ....Mr. Goodman
Villers ....Mr. Woolls
Monsieur ....Mr. Morales
Flutter.......................Mr. Moore
Lady Racket ....Miss Cheer
Lady Frances Touchwood ....Miss Kirk
Miss Ogle ....Miss Storer
Kitty Willis ....Mrs. Hamilton
Letitia Hardy ....Mrs. Morris

This play had been acted first at Covent Garden in
1780, and the book did not appear until 1782. Mr. Hallam must have had means of getting the published script
fresh from the printer.

King and Miller of Mansfield, Dodsley
The cast as before

June 22nd—*Beaux' Stratagem,* Farquhar

Archer	Mr. Hallam
Aimwell	Mr. Wignell
Sullen	Mr. Moore
Foigard	Mr. Goodman
Boniface	Mr. Dermot
Gibbet	Mr. Woolls
Hounslow	Mr. Morales
Scrub	Mr. Morris
Dorinda	Mrs. Hamilton
Cherry	Miss Wainwright
Gipsy	Miss Storer
Mrs. Sullen	Mrs. Morris

Divorce, Jackman

Sir Harry Trifle	Mr. Hallam
Qui Tam	Mr. Morris
Tom	Mr. Wignell
Sambo	Mr. Dermot
Timothy	Mr. Morales
Dennis O'Dougherty	Mr. Goodman
Lady Harriet Trifle	Miss Storer
Biddy	Miss Wainwright
Mrs. Aniseed	Mrs. Hamilton

July 3rd—*Edward and Eleonora,* Hull (altered from
Thompson)

Edward	Mr. Wignell

Gloucester ....Mr. Morris
Theald ....Mr. Woolls
Assassin ....Mr. Dermot
Officer ....Mr. Morales
Selim ....Mr. Goodman
Daraxa ....Miss Cheer
Eleonora ....Mrs. Morris

After this tragedy is inserted a quite unauthorized kind of diversion for the legitimate stage: Signor La Rosa and family, fresh from Sadlers Wells, make their first appearance in the island. Their act consisted of balancing and tumbling and feats of strength and activity.

Definitely their appearances in these bills amount to a rift in the lute. What do Hallam and Henry think of this invasion of their realm? Well, as we shall see later, Henry is not present to express an opinion, but Hallam, who continues to appear on the bills, evidently is acquiescent.

Nevertheless, Mr. T. Wignell apparently scents trouble, and is prepared to take cover. On June 20th he had advertised in the *Gazette* that he did seal engraving of coats of arms, crests, cyphers, etc., on stone, with neatness and dispatch.

And since we have turned aside from the playbook for a moment, let us sympathize with Mr. Morris. In the *Gazette* of July 13th he advertises:

Flew Away
Last Thursday morning from the house of Mr. Morris near the upper end of Orange Street,
A small green Paroquet
Speaks remarkably well.
A handsome reward will be thankfully given on delivering it as above, or at the stage door of the Theatre.

Perhaps Owen Morris and his wife had taught it to
repeat some of their lines! We are glad it wasn't a dog.
A lost paroquet, yes; a dog, never.

Back to the playbook and the company toiling away in
Kingston's soggy heat.

July 6th—*King Henry IV*, Shakespeare, with the Humors
of Sir John Falstaff.

The cast is the same as on January 5th, except that
instead of Mr. Moore playing Falstaff, the role is supported "for this night only, by a Gentleman for his
Amusement, being his First Appearance on any Stage."
Signor La Rosa and his family fill the rest of the bill.

July 13th—*A Bold Stroke for a Wife*, Mrs. Centlivre

Col. Feignwell .... Mr. Moore
Sir Philip Modelove .... Mr. Wignell
Periwinkle .... Mr. Morris
Freeman .... Mr. Dermot
Sackbut .... Mr. Woolls
Truelove .... Mr. Morales
Obadiah Prim .... Mr. Goodman
Mrs. Prim .... Mrs. Hamilton
Masked Lady .... Miss Wainwright
Betty .... Miss Storer
Anne Lovely .... Miss Cheer

The La Rosas added tumbling on a slack rope to the
bill.

August 10th—*Wonder! A Woman Keeps a Secret!* Mrs.
Centlivre

Don Felix .... Mr. Hallam
Colonel Briton .... Mr. Wignell
Don Pedro .... Mr. Goodman

Gibby ....Mr. Godwin
Don Lopez ....Mr. Morales
Frederick ....Mr. Woolls
Lissardo ....Mr. Moore
Isabella ....Miss Storer
Flora ....Miss Wainwright
Inez ....Mrs. Morris
Violante ....Miss Cheer

Then the La Rosa tribe again. Miss Cheer, by the way, must have felt at home in this role of *Violante:* it was that in which she made her American debut years before, at Charleston.

August 17th—*Jane Shore,* Rowe

Duke of Gloster ....Mr. Hallam
Dumont ....Mr. Moore
Belmour ....Mr. Godwin
Ratcliffe ....Mr. Woolls
Porter ....Mr. Morales
Earl of Derby ....Mr. Goodman
Lord Hastings ....Mr. Wignell
Alicia ....Miss Cheer
Jane Shore ....Mrs. Morris

Citizen, Murphy

Young Philpot ....Mr. Wignell
Young Wilding ....Mr. Hallam
Sir Jasper Wilding ....Mr. Moore
Beaufort ....Mr. Woolls
Dapper ....Mr. Goodman
Quilldrive ....Mr. Morales
Old Philpot ....Mr. Godwin
Corinna ....Miss Storer
Maria ....Miss Wainwright

Thank Heavens, we are done with the La Rosa clan

and their tumbling! From now on, the theatre continues relatively legitimate.

September 14th—*Douglas,* Home

Norval Douglas .... A Young Gentleman,
　　　　　　　　　　　　　his second appearance
Lord Randolph .... Mr. Goodman
Glenalvon .... Mr. Wignell
1st Officer .... Mr. Woolls
2nd Officer .... Mr. Morales
Old Norval .... Mr. Moore
Anna .... Miss Storer
Matilda .... Miss Cheer

The bill specifies that "the Character of Douglas to be dressed in the Habit of the Country." The importance made of this matter confirms our view, expressed in a previous chapter, that in the ordinary run of performances, any old breeches and a fancy coat usually made up the costume at the time.

Miss in Her Teens, Garrick

Capt. Flash .... Mr. Wignell
Capt. Loveit .... Mr. Hallam
Puff .... Mr. Morris
Fribble .... Mr. Moore
Tag .... Miss Wainwright
Miss Biddy Bellair .... Miss Storer

This bill was originally advertised for August 31st, and with *The Citizen* for an afterpiece, but Miss Cheer, having had an accident, it was postponed till the 14th of September.

The advertisement indicates that Hallam is having trouble with the young bucks again. The notice reads:

"The Scenes for some time past having been so crowded as in great measure to impede the Performance, it is humbly hoped that no Gentleman will be offended if, for the future, they are denied Admittance there on any Pretence whatsoever. The Duty the Performers owe to the Public renders this Address absolutely necessary."

September 21st—*Fair Penitent,* Rowe

Lothario . . . . By the Young Gentleman
                           who performed Douglas
Rosano . . . . .By a Gentleman
                           for his amusement
Horatio . . . . .Mr. Moore
Sciolto . . . . .Mr. Hallam
Lavinia . . . . .Miss Storer
Calista . . . . Mrs Morris

King and Miller of Mansfield, Dodsley

The same cast as on April 13th

This is the last time Mr. Hallam's name will appear on any Jamaica bill of which we have record. His absence will be explained later.

And since we like to keep track of old friends in the company, we might jot down the fact that Katherine Hughes, her Ranelagh House ruined by the militia, advertises "that she has taken that large, airy, well-known and accustomed Lodging-House, formerly kept by the late Mrs. Todd, which she is fitting up in the most elegant stile, for the reception of those who may favour her with their commands." She has also rented a commodious range of stabling and coach houses, and invites gentlemen from the country.

Military Thespians Again

At this point the theatre is invaded by the Army. The notice reads: "The peculiar distress of a very unfortunate Lady, has induced a few Gentlemen of the Army to perform a Play at the Theatre in this Town for her sole Benefit. The patronage of a generous Public, and the known characteristics of this Island (Charity and Benevolence) are earnestly solicited on the occasion."

September 28th—*The Orphan,* Otway
     Lethe, Garrick

Bucks Have at Ye All came in the interlude. The cast was mainly military, supported by members of the company. This kind gesture gave birth to another. In appreciation of the company's assistance, the military Thespians give a performance for the benefit of the house:

October 5th— *Beaux' Stratagem,* Farquhar
     Lethe, Garrick

October 16th—*Beaux' Stratagem,* Farquhar
     Chrononhotonthologos

For the third time the bill is presented by Army officers, this time at the special request of the Free Masons for the benefit of the late inhabitants of Honduras "who have suffered near Three Years Captivity." The divertissement with the unpronounceable name is listed as "the most Tragical Tragedy that ever was Tragedised on any Tragical Stage." The parts, both male and female, were performed by gentlemen. The whole town turned out for this benefit.

The Provincial Grand Master and his officers and

about sixty Brethren ("they contributed liberally to the charity") escorted the Rt. Hon. Lord Charles Montague in solemn procession to the theatre preceded by the band of the Duke of Cumberland's regiment, "playing grand masonic pieces." The charity by this means collected, free of all expenses, the handsome sum of £271 5s 1d, which was handed over to a committee to distribute among the distressed.

October 29th—*Henry IV*, Shakespeare

The company is back in the theatre again, without aid of the Army. Unfortunately, the afterpiece of this performance is not recorded.

November 2nd—*Edward and Eleonora*, Hull (altered from Thompson)

This cast is pretty much as on July 3rd, except that now Mr. Godwin supplants Mr. Morales as Assassin, and Miss Storer takes Miss Cheer's place as Daraxa.

High Life Below Stairs, Townley

The cast is substantially the same as on April 27th, except that whereas then Hallam played Lovel, now Moore assumes the role. The bill finished with a mock minuet by Sir Harry and Miss Kitty.

November 12th—*Richard III*, Shakespeare

Once again the cast is the same as on April 6th, save that Mr. Roberts plays Richard, which Hallam performed on that date. Mr. Roberts is advertised as playing for his own amusement, "being his second appearance in that character." Let's see: the last time *Richard III* was played was September 1, 1781, and Mr. Godwin played Richard. From the notice, then, we gather that there was another presentation of *Richard III* of which we have no record.

November 16th—*Recruiting Officer,* Farquhar
    Love à-la-Mode, Macklin

This is a benefit by the Army for the American Company of Comedians. In the entertainment, Sylvia is played by a gentleman. And between that and the play came parts of the *Lecture on Heads,* "attempted by an officer."

Before this, on the 14th, at Spanish Town, had been given a concert for a distressed widow and her daughter.

November 27th—*West Indian,* Cumberland
    Spanish Fryar, Dryden

Here we have no casts recorded. It was originally planned to play *The Siege of Damascus,* but it had to be postponed. Meantime, Owen Morris has had another loss. In July, it was the paroquet that flew away. This time it's a watch—but it didn't fly. Read Morris' card in the *Gazette* of November 29th.

Stolen, on the night of the 16th inst. out of the Dressing Room of the Theatre (supposed by a Negro) A Gold Watch, horizontal, capped and jewelled, maker's name, Job Panell (number forgot) the outside case thin. Whoever delivers it at the Royal Gazette Printing Office or at the Stage Door of the Theatre, will receive half a Joe and no questions asked.

But often the sour is followed by the sweet, and a sunny day follows a night of rain. At Spanish Town, on December 6th, a concert and ball is given in the Long Room for the benefit of Mrs. Morris. The tickets were only a pistole each, and we hope lots of people bought them!

On December 13, at King's House in Spanish Town, a ball was given in honor of His Majesty's Birthday. We probably wouldn't take much notice of it except that the advertisement affords the first Jamaican instance of one-way amusement traffic, thus: "In order to prevent Confusion, Ladies and Gentlemen are requested to order their Carriages to come up by the Old Court House, and go off by the Long Room, both before and after the Ball."

That brings us to the end of a year in which we have sat through twenty-five performances and seen thirty-eight plays. We make special note of this fact, because the only previous historian of the Jamaica Theatre, George O. Seilhamer, states: "The American Company in Jamaica had seen its best days. Early in 1782 it disbanded for a time at least. . . . The venture while it lasted was scarcely a profitable one."

Hallam and Henry Depart

It is true that after that September 21st performance of *The Fair Penitent,* Hallam's name no longer appears on the bills, and that at no time in 1782 does Mr. Henry's name appear. Hallam is believed to have gone to England and we shall not see him again until January, 1784, but Henry, we know, went to the States. Not only were the Revolutionary War hostilities drawing to a close, but property rights belonging to the American Company were being invaded. Up in Philadelphia, despite the anti-amusement attitude of officials, the Southwark Theatre had been used by a Mr. Templeman, who put on a slack-wire show. In Baltimore and Annapolis a company headed by Lindsay and Wall had kept plays going right through the Revolution. Henry, hearing of this, resolved to reinstate the theatre in the Northern Colonies. He left Jamaica in 1782 for that purpose.

Henry first put in his appearance at Annapolis, where he secured the passage of an act by the Maryland Assembly confirming to the members of the American Company of Comedians the title to the theatre they had built in that city early in 1771. The bill was passed in May. This accomplished, Henry moved on to Philadelphia where, on July 1, 1782, he wrote a letter to William Moore, President of the Supreme Executive Council of Pennsylvania, asking that property rights in theatres built by David Douglass be secured. He also sounded out the authorities on their attitude toward opening the theatre to dramatic performances. An illiberal policy still prevailed. Henry's plea to be allowed to give moral lectures shattered itself on the rock-ribbed Puritanism of the Philadelphia fathers.

Then he went on to New York. The British were still in that city, and probably he might be able, while waiting for a boat to take him back to Jamaica, to pick up a few pounds. On August 1, at the John Street Theatre he offered an olio—the first and third part of the *Lecture on Heads,* Courtney Melmoth's *Shadows of Shakespeare or Shakespeare's Characters Paying Homage to Garrick.* He had a second night on August 8th, and a third and last on the 16th. In this farewell performance he gave "A Rational Evening's Entertainment," consisting of selections from the *Lecture on Heads,* the *Shadows of Shakespeare,* Dryden's *Ode to St. Cecile,* and Hippisley's *Drunken Man.*[3]

Not until next year does Henry's name appear on the advertisements, and as the papers which printed them were Jamaican, we presume that his passage back to the island was relatively an easy one, even though September is a month generally associated in Jamaican minds with hurricanes.

Henry Andrew Francken, M.R.

The departure of Hallam from Jamaica left open the office of Master of the Revels. Either at the end of the year 1782 or the beginning of 1783, as we learn from contemporary Jamaican almanacs, this post was filled by the appointment of Henry Andrew Francken. Somehow, Jamaican recorders of the great and near-great have failed to give Mr. Francken his due measure of praise.

Born in Holland about 1720, Francken came to Jamaica in February, 1757, where, in March of the following year, he was naturalized an English subject. Lieutenant Governor Henry Moore appointed him interpreter of the English and Dutch languages in the Vice Admiralty Court. After a time he made a journey to the Northern Colonies, getting as far inland as Albany. On his return he was able to communicate to Governor Campbell and Admiral Rowley valuable military information upon the state of the rebelling forces. During the war, like many another Jamaican, he found it hard sledding to support himself and family. Doubtless the post of Master of the Revels helped the family purse over many a crisis. Then in 1784 and 1785 came hurricanes that well-nigh wiped him out. The government made him a customs officer in 1786, but this post being abolished, he was thrown on the charity of his friends, who gave a concert for his benefit by which he was cleared of debts. In 1791 he appealed to the Assembly for assistance, being now seventy-one. The Assembly recognized his services to the public by granting him £200, and in 1793 he was appointed Assistant Judge of the Court of Common Pleas for Port Royal. Francken seems to have been quite a musician, for he took part in at least one concert. He held the post of Master of the Revels in 1782–3, and again in 1785–6. He died on May 30, 1795, at Kingston.

Three-Fingered Jack

Among the readable, but sometimes not altogether exact, memoirs of the early American stage are those by John Bernard, a comedian who played in the States in the first quarter of the last century. Paging over his *Retrospections of America* we come to a fantastic Jamaica yarn, supposed to have been told Bernard by Owen Morris. It concerns a Mr. Herbert, a singer in the American Company of Comedians, of whom unfortunately we have no Jamaica record. Herbert had an extraordinarily sweet voice. He also had a past. Though born of respectable parents, it seems that he "had quitted England owing to an unfortunate attachment." One day in Jamaica, Herbert, so the story goes, wandered out into the country with a companion, and sat down to rest under a palm tree. While his friend went off to get some rum, Herbert passed the time by singing aloud. At that moment, Three-Fingered Jack, an outlaw, driven from his hiding place in the hills by hunger, happened to be near. In fact, he was creeping up toward Herbert to kill and rob him. Hearing the sweet voice, Jack dropped his evil plan, so completely was he overwhelmed by Herbert's singing. The next day Three-Fingered Jack was captured.[4]

It is the part of a cynic to play upon such a pretty legend the glaring light of fact, but it must be confessed that if Herbert was in Jamaica, his time there would be between 1755 and 1758—and Three-Fingered Jack was actually killed in 1781.

However, this outlaw did help make a Jamaican contribution to the stage. The melodrama *Obi, or Three-Fingered Jack* was popular in London at the turn of the century.[5] This seriopantomime in two acts by John Fawcett, with songs and choruses, was performed at Covent Garden, Drury Lane, and the Haymarket and the exploits of the lone robber—whose terrain is still pointed out to visitors in St. Thomas-in-the-East—thrilled readers for three decades.

CHAPTER VIII

1783–1785

Montego Bay Enjoys a Third Season and Mr. Henry Publishes His Play—The Company Departs for the States and We Follow Them—Solitary Showmen Appear

AFTER such a rush of plays in 1782, it might be expected that the company would play a season as usual in Spanish Town during the sitting of the courts and Assembly. Here again we are faced with the unfortunate absence of the press. Indeed, this year 1783 would be a staring blank in our history were it not for the second Montego Bay run. We might blame this unsettled theatrical condition on circumstances in the States, to the fact that hostilities had ceased on January 20th and by April 19th George Washington proclaimed peace. The Company would be anxiously awaiting its chance to return to the States. However, times were bad and commerce closely restricted. Both private and public purses were lean. Moreover, in January there had arrived a large convoy from Charleston comprising 1600 troops, 400 white families—Loyalists glad to leave the States—and 4500 slaves. Many of the whites settled in Kingston, some of them doing well in business, and a few became successful planters. The Government had generously exempted these refugees from taxes for a term of years. Others did not prosper, and had to be supported by private charity.

At Montego Bay Again

We turn once more to the *Cornwall Chronicle* and find the issue of August 30th disclosing Mr. Godwin in town. That inveterate trouper announces the tragedy of *Cleone* to be played on the 3rd of September after a short delay "on account of sending for a Person to perform the Music requisite for the Songs, Dances and Pantomime." Evidently Mr. Godwin has long since closed his evening dancing school at Kingston and the company is anxiously casting envious eyes again on the possibilities for profitable performances offered by the rich planters of St. James's, Trelawney, and Hanover parishes. We continue, then, our little Montego Bay playbook, from its last items, when the company performed here on May 10, 1777, for Mr. Wignell's benefit and in November, 1781, when Mr. Moore delivered the *Lecture on Heads*.

1783

September 3rd—*Cleone,* Dodsley

September 6th—*Douglas,* Home
 Catherine and Petruchio, Shakespeare

This is advertised as being given at the *new* theatre. Godwin offers an interlude of dancing called *The Female Pedlar*. He also respectfully informs his audience that the gentleman who proposes personating Young Norval is indisposed and that he, Godwin, must play the part at short notice. Also that Glenalvon will be performed "by a Gentleman for his amusement," and that of Anna by Mr. Charles Biddle. Here is evidence of amateur ambition at the Bay. We also are meeting Mr. Biddle for the first time. He will figure in American playbills.

September 20th—*Cleone,* Dodsley
Jew Outwitted, Cumberland

Again Mr. Godwin provides a dancing act after the play. In *Cleone,* the part of Paulet is played "by a Gentleman, being his third appearance"; Glenville by Mr. Birmingham, "being his first appearance." In *The Jew Outwitted,* the role of Antonio is filled by the gentleman who performed Paulet and who will sing, "Ah! sure a pair was never seen," and, the advertisement continues, "the other Characters as expressed in the Bills." These bills have not been preserved, so we do not know what members of the American Company are supporting Godwin's venture. That it was his own venture will soon be revealed.

September 27th—*Douglas,* Home
Jew Outwitted, Cumberland

The Female Pedlar is danced again by Godwin. Messrs. Birmingham and Biddle are named in the cast and the characters of Douglas and Glenalvon are by amateurs. The songs are accompanied with a harpsichord.

But we snatch at a footnote to this advertisement:

Mr. Godwin's respectful services wait on the Ladies and Gentlemen of St. James's and begs leave to acquaint them that he has been at a great expense at fitting up a theatre in the best manner the room would admit of. Several theatrical entertainments are ready, within the abilities of his present numbers; but, as he hopes to settle in this parish, he will procure other performers and endeavour to establish a Rational Amusement for the Liberal and polite inhabitants of this respectable part of the Island.

How those eighteenth-century actors could lay it on!

The prices charged for seats in this "room," which Godwin had fixed up as a theatre, also show its arrangement—Side Boxes, Front and Side Seats, 10s, Gallery 6s 8d.

What became of the old theatre erected for the 1779 season we can only surmise. It must have been merely a temporary affair and if it didn't fall down or wasn't blown down after the company departed, it probably was used for storage, or, as the Church would say, passed into secular hands.

October 4th—*Isabella*, Southerne
                Jew Outwitted, Cumberland

Mr. Godwin enriches the program by "an interlude of Speaking, Singing and Dancing called 'The Twelfth of April' "—evidently a creation of his own—and to *Bucks Have At Ye All*, he makes "additions never spoke."

October 11th—*Isabella*, Southerne
                Lethe, Garrick

"Between the Play and Farce, an Interlude called Pantaloon in the Suds (with an additional Scene of Pantaloon in the Sack) to conclude with the Death of Harlequin." Lethe, an old favorite with Army players at Kingston, appears at last here in Montego Bay. And that reminds me: one day, motoring in the hills back of Montego Bay, I found a little crossroads town called Lethe. Another note:

"As the above will be the last Play till the Benefits take place, the outstanding tickets will be of no further use after this night." No Annie Oakleys for the benefits!

October 25th—*A Bold Stroke for a Wife,* Mrs. Centlivre
  Mock Doctor, Fielding

This is Mrs. Godwin's benefit. In the performance he sustains his good wife by dancing *The Female Pedlar* once more, playing Gregory in *The Mock Doctor* and reciting an epilogue. The songs are still being accompanied by that harpsichord.

December 13th—*Isabella,* Southerne
  Jew Outwitted, Cumberland

In *Isabella,* Byron is played by Godwin and Villeroy by a Mr. Dawson, evidently a modest amateur. "An Epilogue written by a Gentleman on this Bay" is spoken by Mr. and Mrs. Godwin and there follows the "Favourite Scene of the Broken Bridge or the Insolent Carpenter." Godwin's dancing interlude this time is called the *Female Fruit-Gatherer* or the *Bird Catcher,* and is followed by a "Minuet in the Italian Manner." Certainly the Godwins are working hard to make this Montego Bay theatre a success. Will reinforcements never come? In *The Jew Outwitted,* Godwin plays Isaac Mendoza, and Dawson, Antonio.

This theatrical announcement of December 13th is accompanied by a notice that Godwin is to open a dancing school at the beginning of January, giving instruction in the Minuet, Hornpipe, and proper steps for Country Dances. He will also conduct a private evening class.

Above the Bay, my masters, stands a famous old house

called Grove Hill. Built about 1750, it has survived all the visitations of hurricane, fire, and riot that have afflicted the town. Its wide verandahs overlooking the housetops and the bay have witnessed many a tragedy and many a romance. Behind the verandah is a house-length ball-room and close by it once stood (so the present owner remembers) a famous orange tree. Into its branches the slaves used to climb to watch the dancers. From these uncomfortable perches they saw Nelson make many a pretty leg. Did Mr. Godwin, I wonder, ever lead the minuet here? Or did the sweet-voiced Storer sisters sing to a company gathered indoors and on the steps of the noble mahogany stairs behind?

We have only one more date in 1783 and it may, or may not, be significant.

December 20th—*Percy,* Hannah More
              Spanish Fryar, Dryden

"The part of Dominic (the Friar) by a Gentleman, late of the American Company in Kingston."

1784

Although we shall be finding a reasonable amount of activity in the theatre during 1784, the year was not exactly prodigal with blessings for the island. A storm on the south shore either sank or damaged every ship in Kingston Harbor. At the same time, Britain's refusal to permit Jamaica to import foodstuffs in anything but British bottoms or from America, threatened a terrible famine, which was averted only when the Governor al-lowed importation of foodstuffs from the United States

for a time. In spite of these difficult circumstances, the
theatre did its share in helping to maintain high spirits.

The Year of Grace, 1783, slipped into the bourne of
time and space and 1784 dawns on the Bay from across
the Reading Hills. Readers of the Montego Bay *Chronicle* of Saturday, January 10th, find a report of an event
of the previous Wednesday, the 7th: "Arrived, the
schooner Polly, Capt. Ogle, from Kingston, having on
board the scenery etc. belonging to the American Company of Comedians."

Meantime, in the *Chronicle* of the 31st we discover the
first item about the musical end of the company:

Mr. Hemmings
(Musician to the American Company)

Presents his respects to the Gentlemen of Montego Bay
and its environs, takes the liberty to acquaint them, he
teaches the violin in a new, easy and expeditious manner.
Terms may be known by applying to him at Mr. Gonne's,
silver-smith, or at the theatre.

N.B. Harpsichords, Piano-Fortes and Guitars tuned.

So Montego Bay has waxed fat enough to support a
silversmith! It still can support only one! And evidently
harpsichords and pianos were quite common. How the
town is prospering!

By January 28th John Henry, back from his futile
effort to revive the theatre in Pennsylvania, announces
that the new theatre, after frustrations from bad
weather and slow workmen, will be opened on February
4th and the gentry of Montego Bay may be amused.

1784—February 4th—*Gamester,* Mrs. Centlivre
   King and Miller of Mansfield, Dodsley

Boxes, 13s 4d. Pit, 7s 6d. Definitely higher than Godwin's prices. Performances are on Wednesdays, Thursdays, and Saturdays. We are in for a regular season. A
puff, published three days later, says that "considering
the short time the theatre has taken in raising from the
foundation, and in fitting up, it has exceeded the most
sanguine expectations of the Public; and, it may be said,
with propriety, to be the handsomest in the Island." So
Godwin's barn has been discarded and a new playhouse
built. This would be Montego Bay's third! We also wonder if the Godwins were discarded. Their names do not
appear in the few available casts.

February 7th—*Love in a Village,* Bickerstaff

Young Meadows . . . . .Mr. Harper
Justice Woodcock . . . . .Mr. Maidstone
Sir William Meadows . . . . .Mr. Morris
Hodge . . . . .Mr. Wignell
Hawthorn .Mr. Woolls
Lucinda . . . . .Mrs. Morris
Madge . . . . .Mrs. Harper
Rosetta . . . . .Miss Maria Storer

King and Miller of Mansfield, Dodsley

The King . . . . .Mr. Henry
Dick . . . . .Mr. Wignell
Lord Lurewell . . . . .Mr. Harper
Joe (with a song) . . . . .Mr. Woolls
The Miller .Mr. Morris
Margery . . . . .Miss Storer
Peggy . . . . .Mrs. Larke (Being her
                                          second appearance)

The curtain for this performance rises at six-thirty.
Thomas Wignell is evidently copartner with Henry or

is serving as business manager, since he asks "Persons having accounts against the theatre" to send them to him.

In these casts we meet with some new names—Mr. and Mrs. Harper, Mr. Maidstone, Mr. and Mrs. Larke, and Miss Storer. The Morrises are still with us, as are Messrs. Woolls and Roberts. Maria Storer is here too. The Miss Storer of the bills, since she was cast for singing roles, was probably Fanny Storer, the one who later became Mrs. Metcheler.

February 14th—*Edward and Eleonora*, Hull
Mock Doctor, Fielding

February 21st—*West Indian*, Cumberland

Belcour ....Mr. Wignell
Stockwell ....Mr. Morris
Capt. Dudley ....Mr. Maidstone
Ensign Dudley ....Mr. Harper
Fulmer ....Mr. Woolls
Stukely ....Mr. Larke
Sailor ....Mr. Roberts
Major O'Flaherty ....Mr Henry
Mrs. Fulmer ....Miss Maria Storer
Louisa Dudley ....Mrs. Harper
Lady Rusport ....Miss Storer
Lucy ....Mrs. Larke
Charlotte Rusport ....Mrs. Morris

Musical Lady, Colman the Elder

Young Mash ....Mr. Wignell
Old Mash ....Mr. Morris
Freeman ....Mr. Maidstone
Rozin ....Mr. Roberts
Lady Scrape ....Miss Storer
Sophia ....Miss Maria Storer

February 28th—*Gamester*, Mrs. Centlivre
             Padlock, Bickerstaff

March 6th   —*Edward and Eleonora*, Hull
             Midas, O'Hara

March 13th   —*Duenna*, Sheridan
             King and Miller of Mansfield, Dodsley

March 20th   —*School for Scandal*, Sheridan
             Gentle Shepherd, Ramsay

March 27th   —*Beaux' Stratagem*, Farquhar
             Devil to Pay, Coffey

April 3rd   —*Beggar's Opera*, Gay
             Citizen, Murphy

After the opera, Mr. Henry recites Courtney Melmoth's monody, *Shadows of Shakespeare*. The public are also informed "that there will be no Play for the ensuing eight days, on account of its being Passion Week." I can scarcely imagine the cockfighting, rum-swiggling planters and their noon-sleeping ladies and the estate bookkeepers with their dusky "housekeeper" mistresses bothering their heads over Passion Week. However, the stage has always been most decorous in respect to religious holidays.

April 13th   —*Clandestine Marriage*, Colman and Garrick
             Thomas and Sally, Bickerstaff

April 15th   —*Chances*, Garrick
             Padlock, Bickerstaff

This is Mr. Wignell's benefit. *The Chances, or the Two Comedians* was altered from Beaumont and Fletcher and adapted to the stage by Garrick.

April 17th—*Cymbeline*, Shakespeare
        Irish Widow, Garrick

"After the Farce (by particular desire) the Manual Exercise by Mrs. Morris. Taken from a Farce called *The Camp* or *A Trip to Coxheath*."

On April 30th the *Chronicle* prints an advertisement of John Henry's attempt at fame by playwriting: *A School for Soldiers or The Deserter*. He speaks of this as a second edition.[1]

May 1st—*Duenna*, Sheridan
        Lying Valet, Garrick

May 4th—*Shipwreck*, Cumberland
        The Register Office, Reed

Mr. Roberts' benefit: "Between the Play and the Farce, the Doctor's Last Examination before the College of Physicians. With Mr. Wignell as President and Mr. Maidstone as Dr. Lost."

May 6th—*Douglas*, Home
        Cross Purposes, O'Brien

"Before the Play a Prologue (written by D. Garrick, Esq.) in the character of a Country Clown, by Mr. Biddle," whose benefit this is. Between the play and the farce comes *The Humours of Mother Cole*, with Mr. Maidstone as Mother Cole. An ominous note is sounded in the *Chronicle* advertisement of May 1st and 8th. "This is positively the last night but one. The Public are respectfully informed that the theatre will be closed on Saturday, the 8th of May. N.B. Wanted, to be ready to sail the 10th of May, a Vessel of 30 or 40 tons, to carry the scenery, etc., of the American Company to King-ston."

May 8th—(Being positively the last night)
       Chances, Garrick
       Lying Valet, Garrick

Benefit for Mr. and Mrs. Larke: "Between the Play and Farce, an Epilogue by Somebody, in the character of Nobody, being a satire on Everybody, without offense to Anybody."

On May 7th Thomas Wignell advertises for his bills. Still the company seems not to have all embarked on that schooner of "30 or 40 tons," for on May 15th, at Miss Williams' Long Room, the two male musicians of the troupe—Woolls and Hemmings—give a benefit con-cert (for themselves) of vocal and instrumental music, followed by a ball. The concert began at six-thirty, just at candlelighting time, a short space after the sun had plopped down into the sea over Lucea way. Evidently Miss Storer had a part in this concert, because in the supplements of May 22nd and 29th to the *Chronicle,* both Mr. Woolls and Miss Storer return their thanks to the parish of St. James and places adjacent, and beg leave to assure them that they "will ever retain the most grateful remembrance of their candour and generous support."

Thomas Wignell, however, seems to have lingered be-hind. Perhaps some of those bills for which he advertised remain unpaid. We find him offering, on August 21st, "A Dramatic Fête in three parts, consisting of a variety of Entertainments Serious, Comic and Satirical, taken from the celebrated Lecture on Heads and Hearts, with suitable Decorations." The scenery gone, he must have been put to some expense to scrape together these decorations. The bill concluded with that hardy favorite, *Bucks Have at Ye All*. This will be played for three nights, "the liberty of renting the theatre being restricted to three exhibitions, T. Wignell respectfully solicits the patronage of his friends to an humble attempt to entertain them."

August 28th finds the "Dramatic Fête" repeated, being followed this time by a "poetic Vision called the Court of Momus, in which will be exhibited a variety of well-known Dramatic Characters—Falstaff, Fribble, Pistol, Miser, John Moody, Lord Foppington, Lord Ogleby, Maw-worm, Mungo, etc." These were old parts familiar to Wignell. The performance brings forth a puff in the *Chronicle* of September 4th, in which Mr. Wignell is lauded for his spirited presentation of the fête which has been "for such a number of years a standing dish with the lovers of true humour and elegant satire." The audience seems to have been numerous and genteel. He is forced to postpone his third and last performance till some later time.

Meanwhile he rides around the coast road, twenty-five miles westward, to Lucea, where, in the court house on September 8th, he exhibits his "Dramatic Fête."

September 25th sees him back in Montego Bay with his fête and on October 9th he repeats it. How extraordinarily patient, those Montegians! Ah, but competition appears. No more does Wignell start on the road to Lucea than—shades of Hyman Saunders!—a magician appears in town. The *Chronicle* for the 11th advertises:

The Young Hollander, sensible to the many obligations he lies under to the public and convinced that his most strenuous efforts have hitherto been exerted to give general satisfaction to those who have honoured him with their presence, has still the hopes of meriting a continuance of their patronage.

By Permission of His Honour the Custos
At Miss Williams's Long Room
The Incomparable Young
Hollander
Will exhibit, this present evening, the 11th instant
Various Surprising
Deceptions

With Cups, Cards, Snuff-boxes, Watches, Money, Handkerchiefs, etc. He will take any Gentleman's snuff-box, and convey it into a small tin box, under three locks and keys, without touching anything.

He will take any Lady or Gentleman's pocket Handkerchief and cut it into as many pieces as the company pleases, and make it whole again with a little of his funny powder.

Two Gentlemen may pick a card each out of the pack, he will put a different card under each of their feet, and convert them into those they have in their hands.

Any Lady or Gentleman may think upon a card, he will throw the pack up toward the roof, and shoot the card flying.

Any Lady or Gentleman may take a card out of the pack and shuffle it into it again, he will scatter them on the floor, and blindfolded will pick out the card on the point of a sword.

He also will perform surprising feats in Tumbling and Leaping.

He will leap over six negroes, two chairs, and a table without touching them.

He will jump through a small hoop held six feet high by two men.

Also many other feats never before performed in this island.

Tickets 6s. 8d.

To begin precisely at Seven o'clock

Mr. Wignell wisely moves to another town: he is amusing the genteel of Trelawny Parish, to the eastward of St. James's. At the court house in Martha-Brae he presents the "Dramatic Fête." First a prologue from the *Lecture on Hearts,* then *Bucks Have at Ye All,* and finally "A Poetic Address to the Ladies in the character of a Mason, in which will be discovered the Grand Secret of Masonry." After the performance came a ball. For all this he charged 14s 4d. However, he warns the populace that he intends leaving Martha-Brae the next Monday noon. The following Saturday in the *Chronicle* he publishes his "sincere acknowledgements to the Ladies and Gentlemen of the parishes of St. Ann, Trelawny, St. James and Hanover for their distinguished patronage of his humble attempts to entertain them."

We have only one more amusement to report in this season and it concerns Savanna-la-Mar. On Tuesday and Saturday November 9 and 13, 1784, Mr. Pool, the noted performer in horsemanship, lately arrived from the Windward Islands, offers a variety of surprising feats. Among them, a "most Wonderful Horse will lay himself down for a considerable time as if dead and afterward groan (apparently) through extreme sickness and pain; he will then rise and set up like a Lady's lap dog. This noble animal will also feign himself lame, so that he can scarcely move." This performance, for which the tickets were a dollar each, began precisely at four o'clock.

Thomas Pool seems to have been a hardened and long-traveled showman. In the autumn of 1786 having played in Philadelphia and Boston, he will appear in New York with his trained horse and use precisely the same advertisement there that he used here. He was from the States originally, for he claims to be "the first American that ever exhibited the following Feats of Horsemanship on the Continent." His New York performance was given "on the Hill near the Jews Burial Ground" in a building with seats raised off the ground. He also had a clown!

It is unfortunate that we must end this season with a regrettable note. At Spanish Town on August 8, 1784, Miss Kirk, "lately of the American Company of Comedians," died. We shall miss her when the company gathers to play again in the States.

Hallam in the States

While Henry and the others were marking time by a short season at Montego Bay, Lewis Hallam, who had gone to England from Jamaica late in 1783 and had played for a brief period in one of the theatres "with tolerable applause," has arrived in New York. There he looks into the company's rights in the John Street Theatre and, after giving "lectures" and "poetic addresses," in January, 1784, he goes to Philadelphia. The ban against plays was still tightly clamped down in Pennsylvania, but Hallam was not to be daunted by it. The war was over and even though things were at sixes and sevens, he saw no need for the populace to be so devastatingly strict about plays and amusements. He petitions the General Assembly for the repeal of its enactment against the theatre.

The best he can manage, however, is to gather together a scratch company and try "lectures." These "lectures" and "concerts of music" were the accustomed subterfuge in England when plays were refused authorization. They were touted as highly edifying.

Both the Allens and Mr. Moore had come along from Jamaica. Hallam advertised Moore as "from the Theatre Royal, Liverpool, late of Jamaica." He also picked up a Mr. Bentley and Mr. and Miss Durang, the latter two being dancers. In Philadelphia a Mr. Lake also joins the company. The playbills now end with the patriotic slogan, "Vivat Respublica!"

In both the New York and Philadelphia tryouts Hallam had Mr. Allen associated with him as partner, and it was under their comanagement that the John Street Theatre in New York was opened in August, 1785. At the same time the papers announced that the old American Company of Comedians would soon arrive in Baltimore.

We shall leave this advice, since it pushes us ahead of our Jamaica dates, and return to the island. What has this "old company" been doing?

1785

After their departure from Montego Bay the previous May, they had gone to Kingston and evidently continued playing. The papers are almost all nonexistent, so we snatch at the solitary hint, published in the *Cornwall Chronicle* of January 15, 1785, which reports a Kingston bill that included *The Maid of the Mill* and *The Lying Valet* on Thursday, January 8th:

During the representation of the play an accident happened, which had very nearly been attended with the most fatal consequences. By some very reprehensible inattention, the lamps in the front of the orchestra, being overcharged with oil, set fire to the wooden channel in which they were enclosed and burnt with considerable violence, when some of the servants belonging to the theatre, with more officious haste than judgment, attempted to extinguish the flame by throwing water over it, which made it blaze up almost to the ceiling, and threw the audience into the greatest terror and confusion, particularly the ladies, several of whom fainted and others were bruised by crowding to get out of the house. The fire was at length happily extinguished, without being productive of any other mischief; though it put a stop to the performance for near half an hour.

Well that it might! The candles used in theatres were bad enough, but whale-oil lamps without chimneys were positively tempting Providence. We regret the incident but are grateful for one more item to our Kingston playbook.

Other items, printed January 22nd and February 26th, lead us to believe that the company had played a winter season at Kingston: "We hear the American Company intend quitting this town for Montego Bay as soon as the benefits are over." Since benefits were given toward the end of a run we can surmise that the company had played a winter season in the fall and early spring of 1784–5 and were about to end it. A fragment of an advertisement for February 26 reveals the play as *The Orphan of China*.

At this time two personalities catch the eye. Thank Heaven for this file of the *Cornwall Chronicle* in the Bristol Public Library; the Kingston papers of the time simply do not exist: "Mrs. Gardner, the celebrated comic actress and Mr. Mahon, a vocal performer of eminence, from the Covent Garden Theatre are arrived in this island . . . January 22nd. Died on Sunday at Port Royal, Mr. John Maidstone, lately of the American Company of Comedians.

The company must have lingered in Kingston, probably hoping that Hallam would send them orders to come north, for not until April do we discover them actually in Montego Bay. The notice states that "some material preparations have unavoidably been the cause of this delay," but the public is assured that "there will regularly be a Play every Tuesday, Thursday and Saturday evenings, during the continuance of the Company here."

At Montego Bay

So we pick up the Montego playbook again and on

April 5th—*School for Scandal,* Sheridan

Sir Peter Teazle .... Mr. Henry
Joseph Surface .... Mr. Wignell
Sir Oliver Surface .... Mr. Morris
Crabtree .... Mr. Haughton
Charles .... Mr. Harper
Maria .... Miss H. Haughton
(Being her first appearance
on any stage)
Mrs. Candour .... Mrs. Harper
Lady Sneerwell .... Miss Haughton
Lady Teazle .... Mrs. Morris

King and Miller of Mansfield, Dodsley

Here are new names—Mr. Haughton, Miss H. Haughton, and Miss Haughton. Miss H. is making her debut. Also, the notice tells us, a Mr. Jackson, from

Berlin, will perform a violin solo at the end of the play. Mr. Pinnock is evidently business manager.

April 9th—*Gamester*, Moore

Beverly ....Mr. Henry
Lewson ....Mr. Wignell
Jarvis ....Mr. Morris
Bates ....Mr. Biddle
Dawson ....Mr. Woolls
Stukedy ....Mr. Harper
Charlotte (first time) ....Mrs. Harper
Lucy ....Miss Haughton
Mrs. Beverly ....Mrs. Morris

Poor Soldier, O'Keeffe

Patrick ....Mr. Henry
Capt. Fitzroy ....Mr. Harper
Father Luke ....Mr. Biddle
Dermot ....Mr. Woolls
Bagatelle ....Mr. Weston
Darby ....Mr. Wignell
Kathleen ....Mrs. Morris
Norah ....Miss M. Haughton
(Being her first appearance
on any stage)

The Haughtons seem to keep on coming. Here's the fourth—Miss M. We also note Mr. Weston as a new name, but shall not have to record him often.

On April 12th the town and the planters from thereabouts cease their labors to celebrate Rodney's victory. For twenty-five years after Rodney conquered De Grasse the day was set apart for island feasting. While we are on the subject we might skip ahead two years and give the report of this day as it was celebrated in this thriving little town on the north shore:

At 12 o'clock the guns at Fort Frederick and Fort George were fired, and followed by a triple discharge of small arms by the Light Infantry, and a royal salute from the field pieces of the Artillery, both companies being drawn upon the Parade for the purpose. In the afternoon entertainments were prepared for different companies in this town to celebrate the occasion, when many loyal and constitutional toasts were drank, and the day spent in the utmost harmony and festivity. The evening exhibited a general and brilliant illumination in the town and neighborhood.

Today Montego Bay can point to one fort decorated with some ancient guns. It is on the road leading to the bathing beach. The guns haven't been fired, I daresay, for nearly a century. However, they are kept neatly painted by the town fathers. And as for troops in town, they also are only a memory.

April 16th—*Douglas,* Home
           Robinson Crusoe or Harlequin Friday

No more casts are found. *Robinson Crusoe* had never been performed in Montego Bay. It was accompanied by "a Dance of Savages, New Music, Scenes, etc." Did they draw those "savages" off the streets and lanes of Montego Bay? The bill also states that there will be a performance every night in the ensuing week. Unfortunately, we have no record of them all.

April 23rd—*Busybody,* Mrs. Centlivre
           Rosina, Mrs. Brooke

April 30th—*Orphan of China,* Murphy
            Poor Soldier, O'Keeffe

This bill is interesting because *The Orphan of China* is advertised as being performed for the first time in Montego Bay whereas the comic opera of *The Poor Soldier* is spoken of as being its third presentation here. Our scant records do not reveal the previous two. It was played with the original overture and accompaniments. At the end of the opera was added "a Display of Scenery representing the Naval Action and Defeat of the French Fleet, on the Glorious 12th of April, 1782, with the burning and blowing up of the Caesar, etc." There's the company playing with fireworks again!

After this April 30th performance the papers abruptly disappear. The American Company of Comedians is left hanging in time and space at Montego Bay (and who could choose a better place?). We have a suspicion that they remained here until July and that it was from Montego Bay that some of them set sail for the States. On August 11th Miss Storer, having traveled up the twenty miles of dusty and twisting shore road to Martha-Brae, gives herself a benefit concert and ball at the courthouse there. "Every Subscriber to pay One Pound, Six Shillings and three Pence, and to have Two Tickets."

The young lady is rather peevish. Read her notice:

Miss Storer begs leave to represent, that she has already been at a considerable expense by the failure of the Concert and Ball advertised before, and as her ill state of health requires she should leave the island in the ensuing month, she respectfully solicits the patronage of her Friends and the Public on this Occasion, which she will ever have a grateful remembrance of.

Well, Miss Storer, we know how hard it is to keep one's head when things are going against one, and July in Martha-Brae *can* be hot, so we forgive you that final use of a preposition at the end of your sentence.

Farewell to the Company

A Charleston, North Carolina, paper of July 2, 1785, in its column of West Indian Intelligence, states that the American Company of Comedians had begun their benefits and "intends to embark for this continent very shortly." The *Cornwall Chronicle* of Montego Bay, in its issue of November 5th, states, "The American Company of Comedians, who left this place in July last, have arrived in Maryland; and were to open the theatre at Annapolis this first of this month."

It matters little from which port the company sailed from the island, but since we are in Montego Bay, let us climb up slowly to the flat terrace on the top of Richmond Hill above the town and talk about them. . . . Far below to the left lie the green patches of the Bogue Islands. On this side, the harbor and then the open sea. On the horizon ridges of the crinkled hills soft with verdure. The town lies at our feet. Like a blinding headlight the sun rests for a moment on the edge of the sea. A little boat catches the breeze. Its sails puff out. It heads toward the westering sun. Good-by! Good-by and safe journey! And years of crowded houses to you! And thunderous applause!

What will become of these old friends?

John Henry, Mr. and Mrs. Morris (how faithful that pair!), Stephen Woolls, Mr. and Mrs. Godwin, Mr.

and Mrs. Allen, Mr. Goodman, Mr. and Mrs. **Harper,**
Charles Biddle, Maria Storer, Miss Fanny Storer, Miss
Tuke (eventually to be Mrs. Hallam), Mr. Moore. Except Moore and the Allens, who are with Hallam in New
York, they will assemble at Baltimore. By November,
1785, John Henry and his troupe has joined forces with
his old-time partner and Hallam and Henry open in New
York on the 21st. On that occasion Henry states, "We
went to the Island of Jamaica, where we were received
with that degree of cordial welcome which so eminently
distinguishes the worthy inhabitants of that truly respectable island." [2]

Of the old company, Dermot is heard from no more.
David Benjamin Roberts and Isaac Morales will remain
on the island permanently and with the latter the erstwhile Miss Wainwright, for she is not seen on the playbills in the States. Mr. Goodman, the Philadelphia law
student turned actor, is dead by October. The *Chronicle*
of November 19th tells his Montego Bay friends the
sad news: "At Philadelphia in October, Mr. Richard
Goodman, so well known in this island for his theatrical
talents; and better known to the discerning part of the
community as the man of science, the scholar and the
gentleman." He had been with the company since 1770.

Mrs. Hamilton, who has appeared in our bills since
June 26, 1779, will join the company and make her debut
in the States on August 27, 1787, at Baltimore as Mrs.
Blanish in Burgoyne's *The Heiress*. She will play, especially favoring old women of comedy, until 1796, when she
ceases being a member of the company. After that we
hear no more of her.

At what time Miss Cheer will join the company the

records do not say. We do know, however, that in November, 1793, she is billed as Mrs. Long in the elder Colman's *The Jealous Wife*. Dunlap gives a plaintive account of this performance: "Time had deprived the lady of all that can attract the spectator's attention to the moving pictures of the stage, and unless that attraction exists, the imagination cannot be enlisted in the service of the actor or author. Mrs. Long was received in silence by the audience, and never heard of more." [3]

Dispirited, she returned to the island. We do not know if Mr. Long still lived, but as Mrs. Margaret Long she had conducted a lodging house at Spanish Town in 1781 and under the same name she kept a tavern at Old Harbour, then a place near Spanish Town, today a forgotten and desiccated village. Like Falstaff she could say, "Shall I not take mine ease in mine inn?" Here she welcomed her guests until February 15, 1800, when she took her last curtain call. The report describes her as "Mrs. Margaret Long, better known by the name of Miss Cheer, many years of the old American Company of Comedians." [4]

It must have been a good tavern and enjoyed a popular reputation—good inns were scarce in Jamaica in those times, for three days after her death, in the same columns—

Michael Burke

Respectfully informs his Friends and the Public that he has taken the Tavern, formerly known by the name of Browne's Tavern, formerly occupied by Mrs. Margaret Long, where he hopes, by his attention to the public, to merit their support.

Thomas Wignell was to win fame both as a clever comedian and as a successful manager. We first encountered him when he was sitting in a hairdresser's chair and someone brought him the news that the Continental Congress had clamped on the ban against the theatre. The ban prevented Wignell's appearing on the stage in the States until after the Revolution. When he did appear, in 1785, he immediately was acclaimed the best comedian so far seen in America. Dunlap describes him as "a man below ordinary height with a slight stoop of the shoulders; he was athletic, with handsomely formed lower extremities, the knees a little curved inward and feet remarkably small. His large blue eyes were rich in expression and his comedy was luxuriant in humour, but always faithful to his author. He was a comic actor, not a buffoon." [5] George Washington was especially taken with him; in fact, Wignell was rated as the President's favorite comedian.

In 1791 Wignell and the Owen Morrises, going to Philadelphia, formed the nucleus of a company to play at the new Chestnut Street Theatre. Two years later he was free from Hallam's control and, as a manager, he went to England to recruit his company. He "brought back the best theatrical company ever seen up to the time of its arrival in America." [6] This troupe also played in New York and Baltimore. Among its members was a Mrs. Merry, whom Wignell married the first week in January, 1803. By February 21st he was dead, the result of an injury sustained from a spring lancet.

For a time Henry and Hallam were successful in their partnership. It is evident that they made money by the venture, but, a greater accomplishment, they reestablished the stage in the States. Eventually trouble arose between them, new managers cropped up, new actors and actresses came into the picture, until both Henry and Hallam were relegated to second place. Their decline was well under way by 1792.

Hallam, who had been unsuccessful in his first marriage, found his second to be troublesome also. In 1792 he will take Miss Tuke for his bride. She was regarded, in her younger days, as being "young, pretty and awkward." When she first played in New York as Cowslip in *The Agreeable Surprize,* the *Daily Advertiser* of March 23, 1787, states that her acting was lifeless and uninteresting and came out flat-footed with the criticism that "a manager's partiality has exposed that girl to a profession which to a woman can never be respected but by talent." On November 20, 1789, when she took a benefit, she was advertised as being an American—"young on the stage but particularly attentive to fulfill the duties of her profession. . . . If she cannot stand foremost in the theatrical list, she at least deserves the appellation of the most industrious and general actress of the company."

However diffident she may have been as to her abilities, she evidently found release from her inhibitions: she took to tippling. In 1795 when she appeared in the principal lady's character in *The Jew,* her condition shocked and disgusted the audience. Hallam said it was opium, but the company and the public knew too much to accept that chivalrous statement. She was withdrawn from the stage. Hallam seems to have straightened her out, however, and after a few weeks she appeared as Lady Teazle in *The School for Scandal,* receiving tremendous applause. This did not satisfy Hodgkinson, Hallam's manager at the time. In 1797, during a scene when Hodgkinson was acting, she walked on the stage, demurely dressed in black, and read a statement of the injuries she had received in being deprived of her means of livelihood. Hodgkinson was hissed off the stage and he retired from acting for the rest of the season.

Miss Tuke played up to 1805 or 1806. In that latter year Thomas A. Cooper was manager and with a young man's insistence on merit, he refused to reengage either Hallam or his wife. Hallam died at Philadelphia on November 1, 1808.

When the company returned to the States, its stock was in the hands of Hallam, Henry, Wignell, Morris, and Woolls; the others were salaried performers. Of these, Woolls and Morris had reached the period of decay. However, Owen Morris will still be alive at the turn of the century, a doddering ancient of days who used to sun his rheumaticky joints in Independence Square, Philadelphia. His name appeared on the bills for the last time in 1805.

Mrs. Morris was in her prime when the company returned from Jamaica and she continued to play until 1815, when she made her last appearance at the Park Theatre in New York. In the days of her prime she received the highest acclaim from the critics. Listen to some of them: "Few women are born with such an happy assemblage of natural requisites for the theatrical profession . . . transcendant genius . . . in *The School for Wives* and *The East Indian,* the surprising ability of this lady in the pathos and energy of tragedy and her unbounded share of humor and comic actions made her the greatest object of attraction in the company."

Little wonder that she received such applause. A tall, imposing, well-formed person, she was the first actress in America to use the device of mystery, now a common stock-in-trade among both our lesser and higher flight cinema stars. Offstage she sedulously shunned the public eye and went to the theatre by side streets and back alleys, and always had her head and face enveloped in a thick veil.

Mr. and Mrs. Allen were first found on the company's bills on March 22, 1777, at Montego Bay. For a time, as we saw, he was copartner with Hallam in New York and Philadelphia. They played at the Southwark in 1784. In December of the next year they opened the theatre in Albany, New York, with *Cross Purposes* and *Catherine and Petruchio*, and Moore giving a talk on Masonry. The company played in Albany until February, 1786, when it went on to Montreal.

In this company Allen was manager and he shared the lead with Moore. Mrs. Allen seemed to be the inspiration and guide of the little troupe. The other claim that the Allens have to fame is that they were the parents of Andrew Jackson Allen, later an actor, for a time Edwin Forrest's dresser, and altogether a picturesque and amusing character.

Stephen Woolls will remain with the company until June 14, 1799, when, after thirty years' association with the stage, Death rings down his final curtain. He was buried in the cemetery of the Roman Catholic chapel in Barclay Street, New York. In earlier years he had been a shareholder of the company, but, during the last few, took very little active part in theatre affairs, the company paying him an annuity. A benefit was given for his wife and daughter on June 19th, with *The School for Scandal* and *Rosina.*

Charles Biddle, whom we met for the first time at Montego Bay in September, 1783, in *Catherine and Petruchio,* made his initial appearance in the States at the John Street Theatre, New York, November 25, 1785, as Archy in *Love à la Mode.* He played Scotchmen and sailors very well. Although he undoubtedly had ability, he was not an actor of the first rank. We will not find his name on the bills after 1790, when he played at Richmond, Virginia, in August of that year under the management of Bignall and West. He died at Richmond on November 27, 1791. His avocation—or perhaps his more profitable vocation—it is said, was tailoring.

The Harpers, who are returning with John Henry and his company, will make a definite contribution to the American stage. He more so than she. They are a young couple: he, modest; she, one of those awfully nice, plain women who are blessed with only mediocre talent, but who work hard, accumulate a broad knowledge of the stage—and attract audiences. She was especially good when cast to play old ladies. Mrs. Harper dies on October 3, 1791—she never did fully recover from the arduous tropics—and he evidently remarries. In 1798 he will be playing in Boston with a Mrs. Harper and later directs the theatre at Newport, Rhode Island. He appears in New York in the season of 1800–1 and 1804–5, the latter being our final glimpse of him. Harper was a sound and useful actor—with "expressive eyes and fine teeth!"

Among the most amusing and worthy figures we encountered in these Jamaica runs was Mr. Godwin, the dancer. We waved a Jamaica farewell to him when he departed from Montego Bay at the end of 1783, for, as we noted in this chapter, his name does not appear in the casts when Henry opened for his final Montego Bay run in February, 1785. Seilhamer calls him "the most complete representative of the strolling player and manager that was ever on this continent." We have noted how, in the very middle of the Revolutionary War, when the rest of the company stayed in Jamaica, Godwin slipped up to the States and joined the New American Company of Comedians, under the management of Dennis Ryan, who continued playing in Baltimore in defiance of Congressional orders. Either before this or after it, Godwin's first wife made her debut in Hallam's production of *Douglas* followed by *The Citizen* in 1779, Godwin dancing *The Drunken Peasant* between the play and the farce.

His first American appearance after the Revolution is at Savannah, Georgia, where, in August, 1785, he opens a theatre, with *Cato* followed by *Catherine and Petruchio,* the company being composed of Mr. and Mrs. Godwin, Mr. and Mrs. Kidd, and ladies and gentlemen "for their own amusement." This was Savannah's first theatre, and Godwin intended locating there permanently. But on January 26th the next year, Mrs. Godwin dies. At the same time Charleston was offering greater inducements. Godwin, moving to that city, advertised his usual dancing school, and in July, 1786, he opened a playhouse called Harmony Hall (perhaps remembering a hall of that name in Kingston) "where may be expected an olio in perfection in folio." Here also he "proposes to establish an Academy for Oratory, Music, Dancing and Fencing." [7]

This Harmony Hall venture did not work out so successfully. Godwin leaves it in March, 1787, and we next find him playing in a troupe at Northern Liberties, Philadelphia. In 1793 he assists in opening a new theatre at Baltimore, and in 1795 is playing in Charleston. After that date he disappears from the stage. It has been a long and checkered career since that day in 1766 when, under David Douglass, he made his debut at Philadelphia as Prince Edward in *Richard III.*

Of the Storer sisters, both Maria and Fanny have appeared on Jamaican bills. Fanny we last saw lingering on the north shore picking up dribblets of coins by a concert at Martha-Brae. She will join the company in late March, 1786, and eventually marry Mr. Metcheler.

Maria Storer's last Jamaica appearance of available record was on February 24, 1784. A year passes, then, as Miss Willis reveals in her *Charleston Theatre in the 18th Century,* the *South Carolina Gazette* of March 11, 1785, gives its reader, reprinting it from the *Jamaica Gazette,* a prologue to a farce called *Miss Out of Her Teens,* performed at the theatre in Harbour Street. It was "written by a Lady and spoken by Miss Storer as Miss Marlove Primrose." This mention of a theatre in Harbour Street adds to our mysteries. The last we heard of a playhouse there was way back in the seventeen-fifties.

That same issue of the *South Carolina Gazette,* under the head of West Indian Intelligence, says, "We are assured that Miss Maria Storer, that celebrated Disciple of Calliope, intends taking her departure for Charleston the latter end of this month and from thence will sail for

Great Britain in order to be in time to get a winter engagement at one of the theatres in London."

The *Gazette* of March 26–30 confirms her arrival, mentioning that she had "performed for several years past at the theatre in Jamaica and one winter in this city with great applause." Her first appearance in Charleston had been in 1774 under David Douglass' management.

She evidently changed her mind about the opportunities in London. On the 9th of May she was given a benefit concert at the City Tavern and on the 25th of June sang parts of the *Messiah* at St. Michael's Church. She may have joined the company of Dennis Ryan, then at Charleston, playing through March and April. By January 28, 1786, we find her sailing that day from Charleston on the sloop *Diana* for New York, "for the purpose of joining the American Company of Comedians." And when, on May 29, 1786, she does appear with the troupe in New York, she is billed as Mrs. Henry.

With this Storer sister, John Henry reached the end of his Storer romances. Through the years he managed to keep this one very much alive. In New York the two became public characters. Henry, assailed by gout, acquired a carriage in which he and Maria drove to the theatre. It was the first coach owned by an American actor. On its side panels he had painted a pair of crutches with the inscription, "This or These." It used to be one of the sights of New York to see John Henry hobbling up to his coach with Maria on his arm—both of them costumed for their parts—she then being lifted, crinolines and all, through the narrow coach door.

These two will remain colorful figures for several years. Then on October 16, 1794, while he and Maria were en route by boat to Rhode Island to play in the theatre there, John Henry died. He was hastily buried on shore, his body later being removed to a vault in the graveyard of St. James's Church at Bristol. His death, it was said, quite unhinged Maria's mind. She died the next year on April 28th, at Philadelphia, in her house back of the old Southwark Theatre.

So we come to the end of those ladies and gentlemen of the American Company of Comedians who have amused the audiences of Kingston, Spanish Town, and Montego Bay through the past ten years—through hard times and good, through blistering heat and torrential rain, through years of fire and famine and high wind and hurricane and earthquake, through wars and rumors of wars and through sickness and death in their ranks. Other actors will come to the island, but we shall never look upon their like again for many a decade. With their departure, we can say that the path from Harbour Street, Kingston, to Broadway, New York, is now fairly defined.

Montego Bay Sings

While we have been sitting here on Richmond Hill telling what will become of these actors and actresses, the night has descended on Montego Bay. Far below us lights twinkle out like "weenies," as the natives call fireflies. From the barracks on Miranda Hill the lights are ablaze. On the horizon, now dark masses, candlelights from the plantation houses flicker dimly. . . . And up from the homes and streets and lanes of Montego Bay comes the sound of singing.

Montego Bay has always been a singing town. In the

great houses of the sugar estates and cattle pens, young ladies for years to come will strum out the songs they heard Woolls and the Storer sisters sing under the directing baton of Mr. Hemming. Busy clerks whistle them as they go about checking sales of slaves and shipments of sugar and rum. Jamaica believes that these songs should never be forgotten. In the *Cornwall Chronicle* of January 14, 1786, there is announced from Spanish Town as just being published

Wilsone's St. Cecilia

Being a choice Collection of those celebrated English, Scottish and Irish songs, which have been so much esteemed in this island by polite companies, both for their excellency of music and beauty of composition.

Most of the favorite New Songs which have been lately introduced here, sung in the much admired *Entertainments of Rosina*, the *Duenna*, the *Poor Soldier*, the *Camp*, the *Maid of the Mill, Robinson Crusoe, Love in a Village*, the *Gentle Shepherd, Thomas and Sally* and other favourite Operas, the editor has carefully inserted; and whatever has tended to suppress Virtue, he has most attentively excluded.

To be had at the Printing Office, Montego Bay, Price 13s. 4d. bound.

I wonder, if in some attic of an old Montego Bay house, could be discovered one of those bound copies. By this time, though, its pages would be pretty thoroughly riddled by bookworms.

CHAPTER IX

Hilarious Market Days—Sable Venus and Sooty Adonis—
Maroon Fun—Negro Dances and Picturesque Musical Instru-
ments—Christmas in Town and Country—Koo-Koo and John
Canoe—The Set Girls

SO FAR in this narrative we have considered mainly the
amusements and high times of only the upper crust, the
very thin upper crust, of the Jamaican social scale—
white Europeans, white Creoles, and those who were so
near white that their fraction of color didn't make any
difference. What fun did the bulk of the population, the
black slaves, enjoy? To what extent did these Cudjoes,
Cubenas, Quacos, Quaos, Cuffees, Quamins, or Quashies
—for thus Gold Coast negroes were named after the
deities of the days of the week on which they were born
—display a merry heart if they had one beating beneath
their ebony hide?

Since the slaves brought their habits with them from
West Africa to the West Indies, certain customs were
early observed. Sir Hans Sloane records the music he
heard Coromantyn slaves sing in 1687 and describes
their dances as consisting "in great activity and strength
of body and keeping time. . . . They very often tie
Cows tails to their Rumps and add such other odd things
to their Bodies in several places, as gives them a very
extraordinary appearance." [1] From these crude dances,
in time, evolved picturesque and amusing masquerades
that were typically Jamaican.

228

Hilarious Market Days

Then, as now, market days furnished one of the bright spots in a week's monotony of toil. The slaves were allowed all Sunday and half of Saturday to cultivate "provision grounds" or garden patches assigned them on the plantation. They were responsible for supplying their own native food or "bread kind"—yams and such—the owner occasionally finding only the salt fish and raw sugar of their meager diet.

In odd moments, too, they managed to raise a few pigs and fowls, gather fruit, catch fish, weave mats and baskets, and such other crude handicrafts. These, together with the surplus from their provision grounds, they toted to market each Sunday. They walked then, as they walk today, incredible distances, carrying the baskets of their stock on their heads, into the nearest town.

The market was their great social event. Here they met friends, here they exchanged gossip—so they made a carnival of it. As many as ten thousand people could be seen at the Kingston Sunday market; other towns were in proportion. Here amid great chattering and merriment, the whites and negroes haggled over the prices of goats, pigs and fowls, fish, vegetables and fruit, mats, baskets, bark rope, yabba bowls, and pottery jars. With the few pennies picked up, the slaves bought extra clothes or trinkets or some delicacy.

Forgetting their miseries in talk and laughter, they made a packed and rowdy crowd in the streets and lanes. Sometimes they fell to dancing, gambling, and fighting, and pandemonium broke out. All too often the menfolk squandered their money for rum—raw rum, potent enough to make them quarrelsome and disorderly.

As afternoon wore on, they hoisted their baskets to their heads and began the long journey back home. Nor was this return to the plantations so orderly as their return is today. There were road fights and squabblings aplenty and a certain amount of drunkenness and rioting.

Eventually the influence of missionaries, with the help of the police, changed this practice to the familiar sight visitors now see. Market day was moved from Sunday to Saturday, so that now the Jamaican Sabbath is estimably sedate and peaceful, and the markets are clean and orderly. Nevertheless, the old markets furnished a needed relief from the six days of hard labor.

One wonders, though, how these poor creatures, after their long walks and exciting day in town, ever managed to do a stroke of work on Mondays. I have yet to encounter in contemporary documents, however, any references to Monday slack work. Once home again, the slaves slept soundly, like the worn-out creatures they were, and awoke refreshed on Monday at dawn when the work horn called them to cane field, sugar-boiling house, stable, and domestic duties.

Sable Venus and Sooty Adonis

Marriage between slaves was unknown. Doubtless plenty of romance waxed and waned between these sable Venuses and sooty Adonises, but it never entered their heads, nor would their owners have countenanced it, to solemnize their attachment with a rite. Besides, the attachment was only temporary. Polygamy was common among the slaves. Most males managed to have half a dozen wives scattered through the neighborhood; their huts made convenient ports of call. Good breeding women gained an added value in the eyes of their owners and lusty males were an asset. If a couple who had been cohabiting grew tired of each other, they cut their cottas, that is, they took the circular pad or ring of plantain leaves worn on the head to give balance to head-borne burdens, and cut it in two pieces. This simple, symbolic ceremony finished, each was free to go the way fancy dictated.

Since polygamy was so rampant, the picturesque marriage ceremonies now observable date from the Emancipation in 1838. Today such a value is placed on the ceremony and the subsequent celebration that many a couple live together for years before the groom is able to save enough money to pay for the ceremony. It is not at all a unique experience for a bride to have as her maids of honor her grown daughters born out of wedlock!

Among the free blacks and mulattos, who numbered about four thousand, the complete lack of marital restrictions were not so prevalent. This was a class of colored people whose numbers increased as the years went on and who, as we shall later see, were even provided for with seats in the theatre. Those highest in the class had been manumitted by private acts of the Assembly and were entitled to all rights and privileges enjoyed by whites, except that they could not sit in the legislature or act as justices or jurymen. A few, especially those left estates by their white fathers, thus being landowners, were entitled to vote.

A certain amount of social distinction grew up between the various kinds of blacks. The Creole blacks—

those born on the island—held the African-born blacks in marked contempt, referring to them as "salt-water negroes" and "guiney birds." Perhaps, on occasion, this distinction influenced their choice of "wife." The Maroons, however, were free rovers.

Maroon Fun

The Maroons, who were not slaves by the way, gained a widespread reputation as gay Lotharios. Their women stayed at home and cultivated the provision ground, while the men, who were adept hunters, ranged the woods and streams. Women on near-by plantations would welcome their arduous attentions. The offspring from such an attachment, following the mother, became slaves. Since in the Maroon clans the males far exceeded the females, this amorous wandering off the reservation may have had a biological excuse. Moreover, the Maroons also practiced the diversions of polygamy. Their women, being a mixture of negro and native Indian, possessed a defiant beauty, not unlike that of an equivalent racial mixture, the "Brass Ankle" girls at Charleston. The men were tall and handsome and well made, and had a wild eye.

It was not to be expected that the Maroons would stoop to the fantastic revelries in which the other blacks indulged. Nevertheless they had their own high moments. Once a year the officers of all the clans trudged the long way to Spanish Town to make their official call on the Governor. That august person received them in state, furnished refreshments and then gave them presents of swords and old laced coats and vests, which they bore home triumphantly, as befitted wards of the King, and which they wore thereafter on all great occasions.

The Maroons, too, had their own rough and sardonic idea of fun. There was that occasion at Montego Bay when Governor Lyttelton stopped off to inspect the town and the Maroons put on a military show for him.

The first act was a demonstration of their fighting tactics: a conch shell blew, whereupon the whole party yelled fearfully, fired their muskets, and then fell to the ground, rolling in all directions to escape the fire of the supposed enemy. This must have been highly amusing to the Governor as he sat, surrounded by his suite, military escort, and local dignitaries at one side of the Parade. After several volleys, the shell sounded again and the Maroons drew their swords. With a wild yell and threatening capers, they rushed on the Governor, some flourishing their swords over his head, others clashing them together before his face, and some laying their naked blades on his neck.

That must have been an anxious moment for Lyttelton, but he never winced. He was relieved, however, when the Maroons laid their arms before him and kissed his feet in abject humility. Their chief made a speech, to which he replied; then the whole company sat down to a feast provided by the Governor's privy purse.[2]

Negro Dances and Songs

Misery aplenty darkened the lives of the slaves and seasons arrived when times were hard for them. In June and July provisions grew scarce—the old yams had all been eaten and the new ones were not in yet. Meantime they subsisted meagerly on sweet potatoes and such fruit as they could gather. Their daily toil, too, was hard, and under the lash of cruel overseers, unceasing. And yet, it had bright moments. At noon they bathed in the sea or rivers, and almost nightly groups of them would gather around their huts for dances and sings.

While the masquerade dances that Sir Hans Sloane witnessed were reserved for special occasions, the nightly dances were no less picturesque. Men and women, boys and girls, they would form a circle around two dancers. Apart from rattles tied to their ankles and wrists, the costumes of these dancers were scant. Drums and a goombah would start pulsing. One of the women began a song—their songs were bawdy or leading that way— and the rest answered in chorus, singing as loud as their lungs would permit. The dancers stamped their feet interminably, circling round and round, twisting their bodies into macabre and lascivious attitudes, each movement following the exact measure of the song and drum, she especially exhibiting a wonderful address, particularly in the motion of her hips and the steady position of the upper part of her person and the right execution of the wriggle.[8] Tired of this, they started another dance. They would stiffen their bodies, throw back their heads, pin elbows to side, legs held firm, and without raising the feet from the ground, slowly approach and retreat, their sinuous bodies writhing and turning, the female dancer all languishing and easy in motion, the man all action and fire and gesture. And so they kept up their animalities until one or both of them fell exhausted to the ground, when another couple entered the ring.

Moonlit nights and Saturday nights were especially

chosen for this revelry. Like the whites, the black slaves didn't cease dancing till dawn. And at "crop-over," when the sugar cane was all harvested, came a big dance and sing. In most of their pleasures the slaves aped their masters, and in most of their vices as well.

The crop-over dance would begin with a big dinner at the great house where the planter entertained his overseers, the local doctors, and other local personages and friends. The bottle passed freely. When they had had enough of that, they called for fiddlers, and the musicians on the place came running, their women trailing behind. They were ready for it—the black, and brown, and *café au lait* girls all wore their finery. And far into the night, white men and their colored people danced and made merry.

At Christmas and at Easter, which they called "Pickaninny Christmas," two or three days' relief was granted the slaves, who usually spent most of the time visiting and dancing, their revelries going on night after night. Of course, they received Christmas presents from the "buckra"—usually salt fish, rum, and sugar for the field slaves and trinkets for the servants. After Emancipation, the dances in which the blacks indulged grew less coarse, as religious teaching began to penetrate their intelligence, and the musical accompaniment grew more elaborate.

Musical Instruments

From the beginning, the drum was the most popular of the musical instruments the slaves brought with them from Africa. Made of native materials, drums were of all shapes and sizes. One, shaped like a barrel six feet long, was called a Gumbie. Another, called the Goombah, was a hollow block of wood or a square box covered with sheepskin at the ends and capable of creating pandemonium: while one player beat it, the other briskly drew a stick along a notched piece of wood laid full length across the drum. Still another type was made of bark leaves and played with two sticks. Other variations were: the Cotter, a block of hard wood cut to the shape of a mortar; the Dundo, a little drum; the Gumbay, consisting of a small square wooden frame over which goatskin was stretched.

The stringed instruments were also various. Sir Hans Sloane described what he called "fiddles"—somewhat like our present-day banjo or guitar—which were hollowed-out gourds covered with skin and strung with horse hairs. These had two strings each. Another was oblong, made of wood, and had eight or ten strings. Other stringed instruments noted by later writers were: the Bangil, which was something like a lute; the Banjar, a crude guitar; the Banjour, quite different from our banjo; the Bender, a crude form of Jew's harp made from bent wood; and the Merry-wang or Banja. Any musical instrument with such a hilarious name as Merry-wang deserves a sentence or two all to itself. It has been described as "a variety of banjo," "a rustic guitar," and "an imperfect violoncello." It was made from a large calabash cut in two and with a dried bladder stretched across the opening. To this was added a finger board and a carved wooden handle decked with ribbons. The strings were plucked.

The only wind instrument of olden times was a flute, presumably introduced by the Coromantyn tribe, as it was one of their favorites. It was made from a hollow branch of a Trumpet Tree, about a yard long. Toward the bottom were three holes. "The high notes were wild but sweet and the lower were deep and majestic." [4] The Coromantyns were a sullen and warlike tribe; all night long they would thump the goombah and sing to the tunes of this flute.

Besides these were several others: the Kitty-katty, a board beaten with two sticks; the Jenkoving, two jars with ordinary-size mouths over which the palms were brought down to make a sucking sound; a Cassand grater, which was rubbed with a spoon to make a cracking noise; Calabash rattles filled with Indian Shot; bones, the jawbone of a horse rubbed with a stick; and the Rookaw, which consisted merely of two jagged hardwood sticks beaten together.

As time went on, these primitive instruments were supplanted by those of European make: tambourines and fifes, guitars, violins, banjos, and flutes. Occasionally one found a bass viol, but this would be owned by a Creole negro who belonged to a dance group.

If the mistress of a plantation great house was to give a dance, she called in the negro musicians of the countryside. They had a quick ear, and could repeat any tune after hearing it once or twice. Some of the bands had a repertoire of twenty or thirty dance tunes for polkas, waltzes, quadrilles, and minuets. Now and then some negro musician could play a sonata without having read a note of it. Of course, none of these slave bandsmen could read a note of music. They had a pretty custom, too; whenever there was a public gathering or a house dance, they would play as they walked along the road to the house and again as they left it. Their tunes must have cheered many a weary guest making her way home through the dawn's gray light.

Negro Songs

In the old days the negro songs at their night revelries were sometimes sad, not unlike the songs of our Southern negroes, but more often they lampooned white folk. While they themselves were sensitive to ridicule, they didn't hesitate to ridicule others. If someone, white or black, incurred their displeasure or some bookkeeper or overseer had a marked mental or physical peculiarity, the slaves were quick to notice it and composed an appropriate song on the spot. The bawdy songs, many of which had an interminable number of verses, rose to the heights of a fine folk art.

There were sung, and still are, ring tunes, used for informal dancing. This was sometimes called "playing in de ring," dancing mixed with horseplay. There were also "digging sings," sung especially in March when the slaves were getting the provision grounds ready for planting yams. A work leader who was usually the wag of the party would raise the tune and the others followed in unison with their work.[5]

Christmas in Town and Country

A number of African tribes were represented in the thousands of slaves transported to Jamaica, and some of them were quite clannish. We have already met the haughty, ferocious, and stubborn Coromantyns. Besides these were the Minnahs, a timid and despondent clan prone to suicide; the Mundingoes, the lazy Ebos, the stupid Angolas, the Aradas, who excelled in agriculture and the Congos, Papaws, Conchas, and Whidahs who made good field laborers. The Congos and Gold Coast negroes were expert fishermen and excelled in making canoes.

At Christmas, when they were given two or three days' holiday, each of these African tribes would form itself into a distinct party, men, women, and children, and elect a chief. She was then dressed in a gaudy costume that covered her from head to foot, and put on a hideous mask. Thus arrayed, she paraded and gamboled through the neighborhood, going from house to house, a band of goombahs, benders, merry-wangs, and banjils accompanying her antics and the shouts and songs of the darkies that trailed at her heels. Each householder, of course, provided refreshments for the noisy visitors and a present for the royalty. The end of the Christmas holidays found the crowd fairly exhausted.

In towns the Christmas revelries provided by the negroes were much more elaborate and followed more closely an African legendary figure.

About 1720 there flourished and fought a noted tribal chief at Tres Puntus in Axim on the Guinea Coast, called John Connu, who originated a famous custom. As copied by the Jamaican negroes at Christmas, it first consisted of a tall, athletic negro wearing a headdress surmounted by a pair of horns and with boar tusks at the bottom, such as Sir Hans Sloane described. He carried a large wooden sword, which he brandished ferociously. Accompanied by a native band and an ever-increasing crowd of friends and children and disreputable women of the town, his party made a picturesque and rowdy sight.

John Connu or Canoe, as he was sometimes called, paraded the streets and danced from house to house, often entering the houses themselves to exhibit his girations, with as many of his followers as could crowd onto the verandah. Friends, especially his disreputable female followers, plied him with liquor between dances, so that John Canoe after whole days and nights of this violent exercise, drunkenness, and other excesses, was worn to a mere shadow. He and many of his followers often paid a fatal price for their Christmas revelries.

Eventually John Canoe assumed a much more picturesque air. Various versions appeared—Jaw-bone John Canoe, so called because of the rattle made from the jaw-bone of a horse that supplied his "music"; House John Canoe, from the style of his headdress; and Butchers' John Canoe, in which the town's butchers participated. Sometimes he was accompanied by another figure, "Koo-Koo or Actor-Boy"; or groups of Actor-Boys paraded the streets alone.

Koo-Koo's costume consisted of a voluminous skirt of muslin, silks, satin, ribbons, and lace and a long loose jacket to his heels, curls dripping down front, behind, and on shoulders, a mask and a fantastic headdress composed of colored beads, bangles, and pieces of mirror "attached to a pasteboard form trimmed round the edges with silver lace, surmounted with feathers." [6] He held a fan in one hand and in the other a whip to keep off pestering urchins. Actor-Boys would spend as much as £15 for this "get-up." At night the costume appeared especially resplendent, for the Actor-Boy was surrounded by a large square wooden frame holding candles and supported by men. This kept the crowd at a safe distance. Inside it he wheeled round and round, singing an unintelligible jargon in stentorian tones to the beat of the goombah and gumbay. By these antics an Actor-Boy might collect as much as £12 a day.

John Canoe's later costume was a nondescript compound, half military, half mountebank. He wore a castoff regimental coat and sash and striped trousers edged with bows. A white mask and a curled wig of false hair was topped by the "house." This was constructed of pasteboard and colored paper ornamented with beads, tinsel, spangles, and feathers. Sometimes it contained little figures. It was placed on a board that John balanced on his head with both hands as he poised and pirouetted, crossing his legs and then suddenly striking a comical posture. Occasionally one of his attendants carried the house, which must have been a relief, considering the weight of the decoration and the wig and the fact that the temperature might be in the higher eighties. He also had his band of native musicians.

In *Tom Cringle's Log,* Michael Scott describes a variation—the Butchers' John Canoe:

He was a light, active, clean-made young Creole negro, without shoes or stockings; he wore a pair of light jean small-clothes, all too wide, but confined at the knees, below and above, by bands of red tape, after the manner that Malvolio would have called cross-gartering. He wore a splendid blue velvet waistcoat, with old-fashioned flaps coming down over his hips, and covered with tarnished embroidery. His shirt was absent on leave, I suppose, but at the wrists of his coat he had tin or white iron frills, with loose pieces attached, which tinkled as he moved and set off the dingy paws that were struck through these strange manacles, like black wax tapers in silver candle-sticks. His coat was an old blue artillery uniform, with a small bell hung at the extreme points of the swallow-tailed skirts, and two tarnished epaulets, one on each shoulder. He had an enormous cocked hat on, to which was appended in front a white false-face or mask, while, Janus-like, there was another face behind, both being garnished and overtopped with one coarse wig, made of the hair of bullocks' tails, on which the chapeau was strapped down by a broad band of gold lace.

He skipped up to us with a white wand in one hand and a dirty handkerchief in the other, and with sundry mop-pings and mowings, first wiping my shoes with his *mou-choir,* then my face, he made a smart enough pirouette and then sprung on the back of a nondescript animal that now advanced capering and jumping about after the most grotesque fashion. This was the signal for the music to begin.

The performers were two gigantic men, dressed in calf skins entire, head, four legs and tail. The skin of the head was made to fit like a hood, the two fore feet hung dan-gling down in front, one over each shoulder, while the other two legs or hind feet and the tail trailed behind on the ground. There were also two flute players in sheep skins, looking still more outlandish, from the horns of the ani-mals' heads being preserved; and three stout fellows who were dressed in the common white frock and trousers, who kept sounding on bullocks' horns.

These formed the band, as it were, and might be con-sidered John's immediate tail or following; but he was also accompanied by about fifty of the butcher negroes, all neatly dressed—blue jackets, white shirts and Osna-burgh trousers, with their steels and knife cases by their sides, and they all wore clean blue and white striped aprons.

Imagine the pandemonium in Kingston and other towns at this time, with literally hundreds of these mummers parading the streets, dancing and singing, and the crowds joining in the choruses at the top of their lungs, from morning to night, day after day.

Even the children had their miniature Koo-Koos and John Canoes and their own gangs of followers. And besides all these were the Set Girls.

The Set Girls

Scarcely had Christmas gone and the town negroes rested from their John Canoe excitement than New Year's and another holiday rolled around. On both these occasions groups of young women, elegantly dressed and divided into two sets, the Reds and the Blues according to the color of ribbon they wore, went from house to house and danced for gifts. Their owners usually furnished the dresses and hats and even provided jewelry. Many of them were domestic servants, so that one householder would wager his Blue Girls against the neighbor's Red. "Monk" Lewis left an account of these Set Girls as he saw their procession on January 1, 1816, at the little logwood center of Black River, all dressed in white. Marching two by two, with attendants and a band of negro musicians and with scarlet flags fluttering, came the Set Girls.

It seems that many years ago, an Admiral of the Red was superseded on the Jamaica Station by an Admiral of the Blue; and both of them gave balls at Kingston to the "Brown Girls"; for the fair sex elsewhere are called "the Brown Girls" in Jamaica. In consequence of these balls, all Kingston was divided into parties: from thence the division spread into other districts; and ever since, the whole island, at Christmas, is separated into the rival factions of the Blues and the Reds (the Red representing also the English, the Blue the Scotch) who contend for setting forth their processions with the greatest taste and magnificence.

This year, several gentlemen in the neighborhood of Black River had subscribed very largely towards the expenses of the show; and certainly it produced the gayest and most amusing scene that I ever witnessed, to which the mutual jealousy and pique of the two parties against each other contributed in no slight degree. The champions of the rival Roses, the Guelphs and the Ghibellines, none of them could exceed the scornful animosity and spirit of depreciation with which the Blues and the Reds of Black River examined the efforts at display of each other. The Blues had the advantage beyond a doubt; this a Red girl told us that she could not deny; but still, "though the Reds were beaten, she would not be a Blue girl for the whole universe!"

On the other hand, Miss Edwards (the mistress of the hotel from whose window we saw the show) was rank Blue to the very tips of her fingers, and had, indeed, contributed one of her female slaves to sustain a very important character in the show; for when the Blue procession was ready to set forward, there was evidently a hitch, something was wanting; and there seemed to be no possibility of getting on without it—when suddenly we saw a tall woman dressed in mourning (being Miss Edwards herself) rush out of our hotel, dragging along by the hand a strange uncouth kind of a glittering tawdry figure, all feathers and pitchfork and painted pasteboard, who moved most reluctantly, and turned out to be no less a personage than Britannia herself, with a pasteboard shield covered with the arms of Great Britain, a trident in her hand, and a helmet made of pale blue silk and silver. . . .

The Blue girls called themselves "the Blue girls of Waterloo." Their motto was the more patriotic; that of the Red was the more gallant :—"Britannia rules the day !" streamed upon the Blue flag; "Red girls forever !" floated upon the Red. But, in the point of taste and invention, the former carried it hollow." [7]

The queen of the Set Girls was elaborately dressed and, instead of a scepter, carried a beribboned cowhide whip with which she exercised authority. In addition to this she had other distinguishing marks—her coiffure and feathered hat were of imposing proportions. Her dress was of the finest muslin trimmed with gold and silver lace and the ribbon of her set. Her jewelry—earrings, quantities of jangling bracelets, and resplendent breastpins—was more extravagant than the others. She also wore stockings, which the rest of the Set did not. Like the others, she carried an opened umbrella, both by day and night. Some of the dresses for the queen were calculated to have cost upwards of £60.

The procession got under way about ten in the morning and the Set Girls continued to parade the town with their bands and flags until night, halting only when invited into houses to dance and sing. As they marched, they sang songs learned for the occasion. Finally at night, they gathered around a booth lighted with variegated lamps and transparencies, where they received their friends, the whites mingling with all the other complexional mixtures, and served them wine and sweetmeats.

The order of the parade was quite impressive and included a figure or two we have yet to meet. Jack-in-the-Green wore a completely enveloping costume composed of cocoanut leaves or flowers attached to hoops and crowned with a large bow and a couple of flags. Sometimes he carried a whip. There was also a "commodore," a very stout woman being selected for this honor.

In the parade, first came four Grand Masters to protect the Set and clear the way. Then a middle group,
flanked by flag bearers, consisting of the band—hand
drums, tambourines, violins, triangles, and the singer or
leader of the chorus—all escorting the queen. Next the
commodore, strutting along by herself. She was followed by the Set Girls, two by two, the tallest first and
the end tapering down to the smallest pickaninnies, all
with the same color and style of dress and parasol. They
danced and sang as they went, chanting at the top of
their voices tropical songs set to popular airs.

In addition to the Blues and Reds were other kinds
of Set Girl. The housekeepers had their own group, but
disdained to dance in their progress through the streets.
Toward the end of the century the presence of refugee
servants from Haiti and Santo Domingo brought out
the French Set Girls. These did not go in for the rivalry
of color, although they fell into three groups that were
jealous of each other—the Royalists, who were Creoles
from Santo Domingo; the Mabiales, who were Congo-
born; and the Americans, who were a general mixture.
They had their queen and their male companions to join
in the dances, and a band composed of drums or "tam-
boos," beaten with the fingers, and rattles called "sha-
kas." They considered it indecorous to dance in the
streets and so confined their efforts to dwelling houses
and walled premises where they would dance for two or
three hours in relays.

Of course the Set Girls of the towns considered themselves superior in taste, manners, and fashion to those on
plantations. And, as we have seen, rivalry between the
Reds and Blues ran high. When their parades met on

the street, a lot of acrimonious backchat ensued and sometimes good lusty hairpulling. Because of this rivalry, the making of their costumes—the choice of material and style of gown, hat, and parasol—was conducted with the greatest secrecy. The preparations began weeks and weeks before the holidays and every penny that could be spared went to them. From the parade and the dances a group of Set Girls would collect from £8 to £10 a day, which was either divided among the Set or used to pay for a ball or party at the end of the Christmas holidays or on New Year's.

In time these Christmas and New Year mummeries lost their fascination or were frowned on. The coming of Emancipation found many of the negroes in the throes of a religious revival that did not countenance such pagan revelries. Moreover very many of them soon were seriously trying to establish themselves as potential citizens—taking up land and forming little villages deep in the mountain districts. What Jamaica gained by their growing stability, it lost in the cessation of these picturesque costume parades. Today one occasionally finds some of the young boys trying to keep the custom alive, but they are usually in out-of-the-way districts. Jamaica now hangs up imitation holly wreaths and goes to the movies.

CHAPTER X

1786–1790

The Stage Rests—Kingston and Montego Bay Diversions—
Frances Barret Woollery—Terpsichore and the Creole—A
New Company on the Island

AMONG the charms of Jamaica—charms to those who
have a romantic urge and can make the dead past live in
their imagination—are the sleepy towns that seem to lie
cushioned on the sweet memories of what they have been.
Glorious old centers of fine living, lavish spending, courteous gallantry, and sometimes bitter warfare, they bask
in the warm sun, refreshed by the "doctor," the daytime
sea breeze, and lulled to deeper sleep at night by the
"undertaker," the land breeze. The ruins of many of
their great houses are overgrown with brush. Their
stone sugar wharfs, which once saw lively commerce,
still stretch into a sea that is gradually eating them away.
Whether by the swift destruction of hurricane or by the
slower crumbling of the elements or the change in trade,
a deadening soporific spreads over these towns. Having
made a great effort and a great show, they doze off, and
so they sleep for years and years.

The Jamaican theatre is somewhat like those "dead"
towns. After a decade of busy seasons under the tireless
American Company of Comedians, the stage apparently
dozed off. Now and then something rouses it to effort—
a faint effort—then it falls back and waits until fresh

blood comes in to take the initiative. The years between
1786 and the end of the century form one of the somno-
lent periods of the Jamaica stage. Our news of plays,
players, and high times comes in meager dribblets.

"What," would Jamaicans ask, "could you expect?
Did we not have trouble on our hands?"

Unrest among Maroons and slaves, those intermittent
interruptions of peace and progress, kept ruffling the waters of orderly daily living. And when these were not
making the population jumpy, storms and hurricanes and
fires and earthquakes were effectively keeping the island
discouraged.

A storm in August, 1785, had left a wide trail of
wrecked homes and crops. The next year a serious
drought, followed in October by another storm, cost fifteen thousand lives. A malignant fever harassed the people and filled the graveyards. The *status quo* of the
Church of England—and the Church of England, stoutly
supported by the planters, always sat stubbornly on its
status quo—was disturbed by the invasions of Baptist,
Methodist, Moravian, and Quaker missionaries who
preached about bettering the condition of the slaves.[1]

By July, 1795, the trouble with the Maroons grew
serious and August saw martial law clamped down on
the island. A bitter, destructive, and expensive warfare
with them dragged on for a year. Montego Bay, so often
a haven for the Thespians, was in the center of it all.

Though sugar was still king and would remain on the
throne for many years to come, Jamaica had begun to
feel acutely the results of absentee landlordship. In the
course of the twenty years that reaches 1772, more than
one hundred and seventy estates in Jamaica had been

sold for payment of debts and ninety-two more were in the hands of creditors. Executions at that time lodged in the marshal's office totaled the staggering sum of £22,-500,000 sterling.[2] By 1792, a petition reveals that "estate after estate had passed into the hands of mortgagors and creditors absent from the island, until there were whole districts—whole parishes—in which there was not a single *resident proprietor* of a sugar plantation.[3]

And so on and so on—economic troubles, slave revolts in Trelawny, England at war with France again and the Jamaican planters digging down into their pockets to the tune of £80,000 to help the old country. Once more Kingston harbor bristled with vessels of war; soldiers and sailors aplenty were seen on the streets and lanes of Port Royal, Kingston, Spanish Town, Port Antonio, and Montego Bay.

Who was there to amuse them? Will those actors left behind by the American Company try their hand at the stage? What ladies and gentlemen of the theatre came from England in this period?

Kingston and Montego Bay Amusements, 1786

Kingstonians, so long accustomed to the professional technique of the American Company, were inclined to be critical of newcomers. Witness their attitude toward amateurs in the report of April 15, 1786, of Mrs. Gardner's benefit. This excellent actress, you will recall, made her Jamaican debut on August 8, 1781, as Mrs. Cadwallader in *Author* and evidently did her share in amusing the theatregoing populace:

On Saturday evening last, a theatrical representation occurred in this town for the benefit of Mrs. Gardner. It commenced with an Occasional Prelude, written by the Lady herself; in the writing and performance thereof, she equally proved the strength of her genius and abilities, in the comic, satiric and initiative veins. It displayed the strongest sensation of favours conferred by this community, without being fulsome, and judiciously discriminated the liberty and licentiousness of newspaper animadversions on stage performances. This was followed by the Comedy of the Lyar, in which Mrs. Gardner very ably sustained the character of Papillion; and some minor effusions, all very well represented, although by novices. And, indeed, it is truly remarkable, the only Defaulter was the only professed Actor who that night trod the stage. The whole was concluded with the Lady's speaking the following expressive lines:—

> For me, whate'er may be my future lot,
> Your gen'rous favours ne'er will be forgot,
> To all my friends, around—above—below—
> A frank return of Gratitude I owe.
> My cordial thanks await you to receive;
> For what is life, without the means to live?
> For this your goodness warmly shewn to me,
> Long may this gen'rous Isle be bless'd and free.

That sounds as though the lady was about to leave Jamaica. We only wish we could say whether she did or not, but no copies of Kingston papers for 1786 exist and the item we have just quoted was culled from the *Cornwall Chronicle* of Montego Bay.

However, we can account for Mrs. Gardner's future movements by one Charleston announcement and two bits of news from New York.

In Charleston, during the opening week of April, 1789, was advertised:

Mrs. Gardner
Late of the Theatre Royal, Covent Garden
At Mr. McCrady's Long Room
A Concert of Vocal and Instrumental music,
with Entertainments
Admittance—5s.

Mrs. Gardner begs leave to assure the public that the room will be brilliantly illuminated with wax lights.

On November 17, 1789, at the City Tavern in New York, Mrs. Gardner offered "an entertainment rhetorical and oratorical, entitled Fashionable Raillery or the Powers of Eloquence Displayed in a Spirited and humorous Touch on the Times." She is making her first appearance in the city and the entertainment she offered was the one "performed by her 47 nights in Dublin and with equal success in Jamaica and Charleston." Interspersed in the entertainment were songs and the whole ended with a mock-heroic afterpiece called *The Mad Poetess.* The price of admission for all this was one dollar.

We gather that the populace did not pack the City Tavern's Long Room, for on December 29th Mrs. Gardner presented herself at the John Street Theatre for a benefit that was given her the next evening. In a published letter she tells how "she was deceived in Charleston by a plausible scamp, brought north, stripped of every penny and left helpless."

A sad circumstance for Mrs. Gardner. What a comedown from the days when, as a distinguished actress, she was playing the heroine in most of the productions at the Haymarket under the management of Foote!

As she does not appear on any of the American play-bills after this performance, we shall have to leave Mrs. Gardner, a sadder and, we hope, a wiser woman, and see if we can cull one more item from the Jamaica amusements of 1786. It is meager, to be sure; but, excepting Mrs. Gardner, we could just as well drop this year out of our account. However, in July the Kingston Assembly takes over the theatre in Kingston "for the first time when about sixty Ladies were present and an hundred Gentlemen, among whom was his Honour the Lieutenant Governor. . . . The company did not separate till about three o'clock yesterday morning." [4]

Over in Montego Bay the *Chronicle* continues printing news of the old Company that once amused that town. It hears that there has joined the troupe a Mrs. Kenna "whose ability in both Tragic and Comic lines, have never been surpassed in the Western World." Also that Mrs. Morris has had a stroke in Baltimore, but her health is now perfectly reestablished. That Hallam and Henry opened the new theatre in Baltimore on the 17th of August with *The School for Scandal.*

Then, just when things are absolutely dead and no news at all is coming through, up pops that ever-present help in time of dullness—Hyman Saunders. He takes over the Montego Bay playhouse, moves in his "Grand Deception Boxes" and on November 6th and 13th and December 2nd and 16th delights the populace of the Bay "without descending to the low tricks of Cups, Balls and Ribbands."

Culture in the musical way seems also to have come graciously on the parish. On November 28th the St.

James's Musical Society announces that its concerts will be on the second Thursday in every month. The Jamaican Creole had and has a fine ear for music and supported concerts with a highly commendable attendance and interest.

And that, my masters, is all the juice there is to squeeze out of the orange of 1786.

1787

Toward the end of March, Kingston reads that the American Company of Comedians has arrived at New York from Philadelphia and will open their theatre. In May, the St. James's Musical Society at Montego Bay elects officers. By the 29th of that month the musical fever spreads to the next parish eastward, to Falmouth in Trelawny. It blossoms out in a concert at Mr. Dumm's Long Room. The songs are by a Young Gentleman—probably a native:

ACT I

Overture—Haydn
Song—"The Topsails"
Oboe Concerto—Hemmings
Guitar Solo—Jackson
Song
Overture—Fritz

ACT II

Overture—Tom Thumb
Song
Violin Solo—Jackson
Harpsichord Lesson—Rodgers
Song
Overture

After the concert there was a ball. The price of admission was half a guinea each—a pretty high figure for a concert even though the Trelawny and sugar planters were wallowing in wealth. Mr. Hemming will be remembered as the erstwhile orchestra leader of the company in Montego Bay. Perhaps the "Young Gentleman" of this evening was one of his pupils.

The hot months pass, the hurricanes avoid the island, and Montego Bay has a concert. The notice reads—

For the Benefit of
Mr. Rodgers
On Tuesday the 27th of November instant, at Mr.
Dauney's Long-Room,
will be performed
A Concert
of Vocal and Instrumental Music.
After the Concert will be a Ball
Tickets 16s 3d each, to be had at the Post-Office, Mr. Giffen's Tavern, of S. Rodgers, at Mr. Mc'Ghee's, near the Theatre, and at the Printing-Office.

S. Rodgers respectfully informs the Public that from the Assistance he has been promised, and having procured a choice collection of new Music, he flatters himself the Performance will be worthy their attention.

The Doors to be open at six o'clock and to begin precisely at Seven.

Two days later the St. James's Assembly moves into the theatre for its monthly dance.

And with those few dribblets of high times and merry hearts, the year 1787 passes into time. However, let us snatch a moment to explain the Jamaican's passion for dancing. That important subject and a Jamaican contribution to the English stage dated from this year both warrant our attention.

Frances Barnet Woollery

Among the worthies that crowd the pages of Jamaican history in the last quarter of the eighteenth century was Edward Woollery, a native Jamaican, of the parish of St. Andrew and member of the Assembly for 1770 and 1771. Of an inventive mind, he is remembered for having made improvements in sugar machinery the value of which the Assembly recognized by voting him £300 worth of plate. His other contribution to the island's annals was his daughter, Frances.

Like many other daughters of Jamaican planters, she was sent to England to be educated. There her talent for the stage first made itself evident, and she succeeded in interesting the manager of the Haymarket Theatre, who, on June 29, 1784, allowed her to appear as Harriet in *The Jealous Wife*. After this debut she tried the part of Sigismunda in Thompson's tragedy and from then on to November undertook several roles with great acclaim.

Her talents coming to the attention of Daly of Dublin, she was offered the part of first tragedienne at the Smock Alley Theatre. Here she appeared in November, 1785, playing a succession of roles—Miss Hardcastle in *She Stoops to Conquer*, Statira in *The Rival Queens*, Jane Shore, Cordelia, and Sigismunda. By that time she had won over Dublin. After this she returned to London appearing at the Haymarket for its usual summer season.

The great promise which she held out was diverted to

another channel: in May, 1788, she married James
Henry Cottingham and retired from the stage. Before
her death in 1810 she had borne six children. Her portrait as Sigismunda was painted by Robert Horne.

Terpsichore and the Creole

Almost with the earliest records we encounter the
Creole taste for dancing. It has always been the chief
Jamaican household amusement, stirring "the most languid Creole, especially ladies, into almost preternatural
activity." In Kingston and the other large towns, public
balls and monthly assemblies were common and no one
objected riding twenty or thirty miles for a dance, even
when the thermometer stood at 80° or 90°.

Now Creole ladies could be languid when they chose,
very languid. Edward Long supplies a colorful description of them:

The ladies who live in and about the Towns, being
often in company with Europeans, and others brought up
in Great Britain, copy imperceptibly their manners and
address: and become better qualified to fill the honorable
station of a wife and to head their table with grace and
propriety.
Those who have been bred up entirely in the seques-
tered country parts, and had no opportunity of forming
themselves either by example or tuition, are truly to be
pitied. We may see, in some of these places, a very fine
young woman awkwardly dangling her arms with the air
of a Negro-servant, lolling almost the whole day upon
beds or settees, her head muffled up with two or three
handkerchiefs, her dress loose and without stays. At
noon we find her employed gobbling pepper-pot, seated
on the floor, with her sable hand-maids around her. In
the afternoon, she takes her siesta as usual; while two

of these damsels refresh her face with the gentle breathings of the fan; and a third provokes the drowsy powers of Morpheus by deliciously irritating the sole of either foot.[5]

It was thought vulgar and ungenteel for the ladies to rise early in the morning.

They sit down to breakfast about nine or past it, have what they call second breakfast at twelve, dine at three or four and drink tea at eight; but seldom eat much, if any, supper. The intervals between these necessary avocations are usually employed in sewing, reading or lounging. . . . The meal called second breakfast is the most favorite of all their meals. . . . It must consist of certain favorite viands, such as black or land crab, shrimps, toasted green Indian corn, pepper-pot (a distinguished dish, made so hot with green pepper, that one can hardly endure it in the mouth), tum-tum, that is, plantains beat into a kind of dough, and boiled in the pepper-pot and several other articles. This must be eaten with the assistance of the fingers alone; for knives and forks are on this occasion *proscribed*.[6]

Nevertheless, no women in any other part of the world could dance with equal spirit and none would work harder to make themselves attractive in appearance or gracious in manner.

The great balls were those given by the Governor in King's House at Spanish Town and they set the standard for luxurious entertainment and apparel. All ranks under him rivaled each other in the brilliancy and costliness of their dances and suppers. Even in the country, refreshments followed the dances—not a finale of eating and drinking, but interludes for cold refreshments—whipped creams, lobster salads, brandy and water and champagne until dawn.

Lady Nugent, wife of the Governor from April, 1801, to June, 1805, in the diary she kept during that period reports several official balls. They all appear to have been rather formal although on one occasion "after supper, I forgot my dignity and with all my heart joined in a Scotch reel. Many followed my example and the ball concluded most merrily." A really brilliant and wearying ball was that of December 30, 1802:

Dress at 7 for the ball given me tonight by the Assembly. Dear little George at my toilet. For the benefit of posterity I will describe my dress on this grand occasion. A crape dress, embroidered in silver spangles, also sent me by Madame Le Clerc, but much richer than that which I wore at the last ball. Scarcely any sleeves to my dress, but a broad silver spangled border to the shoulder straps. The body made very like a child's frock, tying behind, and the skirt round, with not much train. A turban of spangled crape, like the dress, looped with pearls, and a paradise feather; altogether looking like a SULTANA. Diamond bandeau, cross, etc.; and a pearl necklace and bracelets, with diamond clasps. This dress, the admiration of all the world over, will perhaps, fifty years hence, be laughed at and considered as ridiculous as our grandmother's hoops and tissures appear to us now. . . . But, to return to our proceedings; all well here at 8, and we started in high spirits for the ball. We were met at the door by the four stewards, and marched up the room to the tune of "God save the King." I then stood by the state sofa, receiving the compliments of all the company, and making curtesies for near an hour. After which, I opened the ball with the Admiral, danced with a Member of Council and one of the Assembly, and then

thought it dignified to play a rubber of cassino. This
over, General N. and I walked about the room, toadying
and being toadied till supper time. A splendid supper
soon after 12. Transparencies and appropriate devices,
etc. Soon after we had sat down, the company all stood
up round the table, with filled glasses, and drank my
health, with a fine complimentary speech, and three times
three. Then General N.'s health followed, with the same
sort of speech, and applause; and last of all, our dear
child's health, with blessings and good wishes, most grateful to our hearts. General N. thanked them, and I curte-
sied and looked my thanks, but I could not speak, and
really felt so much overcome with the whole thing, that
I was glad when the uproar ceased, and the attention of
the company was drawn to some other toasts, proposed
on the part of General N. about the concerns of the Island, Kingston, etc. Got back to the Penn at three.[7]

Country assemblies, of course, were not so formal as
those at King's House. Dinner came first, then more
guests arrived for the dance to follow and the supper
supplied throughout the evening. It was customary to
decorate the first floor of the great house with branches
of fragrant orange, lemon, lime, mango, pomegranate,
with dozens of others all hanging rich with fruit or in
blossom, besides innumerable native flowers and shrubs.
"The fragrance which pervaded the apartment was de-
lectable and, when joined with the sumptuous appearance
of the fruit, the blossoms and the flowers hanging in clus-
ters, amidst the dark green leaves to which they belonged, illuminated with transparent lamps of every hue,
from the most modest to the most gaudy, the spectator
must have admitted that the splendid scenes in the Ara-
bian Nights were not altogether fabulous."[8]

Country dances—reels and such—seem to have been

the favorites. And the Creole lads and lassies were inde-
fatigable in them, for there's scarcely a record of a dance
in Jamaica but states proudly that the party didn't break
up till dawn. Negro fiddlers, accompanied by the lively
sound of the tambourine, in lieu of the bass viol, furnished the music. Some of these negro bands had a repertoire of twenty or thirty pieces, so that the music at
dances was not half so monotonous as it is today when
the "Black Bottom Boys" try to imitate American jazz
and swing music.

1788

A very patchy mosaic we are forced to make of this
year 1788, but it does finally afford us news of the theatre. From a few copies of the Jamaica *Gazette* preserved
in the Royal Empire Society in London, we extract the
bills of a short Kingston run. What happened before
July 19th, and what happened after July 30th, we have
no way of knowing. However, we are thankful for these
few fragments to add to our playbook.

Never performed in this Town,

ASSEMBLY ROOM IN THE PARADE.

(By Permission of the Master
of the Revels,)

THIS PRESENT EVENING

Will be presented,

THE COMIC OPERA OF THE

AGREEABLE SURPRIZE.

Sir Felix Friendly, by Mr. Mahon,
Compton, by Mr. Nelson,
Eugene, by Mr. Cross
Chicane, by Mr. Hynes,
Thomas, by Mr. Phelps,
And, Lingo, by Mr. Morales,
Laura, by Mrs. Mahon,
Mrs. Cheshire, by Mr. Roberts,
Fringe, by Miss Muligin,
And, Cowslip, by Miss Quin,

A Flute Concerto by Mr. Salomons,

Part II

and Interlude, Called

THE VINTNER TRICK'D.

Mixum, by Mr. Hynes,
Mrs. Mixum, Mr. Roberts,
and Vizard, Mr. Morales.

Part III

The Comic Opera of

THE PADLOCK

Leander, by Mr. Mahon,
Don Diego, Mr. Nelson,
And Mungo, Mr. Morales,
Leonora, Mrs. Mahon,
Ursula, (first time) Miss Quin.

The whole to conclude (by particular desire) with
the favourite song of

VAUX-HALL WATCH,

by Mr. Mahon.

Between the interlude and Farce, a new Hunting Song,
called,

THE FOX CHASE

by MR. CROSS.

Tickets for the Ball Room, 10ss.—Upper Boxes
6/8; to be had of Mr. Mahon, and at the
Coffee houses and Printing-Offices.

N.B. It will be strictly observed that no person will be
admitted behind the scenes, either at Rehearsals or the
Performance. Places to be taken on the days of performance from nine till five at the Theatre.

The bill brings a whole company of new names to us.
Only Morales and Roberts are left over from the Hallam and Henry troupe. The advertisement also informs
us that this was the first presentation in Jamaica of *The
Agreeable Surprize*. Likewise we note that this performance is "By Permission of the Master of the Revels."
Hitherto it has been the Governor or the Lieutenant
Governor or the Custos of the parish who gave permission for the plays. And yet the office of the Master of
the Revels had existed in the island now well over thirty
years. Evidently Mr. William Smith, the present Master, was taking his post seriously and insisting on his
rights.

In the *Gazette* of July 23rd Mr. Mahon, who was evidently manager, was publicly told why this company
lacked public support:

Theatre

ON Saturday last Mr. Mahon made a second attempt to
entertain the community in the line of a *Theatrical Fête*,
and, we announce with no small degree of concern, without that pecuniary encouragement his ability and industry
merited. . . . The business of the Theatre is an arduous
undertaking . . . the ability of a *Garrick*, a *Siddons*,

or any hero or heroine of the Buskin and Sock, if un-supported, might, with propriety, be compared to a *Mal-borough* without soldiers . . . the bravery of the latter, with the excellence of the former, being, equally depend-ent upon a proper support of subordinate character. The *Agreeable Surprize* was lopped of the latter part of its title . . . *agreeable* it certainly was, but the *Surprize* was totally lost by the unaccountable want of feeling and indifference of the Actors upon the principal incident, by which the idea *surprize*, in the last act, is founded, i. e. *explanation*. Two supposed mendicant Orphans, are, in a moment, restored to affluence and honourable parents. . . . Should this be marked with the coolest indifference? Our Correspondent forbears a further comment. . . . The music was wretched . . . the leading Gentleman seemed a foreigner, if so, the ignorance of our language may, in some measure, account for the *concordia discor* being the leading feature of his performance; on the flute he seems to possess ability, but we cannot recommend to him, as a leader, the further public use of the violin. . . . The dresses, particularly of Crompton, were *outré* in the extreme . . . the character of a *friendless, young imprudent Midshipman,* was substituted in lieu of the honest *old Captain* . . . the Gentleman who took this part as well as *Diego* in the *Padlock,* must have sacrificed at the shrine of Bacchus, or otherwise imbibed an unac-countable stupor; nature has been bountiful to him in a voice, and, with a proper attention to dress and address, he would be an acquisition to any stage. . . . *Mrs. Ma-hon,* notwithstanding her embarrassment for want of a bird, compensated for the deficiency, and warbled to ad-miration. . . . *Miss Quin* was everything desirable in *Cowslip,* and wanted nothing but age and deformity in *Ursula* . . . *Fringe* is an insignificant character. . . . *Morales* and *Roberts,* were, at least, decent.

Nevertheless, Mahon and his troupe persist, for on August 22nd appears the advertisement:

THIS PRESENT EVENING,

AUGUST 2,

Will be presented,

An OPERA CALLED,

INKLE AND YARICO.

Inkle, by MR. MAHON,
Sir Christopher Currey, by MR. CRASTO,
Medium, MR. ROBERTS,
Planter, by MR. HYNES,
Campley, by MR. NELSON,
And Trudge, MR. MORALES,
Yarico, by MRS. MAHON,
And Wowsky, by MRS. OLIPHANT,

Between the Play and Intertainment,

"THE SKEATING DUET,"

by Mr. Nelson and Mr. Crasto.

A SOLO CONCERTO by MR. PATCH.

To which will be added,

(By Particular Desire), The

AGREEABLE SURPRIZE.

Sir Felix Friendly, by MR. MAHON,
Compton, by MR. NELSON,
Eugene, by MR. CROSS,
Chicane, by MR. HYNES,
Thomas, by MR. PHELPS,
And, Lingo, by MR. MORALES,
Laura, by MRS. MAHON,
Mrs. Cheshire, by MR. ROBERTS,
Fringe, by MRS. OLIPHANT,
And, Cowslip, by MISS QUIN.

The Orchestra will be conducted by Mr. Patch.
First Fiddle, MR. WELDEN,
Flute, MONS. SALOMONS.

Another old name appears on this bill—Mr. Patch.
We recall him going into bankruptcy years back. He was
a musician or orchestra leader for Hallam and Henry.
This is the first time we can remember Mr. Morales
listed as a singer.

The following are some of the most favourite AIRS,
in the Opera of Inkle and Yarico, intended to be performed
this Evening at the Theatre in this Town.

> SONG.—Mr. Morales.
>   "Last Valentine's Day".
> SONG.—Mr. Mahon.
>   "O say, Bonny Lass".
> SONG.—Mr. Mahon.
>   "One day I heard Mary say".
> DUET.—Mr. and Mrs. Mahon.
> SONG.—Mr. Morales.

Note: The words of the songs are set out in the Gazette.

With those two performances, we conclude all that
the existing newspapers say about the theatre in Kingston in the Year of Grace 1788. Except that the *Gazette*
of August 6th gives us a review of the last performance.
Note how modern the critic—he didn't stay for the afterpiece, but rushed back to the newspaper office to write
his review! Or, perhaps, he was too utterly bored to stay
any longer!

On Saturday evening Mr. Mahon and his *young* troop,
used their best endeavours to entertain the town, at the
Quondam Theatre, with the Opera of Inkle and Yarico

and the Agreeable Surprize. The house was sufficiently honored with respect to gentility, but, in point of numbers, it was very indifferently distinguished. The Opera, however, in spite of such a draw back upon the spirits of the performers, as half filled boxes and a thin gallery, was played with considerable vivacity and judgment, and was much applauded by the audience. Mr. and Mrs. Mahon were particularly happy in personating Inkle and Yarico, and the House was full of their praises . . . most of the other performers also did justice to their respective parts, and received a proportionate tribute of applause. As our correspondent did not wait for the representation of the Agreeable Surprize, he cannot speak with respect to its reception.

The only one of this troupe who eventually figured in American playbills was Mr. Nelson. We discovered him playing in 1794–5 under the management of Hallam and Hodgkinson at New York, in the role of Apathy in *Children in the Wood*. A local critic said he "is not brot forward as his merits as a singer and an actor deserve." He suffered from rheumatism, apparently the result of his stay in the tropics. Well, even rheumatism could not account for the withering scorn of another critic who said of him in *The Witches' Dance* that his grimaces and gestures were so ridiculous and disgusting that he should have been hissed off the stage. Little wonder that he ended his engagement on July 27, 1795, after a few months with the company.

Two musical events happen in August. There is first the announcement regarding Mr. Henry Jackson, in the *Gazette* for August 6th. He, it will be recalled, played the violin in the April 5, 1785, presentation of the *School for Scandal* and *The King and the Miller* at Montego Bay.

The *Amateurs of Music,* will doubtless felicitate themselves on the arrival here of Mr. *Henry Jackson,* from Montego Bay, whose celebrity, on a variety of instruments, ranks him among the foremost of his profession, either at home or abroad. . . . As a *Piano* performer and on the Violin, he perhaps outstrips every competitor in this country, and the countenance formerly shewn him, seems to promise a continuance of public encouragement.

On the 9th the readers of the *Gazette* also learned that—

For the Benefit of

MR. DE SALOMONS,

This present evening,
At Mr. Byrn's House, by the Beef Market,

(Formerly Mr. Bradford's Concert Room)
Will be Performed, A

CONCERT

Of Vocal and Instrumental Music,

Act I

Overture, Van Hall,
Song, "Charmante Fleur," Miss Quin,
Concerto, Le Cot, Mr. Salomons,
Song, "When ruddy Aurora awakens the day,"
Mrs. Mahon,
3rd. Symphony, Opera 13, Stamitz,

Act II

Favourite Overture, Haydn,
Song, "Let Fame sound the Trumpet," by a
Gentleman,
Organ Concerto, Mr. Patch,

Song, "The Twins of Latona," Mr. Mahon,
Violin Solo, accompanied by Tenor, Mr.
Jackson,
Eccho Casch,
Favourite Symphony, Carlo Ditters.

After which, there will be a BALL for the
LADIES.

Tickets, at Half a Guinea each, to be had of Mr. Salo-
mons, at Mrs. Van Backman's Lodging House, Church
Street, at Mr. (?) die's Coffee House, and at the Jamaica
Gazette Printing Office.

The concert was evidently an artistic success. At least
the *Royal Gazette's* musical critic was less harsh than the
writer of the dramatic reviews. It will be noted from the
following worm-eaten newspaper review that several
members of the company, "in the singing way," take part.

The concert for the benefit of Monsieur Salomons,
on Saturday last, was such as (?) called a feast of music. The Company was very respectable and genteel,
though not so numerous as the occasion seemed to require. . . . The lively and charming overture of *Van-
hall's,* was performed with incomparable taste and execution, and highly delighted every votary of Apollo. . . .
Miss Quin sung the fine song of *"Charmante Fleur"* in
a very pleasing manner, and received the universal approbation of the audience. The Flute Concerto, by Monsieur Salomons, was an admirable specimen of the sur-
prizing powers of harmonious sounds, and rivetted the
attention of the company to a very extraordinary degree.
. . . *"When ruddy Aurora awakens the day"* was given
by Mrs. Mahon in the happiest and most charming style.
. . . The gentleman who sung the song of *"Let Fame
sound the trumpet,"* acquitted himself with great feeling
and judgment. . . . The Concerto on the Piano Forte,

by Mr. Welden, was performed in so pleasing a manner, as gave us no room at all to regret the (?) of Mr. Patch, whose name was placed (?) to this part of the Concert in the bills (?) day. . . . "*The Twins of Latona,*" by Mr. Mahon, was extremely well sung, and drew forth reiterated plaudits. . . . And (?) (Haydn's) Periodical Overture was most bewitzhingly executed, and reflected the highest credit upon the performers. . . . The company retired between 10 and 11 o'clock, highly pleased with the entertainment.

Plays at Spanish Town

In this year the theatre at Spanish Town aroused to life, but we have to wait until June before it rubs its eyes and gets into action. On June 14th, *The Beaux' Stratagem* and *The Agreeable Surprize* are performed by Gentlemen of the Army for the benefit of Mrs. Mahon, "to an audience the most crowded and brilliant we ever recollect to have seen in this island." Two days later comes the comic opera of *Rosina* with a repetition of *The Agreeable Surprize*. This is for the benefit of Mr. Patch. By August the urge for the theatre is sufficiently strong at the capital to establish a Theatrical Club. On the 30th it presents *She Stoops to Conquer* and on September 10th *The Comedy of Errors*. The company plays on through the September sitting of the Grand Court.

The building which the Spanish Town players used was evidently the old theatre built by subscription in 1776–7. The troops had not yet arrived to use it as a barracks. The *Cornwall Chronicle*, of August 16, 1788, reports that the theatre had "undergone a thorough alteration . . . the ornamental parts executed by gentlemen, are in a high stile of taste. A number of new scenes

have been painted and the dresses, we are informed, are
entirely new."

From that source, then, we make up a little playbook
for Spanish Town:

June 14th   —*Beaux' Stratagem,* Farquhar
             Agreeable Surprize, O'Keeffe

June 16th   —*Rosina,* Mrs. Brooke
             Agreeable Surprize, O'Keeffe

August 27th   —*She Stoops to Conquer,* Goldsmith
             Rosina, Mrs. Brooke

September 4th —*Wonder,* Mrs. Centlivre
             Poor Soldier, O'Keeffe

September 3rd—*Comedy of Errors,* Shakespeare

This appears to have been performed on the Old Harbour Road and a Mr. William M'Taggart was a principal actor.

September 9th   —*Beggar's Opera,* Gay
             Miss in Her Teens, Garrick

September 11th—*Beggar's Opera,* Gay
             Agreeable Surprize, O'Keeffe

We also learn, from the *Cornwall Chronicle,* that
"after discharging the heavy expenses of fitting up the
theatre and the nightly charges, which were considerable,
they found themselves able to devote a very handsome
sum (£100 we hear) to the relief of an officer's widow."
Worthy warriors!

On September 20th Mr. Mahon advertises in the
Kingston *Royal Gazette:* "Any Lady with Talents and
Inclination for the Stage, and willing to make that her

profession, will meet with Encouragement, by addressing a line to R. M. at the Editors of this Paper, where and when She may be spoken with." Mahon evidently is anxious to corral talent, for he repeats the advertisement in the *Royal Gazette* of September 24th and October 1st. There is one final item:

> October 7th —*Lyar*, Foote
> *Quaker*, Dibdin

The court had risen and Spanish Town was fairly deserted. On this occasion "the audience, tho' not numerous, was composed of the first characters. . . . The scenery, executed in a masterly stile, is, we understand, the production of Ensign Schroeter of the 14th, a gentleman whose ability in drawing are deservedly admired." So Ensign Schroeter was to the Spanish Town theatre of his day what the ill-fated Major André and Colonel Delancy were to the British military Thespians of Philadelphia and New York.

On October 4th is announced a musical event of major proportions. First, its purpose is to erect funds for a statue of John Wolmer, the Kingston goldsmith, who had died in 1729 leaving his estate to establish a free school. After all these years Kingston was just getting around to honoring his memory with a statue.

Sure enough, on the 5th of November, in Kingston Parish Church, starting at ten o'clock in the morning, the following ambitious program was given by a combined group of professional and amateur musicians:

Overture   —Occasional Oratorio
Song   —Judas Maccabæus
                     "Pious Orgies"

Song	—Messiah
	"Why Do the Nations"
Chorus	—Messiah
	"Oh! Thou That Tellest"
Song	—Joshua
	"Oh! Had I Jubal's Lyre"
Chorus	—Jonah
	"Tune Your Harps"

*   *   *   *   *   *

Magdalene Ode	—"Grateful Notes"
Song	—Jephtha
	"Ye Sacred Priests"

Voluntary on the Organ, Mr. Patch

Anthem	—Solomon's Song
	"Rise Up, my Love"
Coronation Anthem	—"Zadock the Priest"

The "band consisted of upward sixty vocal and instrumental performers, who have made themselves perfect by repeated rehearsals, and the organ has been thoroughly repaired, so as to bring into full use a number of stops that were formerly very much out of order." Little wonder that the critic acclaimed this concert as "a concord of the most melodious sounds that ever floated in the Temple of Deity in this town."

The Wolmer concert over, let us start round the west end of the island. We arrived in Savanna-la-Mar and in the *Gazette* of that town read, on September 9th, this merry note:

It is recommended to the Gentleman whose exhibitions in the Slight of Hand way astonished and drew together such numbers not long since in this Parish, to be less nimble with his fingers, which he wishes to keep in prac-

tice by sliding off handkerchiefs of the heads of poor de-
fenseless negroes, as they are passing and re-passing the
streets. Though no Beadle happens to be in the Parish,
he might still find there are not hands wanting to apply
the whip, should he fall into the hands of justice.

Surely this couldn't have been our esteemed friend,
Hyman Saunders. Perhaps it was the Young Hollander,
or Mr. Bernard, or his Venetian? The *Gazette* does not
tell us, so we ride on to Montego Bay.

All this time Montego Bay seems to have been satisfied with its monthly assemblies and local concerts, the
only break in their steady cultural succession being a
cockfight. The announcement in the *Cornwall Chronicle*
of March 15th deserves printing in full if only to show
what splendid sporting competition existed between the
parishes on the north shore: "On Saturday next will be
fought a Grand Main of Cocks, being the First Subscription Main for Five Years, at Mr. Dauney's Long Room,
between the Gentlemen of St. Ann's, Trelawny and the
Island, and the Gentlemen of Westmoreland, Hanover
and St. James's. Thirty-one Cocks to be shown in the
Main and Twenty-one in the Byes. The Bye battles to be
fought on Thursday."

The *Chronicle* of April 4th reports Westmoreland,
Hanover, and St. James's leading by 7 to 6. Then, the
next day, after twenty-one battles were fought, the main
proved a draw.

Did the gentlemen of the parishes, I wonder, sit around
a semicircular port table to watch the fight? And was
there a "roundabout" to display the hackle and tail feathers? And did each fighting-bird have his little red carpet
and leading string and did they spin tops in front of the

cocks to raise their anger to a fury?

These interparish cockfights were generally occasions for prolonged gentlemanly drinking. Of course, side bets were laid on the birds after each encounter started and not inconsiderable sums changed hands. Often they bred hard feeling; sometimes they led to duels. There's one tale of a Jamaica cockfight that ended in a duel because one contestant called another a Yankee. This was a term no gentleman could accept without fighting. However, the aristocratic honor was preserved and amply satisfied, even if the pistols—unbeknown to the duelers—were loaded with nothing more deadly than dried peas!

In October of this year we have a touch with the old company. Its advertisement in the *Chronicle* from October to April, 1789, dated from Spanish Town states:

> Proposals for publishing by subscription
> The Contrast
> A Comedy
> Written by Major Tyler
>
> And performed at the theatres of New York and Maryland with universal approbation.

Twenty copies, we find, were reserved for Jamaica, being subscribed for by Mr. Aikman, and one for Barbados. *The Contrast or The American Son of Liberty* was written by Royall Tyler, who had given Wignell the copyright of the play. It was introduced to the public at New York in June, 1787, where it ran for five nights—an unprecedented mark of its popularity—and was played also in Philadelphia, Baltimore, and Charleston. The play holds up to merry laughter the fashions and foibles of New York's gay set.

1789

Since it was Montego Bay that we last heard from in the old year, we shall give the town first place in the new. The Bay gets its theatrical thrills vicariously, by reading the reports of what is happening at Kingston and Spanish Town. However, it manages to create a few amusements of its own.

On the occasion of the last amusement, Mr. Dauney's Long Room housed a Grand Main of Cocks. It now assumes a more respectable air. On June 6th, it witnesses a stag dinner of one hundred plates. Afterward the gentlemen join the ladies at the theatre for a subscription ball to celebrate the King's birthday—George III—and "especially His Most Gracious Majesty's Recovery from his late indisposition." Our account pictures a full evening and doubtless the dawn saw many a fuzzy head:

At five o'clock near an hundred gentlemen sat down to an elegant entertainment at Mr. Dauney's New Room. "Long live the King," "The Queen," "Prince of Wales and the rest of the Royal Family"; "Navy and Army"; "Lord Thurlow"; "Mr. Pitt and the Constitution"; "The Governor"; "Commodore"; and many loyal and constitutional toasts were drank.

The evening concluded with a general Illumination and a Ball. . . . The ball opened at the Theatre at a little after eight o'clock; nearly 200 Ladies and Gentlemen were present. The room is considerably enlarged by the judicious removal of the side-boxes, and was handsomely illuminated by three elegant glass lustres. At the upper end was a transparency of Britannia on her knees receiving from the hand of Providence a medallion of the King, an inscription above, Restored to Health and Us.

The Ladies were elegantly dressed; and most of them had inscriptions of "God Save the King"; "Long Live the King" etc., neatly ornamented. The minuets were over at ten, when the country dances began, which did not break up till five o'clock yesterday morning, when the company retired very much pleased with the entertainment of the night.

The town of Lucea, to the westward of Montego Bay, was not to be outdone. It, too, had a dinner and a ball on this occasion, but we are sorry the high wind played such havoc with the illuminations. High winds in Jamaica are no respecters of king or commoner. The party was composed

of the gentlemen of the parish of Hanover and several gentlemen of the Army, who dined at the tavern of Mr. Isaac Lyon, as a joyful testimony of their happiness on the recovery of our Sovereign. The day was spent with the utmost harmony, and every mark of loyalty distinguished the dispositions of the company and the inhabitants of the place. Many local toasts were drank, and a very beautiful illumination of nearly the whole town, the neighbouring houses and a part of the shipping, concluded the evening. The next evening a very elegant entertainment was given by Capt. Skerrett at the new house at Fort Charlotte, at which were present about sixty ladies, who made a very brilliant appearance; there was also a very grand illumination of the Fort and Barracks, but from the violence of the wind, it could not be supported as long as it was wished.[9]

Into this untheatrical succession of assemblies, concerts, cockfights and patriotic dinners comes a fresh amusement. At the theatre in Montego Bay is announced for Saturday, July 11th:

Mr. Bernard
and
The Venetian

Various Performances upon the Tight and Slack Rope, Also Tumbling, Leaping and Balancing.

Likewise will be performed various Deceptions with Cups and Balls, Money, Snuff-Boxes, Cards, Handkerchiefs, etc.

Mr. Bernard amuses the Bay folks on July 11th, September 2nd and 4th, and October 27th, quite an extensive run. Not since the Young Hollander was here has the Bay seen a magician and tumbler.

Kingston and Spanish Town

Lacking theatrical news for these two important towns in the year 1789, we can only jot down notes of culture and merriment.

After the Wolmer concert, Kingston seems to have taken up music in a big way. On January 10th at Thompson's Tavern was held "a very respectable meeting of the musical amateurs and professionals for the purpose of establishing a regular concert in this town. Harmony Hall was selected as the place, and the concerts were to be supported by subscription." Listen to the array of talent— "the ability and number of the professional men, the assistance of the Dilletante and the powerful [sic] aid of the respective regimental bands."

In February we hear "that the theatre in Spanish Town will again be opened and that amongst other new entertainments the comedy of *The West Indian* will be performed and that Mr. O'Keeffe's new favorite Opera called

Peeping Tom is now in rehearsal." This short run for the amusement of the February Court finished February 15th with Mr. Home's much-esteemed tragedy of *Douglas*, which was performed with all the ancient dresses and the Scotch music between the acts. It was a benefit of that veteran son of Thespis, David Benjamin Roberts, "whose distresses, abstracted from some little pretentions to a place in the train of the comic muse, present him as an object worthy some attention."

In this run were played:

> *West Indian,* Cumberland
> *Beaux' Stratagem,* Farquhar
> *Peeping Tom of Coventry,* O'Keeffe
> *Mayor of Garratt,* Foote
> *Douglas,* Home
> *The Waterman,* Dibdin
> *Padlock,* Bickerstaff
> *Tom Thumb,* Fielding
> *Padlock,* Bickerstaff
> *Quaker,* Dibdin

Although the announcement of that last evening's performance speaks of the curtain dropping "forever between the public and their obliging entertainers," we find the Gentlemen of the Army exhibiting on May 30th to an "assemblage of persons of the first rank," Colman's comedy of *Ways and Means* and O'Keeffe's *Peeping Tom*.

Seven days before this last curtain, Spanish Town had celebrated the royal birthday. We shall let the papers tell it:

Upon this auspicious occasion his Majesty's Attorney-General, with the spirit and liberality of a Prince, gave a most sumptuous entertainment to a select party of his friends, and kept open house until near day-light. The Theatre in Spanish Town was illuminated in a very superb manner. A fine transparency of the King's Arms graced the centre of the West front; on one side of which were the words, "Pitt, the Guardian of England," and on the other side, "Success of Jamaica." Over this painting was a white transparency with a suitable inscription, on the right of which was the word "Navy" encircled with naval trophies, and on the left the word "Army," surrounded with trophies of war. The whole was arranged and executed very handsomely by the ingenious Mr. Schroeter.

Kingston was not to be outdone on this occasion, for it holds a concert and assembly and the front of the theatre is illuminated.

We close these fragments of the year 1789 with a note that brings us back to the old American Company of Comedians: "Kingston, August 1st, Married: Thomas A. Woolls, Esq. to Miss Lewis of this island." Already that lad's grown up and taken a wife. How time does fly!

CHAPTER XI

1790–1808

Troubles in Santo Domingo Bring an Invasion of Foreign Talent—The Last Decade of the Century Drags on in a Welter of Singers, Tumblers, and Nondescript Showmen

IN 1790 there was living in Paris a young man under thirty years of age, by name George Ogé, a native of Santo Domingo, son of a white planter of considerable standing and a mulatto woman. The father had long since been dead; the mother was still alive, and possessed and managed a coffee plantation about thirty miles from Cape François. A successful agriculturist, she was able, from the profits of the plantation, to educate her son at Paris and to maintain him there in a certain degree of affluence.

While there, he fell in with a society called Les Amis des Noirs. Its leaders were Grégoire, Brissot, Lafayette, and Robespierre, who pursued arduously the new doctrine of equality and the rights of man. At the meetings of this society James Ogé began to realize the miseries of his class—how, because of the color of their skin, he and his fellow mulatto and negro Santo Domingans were exposed to cruel wrongs and contumelies.

The patrons of this society were not above inciting to revolution in various parts of the French empire. Ogé gathered the notion that the colored people in his native island were ready to rise against their oppressors. All they needed to stir them into action was a leader. It took very little persuading to make him believe that he was the man.

With the intent secretly to collect arms and smuggle them into Santo Domingo, he embarked for New England in July, 1790. The whole plot, however, was known to the authorities on the island even before he left France. That he was allowed to land secretly, bringing with him arms and ammunition, was merely inviting him into a trap. When he demanded that the Governor extend to negroes and people of color the same statutes and privileges enjoyed by the whites, he forthwith became the leader of the mulattos and other malcontents. If the governor did not act, announced Ogé, he would take up arms in their behalf.

Unfortunately for his dream, Ogé was able to rouse only two hundred followers, chiefly raw, ignorant, and undisciplined youths. They pitched their camp near Cape François and began massacring men and families who refused to join their cause. A body of regular troops and militia was rushed to the rebels' camp, and, meeting but weak resistance, they slew some, captured others. Ogé escaped. His misguided efforts aroused the white inhabitants, who armed themselves and began threatening all mulattos on general principles; and the mulattos, in turn, took up arms in their own defense. Eventually, Ogé was captured. He made a full confession, implicating many of his followers, and disclosed the measures which the colored people had used to incite negroes to rebel. Twenty of his followers were hanged, and Ogé was "Broken alive and left to perish in that dreadful situation on the wheel." [1]

At first glance, it might seem the farthest possible cry from the miserable Santo Domingan, James Ogé, to our record of high times and merry hearts in Jamaica. His rebellion, however, was the forerunner of many uprisings in which great numbers of the white population were slaughtered or driven from the island. Some sought refuge in the Southern States—at Charleston and Savannah especially; some found their way to Jamaica and other British-controlled islands. To Charleston they brought a fresh culture that ultimately, with the aid of refugees from the Reign of Terror in France, blossomed out into the French Theatre at Charleston; and at Philadelphia, plays acted in French. During the last decade of the eighteenth century, Jamaica benefited to the extent of welcoming and enjoying many Santo Domingan and French émigrés who were musicians of more than ordinary merit.

1790

In this decade, while Thalia and Melpomene may seem to have deserted our island, Calliope offered the best of her charms—at least, the best she could offer under the circumstances. Musicians and show folk naturally came first to Kingston, as it was the most thriving town. In 1790 it was a full mile square, containing about two thousand houses, besides the huts of the negroes. The whites numbered about 3000; free people of color, 1200; and slaves, 8000. Says a contemporary description:

The theatre is a little, mean, narrow, close fabrick; there is also another public building called Ranelagh House, in which ladies and gentlemen hold public balls and assemblies; there are also two Free Mason Lodges, to wit: Saint Andrew's and Saint Patrick's; both Scotch and Irish keep up that ancient honourable and friendly society monthly, and celebrate Saint Andrew's and Saint Patrick's days yearly, by going in procession to church, and having sermons preached on the occasion, and afterward dining all together, and passing the evening in mirth and chearfulness.[2]

This "little, mean, narrow, close fabrick" changed hands on March 4, 1790. The *Daily Advertiser,* reporting the sale, speaks of it as the "Royalty Theatre." We surmise that by this time Hallam and Henry had now ended all their contacts with the island. The building could not have been too little or too mean, as it sold for £1600.

Before we begin listing the scant amusements of 1790, we must report the passing of a member of the Mahon troupe: in January, on her way home to England, died Miss Quin, "formerly of the American Company of Comedians."

The next month the *Daily Advertiser* reports a fresh diversion:

Mr. Ullman

An Artist lately arrived from the city of Augsburg in Germany, begs to inform the Ladies and Gentlemen, that he exhibits many curious exercises by living Birds as performed before the Emperor of Germany, and His Most Christian Majesty Lewis the XVI and other European Courts. . . .

He also performs with little dogs. Admittance 3s. 4d each. **Only white persons will be admitted to the above performance. Tomorrow he intends exhibiting to persons of colour.

That is the first indication of the color line being drawn in amusements here.

On February 22nd Mr. Ullman is obliged to inform "the Ladies and Gentlemen of this town that the indisposition of one of his Birds will prevent his exhibiting." We have seen performances postponed by indisposition of actors and actresses, when fever or dysentery swooped down upon the company, but never before has a trained bird held up the show.

On March 16th the *Advertiser* reveals old friends —Mr. Bernard and the Venetian doing their stunts at "the Long Room, late Dallas's Lodging House, in Church-street." We first met this pair at Montego Bay in 1789. You will recall that Mr. Bernard claimed, after the extravagant manner of his kind, that he had "had the honour of exhibiting before most courts in Europe." And here they are, leaping, tumbling, balancing, and performing "Wonderful Dexterity upon Tight and Slack Rope," for the amusement of both the élite and commonalty of Kingston and its environs.

By the 13th of April we have a concert in Kingston and on April 29th the *Advertiser* enlightens its readers with the news that "Mr. Felix Byrne, late of this town, is now actually under the tuition of Dr. Arnold,[3] and is to make his first appearance on a London Theatre in the character of Young Meadows in Love in a Village." Because of this, or merely after it, the *Advertiser's* readers of May 8th are stirred by the following complaint:

It is somewhat astonishing that in this town, which can boast more Musical People than almost any other place of its size and population, there should be only four Public Concerts in twelve months, and that a performer, hitherto unrivalled in excellence, should depart for want of encouragement. *Sic transit Gloria Musicorum.*

Well, Mr. Byrne was gone and the rebellion in Santo Domingo hadn't gotten under way to send musicians here, so the best Kingston can do is to enjoy the remaining home talent. On June 30th the Kingston Subscription Concert was held at the Assembly Room and "very genteely, tho' not numerously attended. The selection of Music was much approved and the performance of a young lady, an amateur, in a duet composed for two performers on one instrument, greatly admired. Many of the military were present but very few of the navy."

How, I ask, could you expect hairy-chested and tatooed sailors to sit through a piano duet by a lady amateur? They probably would have started a riot loud enough to bring out the Town Guard.

July 7th sees Mr. Ullman and his trained birds (all well and willing) in a performance "at the Dancing Room of Mr. Sequira in Orange-street." He also adds good measure "with little Dogs dressed in uniform." The charge for this is 1s 8d for ladies and gentlemen, and 1s 3d for children—with no mention as to whether they be black, white, or intermediate shades.

At the beginning of August we catch our first whiff of the stage—Mr. Mahon is offering "A Miscellaneous Entertainment of Music, Scenery and Machinery, selected from the favorite Entertainments of the Eidsphusikon, Fantocconi and Les Ombres Chinoises." The bill is diversified:

I

The much admired scene of the Broken Bridge. The Dialogue and Song by Mr. Mahon.

II

A Rural Prospect descriptive of a Waterfall in motion, a Mill-work, a Miller's House, Carts, Horses, Servants, etc., employed about the mill, and in motion. Dialogue and Songs by Mr. and Mrs. Mahon, and a Young Gentleman.

III

A Beautiful Representation of the Public Gardens at Paris, with the different Companies, Attendants, etc., in motion, equal to life. In this Part will be exhibited a Representation of a Real Storm, Thunder, Lightning, Hail, Rain, etc. with the ludicrous effect upon the Company. The Storm subsides, a Calm succeeds. A Hornpipe in the English taste. The Dialogue by a French Gentleman and a song by Mrs. Mahon.

IV

A Musical Entertainment never performed here, called The Recruiting Serjent, Composed by Mr. Dibdin; Serjent, Mr. Mahon; Recruit, by a Gentleman; Countryman, Mr. Roberts; Kitty, by Mrs. Mahon. With Scenery, Machinery, etc.

V

A Representation of a Foreign Robbery, with the detection of the Thieves by a faithful Dog, with sundry curious figures of moving animals, etc.

VI

A view on the Coast of Africa, with the method of taking the Lion in the Toils and the efforts of that noble animal to extricate himself.

The whole to conclude with a Transparent Likeness of the Gallant Lord Rodney, descending from the Clouds,

supported by Victory and Britannia, and accompanied by
the Brave Admirals and Officers who supported him on
the Memorable 12th of April, 1782, with a full Chorus
of Rule Britannia.

Admission to Ball Room, 10s. Gallery, 6s. 8d.

The vision of Rodney descending from the clouds
doesn't seem halfway ridiculous when those who have
been to Spanish Town and seen the Rodney Memorial
recall how that bluff hero is portrayed. No Roman ever
wore his toga with more chic. Jamaica did not quite recover from Rodney's victory until Nelson's triumph at
Trafalgar overshadowed it in popular remembrance and
celebration. Incidentally, we note that Mr. Roberts is
still picking up a few pennies with an occasional part.
Mahon repeats his entertainment on August 5th, but
by the 7th the town is lured away to see another troupe:

The performance of Mr. Curtis and his Troop at
Dallas's Long-Room in Church-street on Saturday night
was truly pleasing and surprising. The inimitable performance of Mr. Curtis himself upon the Tight Rope is
too well known to need any commendation. They spoke
for themselves, in repeated plaudits from the Audience,
who testified their pleasure and surprise, especially at
his Fandango on the Rope without the assistance of a
balance pole.

An inspired puff, to be sure, but it piques our curiosity
to learn just what it was that Mr. Curtis offered his
Kingston public. Here's the bill:

A Minuet upon the Tight Rope by Mrs. Maltese.
Mr. Florentine will Dance upon the Tight Rope in a
variety of ways, and will sit upon the Rope in a Chair,
as at Breakfast, with Table, Cups, Saucers.
Mr. Curtis will dance an English Hornpipe and a

Spanish Fandango upon the Tight Rope without the assistance of a Balance Pole.

The same will be performed in a comical manner by Signor Piazachao.

Balancing upon the Slack Wire by Mr. Florentine.

Second Part

A Divertemento

will be presented, in which will be Exhibited a Magical Spanish Pantomime

Pantaloon by Mr. Curtis,
Harlequin by Mr. Florentine,
Colombine by Mrs. Maltese,
Perot by Mr. Meanwell,
Anatomizing Doctor by Mr. Brigella.

With several amazing Deceptions too tedious to mention.

Front Seats, 10s.   Back Seats, 6s. 8d.

On the 10th Mr. Curtis offers another bill, in which a Holland Lady tumbles to great perfection on the tight rope. Mr. Florentine not only jumps through hoops and dances a jig on the wire, but also plays a violin while standing on his head, and Curtis dances on a parcel of eggs blindfolded, with sundry jumps and tumbles. The evening concludes with a pantomime called *The Barber à La Mode*.

After this a subscription concert introduces a more cultural note on October 6th; then, in late November, appears a professional musician:

Signor Fallotico

Who has had the honour of performing before the different Courts in Europe, is just arrived from the Cape and solicits the patronage of the Ladies and Gentlemen of this Community to his Concert of Vocal and Instrumental Music to be performed shortly. Sig. Fallotico means to exhibit an Instrument (entirely novel to the natives of this island) called the Harmonica. . . .

In a community that is still scanning the sky, as Jamaicans do in late summer, for hurricanes that may bring disaster to the island, this introduction of a weird instrument would surely arouse as much interest as though a camel walked unaccompanied up Harbour Street. Although we don't mean to peep under Signor Fallotico's curtain, we do, somehow, remember that Benjamin Franklin invented a musical instrument that he called the Harmonica. However, we shall see.

December 18th is the day Signor Fallotico selects for his first concert, and the Assembly Room on the Parade —Ranelagh House—is the place.

Act the First

Overture . . . . De la Bella Arsena
Italian Ariette . . . . Sig. Fallotico
Grand Concerto; the Solo parts on the Harmonica
    by Sig. Fallotico.
This Instrument (never before exhibited in this island) is composed of forty-five glasses of various dimensions, the tones of which are admitted by all judges to be the most exquisite of musical sounds produced by art.
Italian Ariette, Composed and sung by Sig. Fallotico.
Haydn's new Grand Symphonia

Act the Second

Italian Ariette, Rondo, by Sig. Fallotico.
Sonata on the Harmonica, accompanied by a Violin.
Italian Ariette descriptive of a Musician disgusted

with the several Performers, by Sig. Fallotico.

Various Airs and Variations on the Harmonica composed and performed by Sig. Fallotico.

Grand Overture, called The Battle of Ivere.

After the concert came a ball. The tickets were 20s each—quite steep!—and could be obtained, among other places, at the home of Mr. Morales. This may have been our old friend Isaac Morales of the American Company. Note, too, that almost invariably these Jamaican concerts were followed by a ball. It was as though the audience was being subjected to nursery discipline—you simply had to eat your meat and potatoes before you could have dessert!

This concert is repeated on the 22nd of December, and with it, the recorded amusements for 1790 come to an end. Jamaicans in general and Kingstonians in particular have had a pretty full course of concerts, tumblers, and slack-rope artistes. Apart from them, they had to get along as best they could with an occasional festive dinner and the more genteel assemblies, even though the latter did start at eight in the evening and wind up at three in the morning.

The entertainments of this year were generally frivolous. They did not require any extraordinary cerebration on the part of the populace. Gone were the days when an audience would crowd in to see Shakespeare and Farquhar and such "high-brow" plays. For a matter of fact, the island was waxing too fat. Although the previous five years had seen it pass through an almost uninterrupted period of stress and strain, it was now definitely on the way to recovery. Its products were finding more favorable markets and crops were abundant.

1791

We open the new year with echoes from the past—occasional business notices regarding Mr. Douglass, the printer, who resides in Spanish Town. His house was "opposite the North Corner of the Public Buildings." This was David Douglass, Jr. In his father's will the printing business was left to him and for some time after the death of David Douglass, Sr., the son carried it on. This house may also have been his father's too; it is mentioned in the will.

The year of 1791, so promising for Jamaica, so ominous for Santo Domingo, opens with a concert on January 26th for the benefit of H. A. Francken. The erstwhile Master of the Revels has fallen on hard times and his friends gather about to extend the commendable hand of charity.

In those days it was customary, when a concert was being planned, to give notice of this activity some weeks in advance. Something like publishing banns of marriage. Thus, on April 8th, George Edward Salimen announces in the *Royal Gazette* that he intends giving a concert on the 28th. The concert, which began at seven, was followed by the usual ball. It was "at the Theatre on the Parade," and the program, in two parts, shows Mr. Mahon of the erstwhile theatre singing a song, his good wife doing likewise, Mr. Evans and Mr. Weldon playing solos on the harpsichord, and an unnamed gentleman offering two songs and Mr. Salimen performing two flute concertos.

At the end of March, before Salimen's program was completed, Signor Fallotico not only tempted the public with a concert (at two dollars a head) but also offered an added attraction called Representatione Perique. The place was the theatre. After the concert—instead of a ball —he advertised:

An exhibition of artificial Fireworks, in which neither fire, powder or phosphorus will be used: but to the eye of the spectators will have the appearance of real Fire. He will display the Arms, Flags and Trophies of the different Nations of Europe; also an exact representation of the famous Battle of April 12, between the gallant Lord Rodney and Count de Grasse; where will be observed the two fleets in regular line of battle engaged, the report of the guns heard, the destruction of some of the enemy's vessels, the agitation of the seas, in short, every circumstance attending that celebrated action.

I wonder if the Kingstonians didn't weary a little of these Rodney displays; here, within six months, is the second of them.

At the end of May Montego Bay stops its bustle of trade in slaves, pimento, sugar, and rum to watch a new tumbler; and with his announcement, we again realize that Mr. James Fannin,[4] editor of the *Cornwall Chronicle* in that town, was a more careful compositor than the printer of the Kingston *Daily Advertiser*. In the latter paper we read about a "Mr. Curtis" and a "Mr. Florentine." Here in Montego Bay we learn the facts:

Mr. Cortes and Company (from Rome) will exhibit various Feats of Tumbling, Dancing, etc. on the Tight and Slack Rope and Wire, in the Venetian Stile, The Famous Florentine Lad will show many surprising Feats.

Mr. Cortes will mount the Tight Rope and dance a Hornpipe and show several Antics in Dancing, Leaping, etc. The Buffoon, with Don Piaffo (who has performed in London) will show many pleasing and diverting Antics.

Mr. Cortes has performed with great Applause in London, Paris, Madrid, Lisbon, etc.

A bit of a comedown for Montego Bay, this, after those crowded seasons with the American Company, and *The Beggar's Opera* whistled by every errand boy on the streets. However, they had to accept what came to them. And in August, they troop out to Bradley's tavern to see

William Powers Knight

Lately from Charleston, in America.

1. He will go a row of fore springs and back springs.
2. He will stick two pins in the floor, in front of his feet, throw his head backward between his legs, and take up the two pins, one on each eye-lid.
3. He will lay down a snuff-box in front of his feet, throw his head backward between his legs, and put his finger, his nose and his toes all in the box together.
4. He will stand on his head on the small nob of a chair, with his heels up, and dance a hornpipe.
5. He will let a strong man take him by his right hand, and another by his left foot, and lift him from the floor, when he will turn his body round several times, and without his hand or leg turning in the men's hands.
6. He will lay a quarter-dollar on the floor, throw his head backwards between his legs, and take up the quarter-dollar in his mouth without using his hands.
7. He will walk upon his hands, with both feet under his arms.
8. He will lay four quarter-dollars on his feet, throw his feet backwards and forwards over his head, without the pieces of money falling.
9. He will put his head opposite to any person in the

room, and walk round his head several times without moving it out of the same position.

The prices are interesting: "Ladies and Gentlemen, 5s. each, Children and People of Colour, 3s. 4d." This is the first time we have encountered a special price for mestees, octoroons, and all the other complexional variations.

Back in Kingston once more, we meet again David Benjamin Roberts, almost the last leaf left on the tree of the American Company of Comedians. On September 3rd, by particular desire, he opens "an Exhibition (at his last retreat at the back of the Theatre) of pieces Historical, Pastoral and Comic Medleys. . . . Care will be taken that no improper company is admitted." Now, just what did Mr. Roberts mean by that? And what are we to surmise by his phrase "last retreat at the back of the theatre"? Was he reduced now to being merely a watchman and janitor for the building?

He fairly spreads himself with the program that he gives on October 3rd, 10th, 17th, 22nd, 27th, and 29th, with variations. His sole support in the bills is a ubiquitous "gentleman." They are his imitation of Loutherburgh's *Eidophusikon:*

Mr. Roberts's address to the audience
Perseus and Andromeda
The royal fort, ships at anchor, fire-ships, etc.
A tempest with shipwrecks
A calm—ships in chase
The flaxen-headed cow-boy returning home with sheep
Mr. Garrick's drunken sailor, by Mr. Roberts
The sailor's return to the house of Rendezvous at Portsmouth
Mr. Garrick's country boy, by Mr. Roberts

And Bonnyface in the Beaux-Stratagem, by Mr. Roberts
    also Reflecting Scenes
Garden of Eden
Stag hunting, the hounds in full cry
Hob in the well
Hudibras's drollery
Councellor Puzzle and the boxers
The magician, man, wife and child
Razer, in the Upholster, by Mr. Roberts
Horse guards
The King going to the Parliament-House
Cuckolds going to Horse Fair
The dishonest baker caught at short weight
Noah's ark, etc.
An epilogue by Mr. Roberts.
    To which will be added a Pantomime called—
      The Witches; or the Birth of Harlequin
        In twelve different parts.
    The whole to conclude with the Gods in Midas and
the Grand Chorus.

Coming on the tail of Roberts' last performance of
this bill is a concert, at the Assembly Room, for the
benefit of Monsieur Pieck and in the same room on December 5th a benefit concert for Mr. Weldon. In the
latter program we find the name of a Signor Pepe, who
tells the town that he is back on the Island after fifteen
months' absence and, if he receives enough encouragement, hopes to settle down there for good. The encouragement will be measured by the extent to which the
genteel populace patronize his offer to teach them singing, the violin, mandolin, and Spanish guitar.

So far this year we have neglected the capital, and
for the simple reason that not until its issue of July 14th
did the *St. Jago de la Vega Gazette* announce Spanish

Town's first attraction. On the 16th Mr. Cortes gives his tumbling show there. Its next recorded amusement is a concert for the benefit of Mr. Patch, the other lingering leaf on the Hallam and Henry tree, at the theatre, the same that David Douglass and others built years ago. The Mahons take part in this.

Meanwhile, on the 3rd of December, certain gentlemen of Spanish Town rouse sufficiently from their lethargy to attend the dinner of the Eton Club, held at the theatre: "Dinner to be on the Table at four o'clock." The president of this organization (were they old Etonians?) was Speaker of the Assembly, and the stewards were: the Honorables John Scott, George Scott, John Lewis, Thomas Murphy, William Bullock, and Oliver Herring. These robust names come as a relief after the procession of those of Italian and French origin with which these past two years have been crowded.

From 1792 Onward

Although they will crowd them, we have no intention, having already given samples, of filling these pages with the programs of all the concerts given by foreigners in this last decade of the eighteenth century.

Signor Pepe leads the way with a concert in March at the Kingston Theatre, and in April, Henry Andrew Francken, Master of the Revels, has another benefit concert given him in the same building. The Mahons take part in these. By May, a whole coterie of refugees offer their musical talents—Mons. Petit, Foucard, Boullay, and Guenin. In that same month appears a long report, surely nostalgic reading for actorless Kingstonians, about

the progress Mr. Wignell is making at Philadelphia with
his new Chestnut Street Theatre. Even New Orleans
catches the fever and begins to build a theatre. Both of
these are faithfully reported in the *Royal Gazette.*

The next year more refugee names and concerts creep
into the newspapers—Mademoiselle Dubourg and Mes-
sieurs Biffari and Michaut. By September, 1793, our
friend Henry Andrew Francken is appointed assistant
Judge of the Court of Common Pleas for Port Royal—
probably a sinecure for the old man. He is dead by the
end of May, 1795. And in November of the previous
year, Jamaicans had read of the death of another friend
—"On his passage from New York to Rhode Island,
John Henry, Esq. of the American Company of Comedians, formerly in this island."

But while we have death on one hand, on the other
is life; in 1793 Captain William Bligh of *Bounty* fame
introduced into Jamaica the breadfruit tree, and in 1794
William Ricketts Johnson introduced the Otaheite or
Bourbon sugar cane, agricultural contributions destined
to prove of great aid to Jamaica's progress.

The days have scarcely turned into 1795 when Mr.
Roberts makes what he declares will be positively his
"last Farewell Address to this most generous and humane Public." It is an "Attic Entertainment of a great
variety and a grand representation of Transparent Paintings of Shades and Scenes with great Illuminations." He
has served the island folk faithfully for twenty years.
There is something pathetic about the old man, working
away in his "last retreat" at the back of the theatre,
painting those "Royal Arms of Old England" and a representation of "A Grand Knight of the Bath" and "A

Grand Triumphal Arch in China."

The old playhouse on the Parade has been put to many uses, and by July, 1796, it serves still another— a church, when the Reverend Dr. O'Brian, chaplain to the 3rd Irish Brigade, used it for divine service. Perhaps this was an unwitting requiem on amusements, for, search through the local papers of 1797, you'll not find a single record of a play, a concert, or even a tumbler.

There were reasons for this dearth of high times. When Lord Balcarres, the newly arrived Lieutenant Governor, looked over the population of Jamaica, he found the island harboring three classes of foreigners. There were French refugees of all ranks, qualities, and colors, who had fled from the horrors of Santo Domingo. Besides these were "many noblesse of France, ladies of the highest consideration, accustomed to every delicacy and luxury." These two formed the aristocrats of the refugees. Next came "a multitude of slaves and handicraft men of colour, with great numbers of brown women." The third class comprised the French prisoners of war confined aboard hulks moored near shore. France had declared war against Great Britain, Spain, and Holland in February, 1793.

Among the latter were incendiaries sent to Jamaica by the French Directory of Santo Domingo, with the intent to stir up revolt among the negroes and set fires. They were supplied with plenty of bribe money, and some did manage to get ashore. An attempt to fire Kingston was discovered and stopped. Shortly thereafter, in June, 1795, Montego Bay was almost wholly destroyed by fire. Some insist the fire started from sparks from a forge that caught to some straw, others that French incendiaries set the blaze. It soon ran through Harbour, North, West, and South Streets and the wharves and part of Market Street. The courthouse and several other buildings were blown up, but this did not check the fire. In all, 110 of the best houses were destroyed, together with 155 hogsheads of sugar and 100 puncheons of rum—a total loss that ran between £300,000 and £400,000. Islanders subscribed liberally, the town was rebuilt, with many improvements—streets widened and straightened, and many new ones laid out.[5]

This same year, 1795, saw the terrible Maroon revolt in St. James's Parish, with Montego Bay the center of the troubles. Eventually, after much bloodshed, it was crushed and five hundred of the Maroons were transported first to Nova Scotia and thence to Sierra Leone, Africa.

By July, 1795, the peace of Basle brought the exterior troubles to an end.

Meantime in Jamaica had been left a few Haitian planters and their families, from whom have descended some of the island's present aristocracy.

The last year in the century is fairly deluged with refugee concerts, bringing in such names as De Poincy, Remondet, Du Metz, Touthemoulin, and Morriseau, St. Clair, Gerard, De Barthe. The price of tickets has now risen to four dollars each. Peter Du Moulin appears on February 16th with tight- and slack-rope acts, but the most important item in his announcement is that it will be held "at the New Theatre in Church Street, near the Parade, a house formerly known by the name of Dallass's Lodging House." Evidently some enterprising citizen thought there was money in this show business. His investment thereupon stings into action the owners of the old theatre. By July comes the news that the theatre on the Parade "will be opened in the course of the ensuing month for Dramatic Performances. It has been fitted up in a very elegant manner and so conducted as to answer occasionally for a Concert and Ballroom."

Let Du Moulin dance on the tight rope with two children tied to his feet and go through military exercises high in the air, and "turn like a windmill, having fireworks fixed to his feet," nevertheless the old theatre that knew the tread of Hallam and Henry and Miss Cheer and the Owen Morrises will go on. Also, it seems that Mr. Du Moulin and his fellow showmen have been going on for some time. At the Northern Liberties Theatre in Philadelphia, "a Company of French Dancers on the Tight Rope, including the Young Florentine and Mr. Du Moulain" played from November 26, 1793, to July, 1794. They apparently separated, for the Young Florentine joined up with Cortes, and the two separate troupes, Cortes' and Du Moulin's, appear here in Jamaica.

In this final year the subscription concerts not alone afford opportunity for both foreign and local talent, but also bring forth Jamaican child prodigies, such as the young lady of ten and a half years who plays a piano concerto accompanied by two violins, a violoncello, and two horns. We also note that Mr. Felix Byrne, back from the London theatres, is on the island again and delighting audiences with his songs.

After this decade of foreign talent, it was to be expected that the Jamaican worm would turn. The new century had scarcely run four months when a terrific blast, signed by "Theatricus," gave the population food for thought:

From the sterility of public amusement in this town, the community must necessarily confess itself highly obliged to the present Manager of the Theatre for his endeavours to supply the deficiency, by satisfying at least one of the senses, namely the eye. It is not to be presumed that a truly British house, such as the generality of this community serve to compose, can be entirely gratified in this department of Amusement by the hasty contemplation of French taste and the ear-lulling unintelligibility of French sounds.[6]

He runs on for several paragraphs in this style, making pointed digs at the French "clopping" and the "dumb shows" that are called pantomimes, and laments the shortage of English actors available in Jamaica.

One might think that such a tirade would bring forth local aspirants by the score. None appeared in 1800. What is happening in Kingston is almost a counterpart of what happened at Charleston in this era, when that thriving center of culture was able to support both an English-speaking and a French theatre. Here is a bill from the Kingston *Daily Advertiser* for December 20, 1800, which shows that Theatricus was right—the French are dominating the stage.

Kingston Theatre

For Mr. Villeneuve's Benefit

Mr. Villeneuvi most respectfully informs the Public that the present evening, the 20th instant, he will have the Honour to give the first Representation of

Servant Mistress

A Comic Opera in two acts, the music by the famous
Peigeonese

Characters

Pandolphe ....Mr. Villeneuve
Zerbine (the Servant Mistress) .. Miss Franscisqui
Scapin .... Mr. St. Just

And the First Representation of the Marquis de Tulipano

A Grand Comic Opera in two Acts; the music by the
celebrated Pasiello

Which will be concluded by the most Laughable Fight
with Daggers by the Marquis and his son against two
Squires of the Countess Olympia

Characters

Le Marquis .... Mr. Villeneuvi
Georgine .... Mr. Hensant
Countess Olympia .... Mrs. Villeneuvi
Veibana .... Miss Fleury
Squires attached to the Countess
Peasants armed with sticks and daggers

Between these two operas, Mr. St. Just will dance a hornpipe.

From this sample of the French run, we turn into 1801
and find some local talent shining forth. In February,
J. Scott, organist of the Spanish Town Cathedral, gives
a concert at the new room in Kingston, and the same
month Mr. Lailson opens a circus in the riding school at
the Dragoons' Quarters at Spanish Town. For this circus ladies and gentlemen will pay 20s admittance, and

people of color, 13s 4d.

Lailson's name, new to Jamaica, was already familiar to circusgoers in the Northern Colonies. We first find him in New York, with a circus building on Greenwich Street, opening in the autumn of 1797. In his cast are Sully, a clown, Messrs. Joseph, Herman, Langley, Pouble, Mr. and Mrs. Douvilliers, Constant, Mrs. Rowson, Miss Venice, Miss Lailson, and Miss Popette. Lailson left New York in 1798 and moved down to Philadelphia. There his circus collapsed, so he packed his traps and went to Charleston for a winter season, where his circus proved a counter attraction to the theatre. From Charleston he must have come on to Jamaica.

Two other notes catch the eye—Felix Byrne is settling down; in January he marries a Miss Jane Wilson and begins teaching music and selling musical instruments. In October, 1801, when the Governor gives a ball at King's House, Spanish Town, to celebrate His Majesty's birthday, it was determined to make the party decorous; "No Gentleman can possibly be admitted in Boots or otherwise improperly dressed." A new Governor had arrived, Lord Nugent and his lady, and the town was putting its best and unbooted foot forward.

There are balls aplenty. At one given by the Privy Council in November, the company was "more numerous, brilliant and respectable than we recollect to have seen on a like occasion." Doubtless, no gentlemen in boots!

Another reason for island rejoicing toward the end of this year was the news of preliminaries of peace being signed. At Montego Bay the populace crowds into the courthouse for a band concert led by Messrs. Millar and Carnaby, local celebrities. The men then dine—a hun-

dred of them—at Griffin's Tavern, where many toasts
are drunk, and a ball follows. The town is illuminated
and the adjoining hills are ablaze with beacon fires.

That same month, Signor Falconi, who cautiously advertises himself as a native of Italy, gives the inhabitants
of Spanish Town a new kind of entertainment—"philosophical and entertaining experiments." Probably tricks
with the newfangled electricity. He must have set the
heads of the proper people nodding with approbation
when he advertised: "In a community like this, such
things ought to be encouraged; it fills up those hours
after dinner too often devoted to the pernicious pleasures
of the bottle." Signor Falconi gave this same entertainment in New York in 1787.

Then in December a really new and exciting attraction
comes to the capital:

An Air Balloon

Will be let off at the Dragoons' Riding School on Monday evening next. In a few seconds after the ascension
of the balloon a cat will drop from it, carrying in her
paws an umbrella and will fall to the ground without
receiving any injury. . . . Also at the same time a report of a pistol will be heard, immediately on which a
number of cards will descend from the balloon in various
directions, having a very singular and curious appearance.

The French Theatre is still playing at Kingston. By
February, 1802, Augustus Tessier, who was now manager, advertises in the *Daily Advertiser* of the 11th that
he is reopening the theatre. He has "erected a vast and
most commodius amphitheatre for the accommodation
of the people of colour, to which he has added a row

of the second boxes adjoining the circus, by which means the people of colour will have a very spacious, airy and distinct place to which they ascend by a separate passage."

He intends giving pantomimes and operas. Thus on the 15th the bill includes *Don Juan or Peter's Banquet,* a grand pantomime and ballet in three acts, and *The Blacksmith,* a comic opera in two acts, with a hornpipe between, danced "by a performer lately arrived from Europe." The casts are:

Don Juan, Delpini and Oulton

Don Juan .... Mr. Tessier
Don Fernando .... Mr. Villegrain
Commandant .... Mr. De Mossie
Scaramouch .... Mr. Remondet
The Statue of the Commander .... Mr. Incent
The Daughter of the Commander ... Miss Tessier
Her Chambermaid .... Miss Popette
A Fisherman .... Mr. Villegrain
His Two Daughters .... Miss Francisqui
                                Miss Popette

Blacksmith, O'Keeffe

The Blacksmith .... Mr. Tessier
Labride .... Mr. Incent
Eustache .... Mr. Villegrain
Bastien .... Mr. Brelet
Colin .... Mr. Remondet
Jeannette .... Miss Francisqui
Caludine .... Miss Tessier

The performance concluded with "a ballet of Furies armed with torches and flambeaux, executed in Hell, in which Miss Francisqui performed the character of Tisiphone." As in the American Company, there was some doubling-up in this French troupe.

On March 4th Miss Eloise of the company takes a benefit in

Barber of Seville, Mrs. Griffith

Count Almovina .... Mr. Remondet
Don Baizile .... Mr. Nau
Figaro .... Mr. Tessier
An Alcalde .... Mr. Legrand
A Notary .... Mr. Villegrain
Rosine .... Miss Francisqui

March 4th, at the Kingston Theatre, sees Mr. J. P. Cussans delivering passages from approved authors. He also sings several songs. What a mixture is his program:

Part One

Alexander's Feast, Dryden; Song—'Some Talk of Alexander'; The Dead Ass, Sterne; Song—'I Have Looked into Life,' G. S. Carey; Letter from a Young Country Gentleman on his Travels, to his Father; An English Song in the French dialect; A short anecdote of a French Gentleman; Song—'Polly of Bethnal Green'; An extract from Dr. Smollett; Song—'The Little Rolling Sailor'; The Seven Ages, Shakespeare; Song—'The Mulberry Tree,' Brush Collins; Song—'The Heart of a Lamb,' Dioden; A few lines of Poetry from Gay; Song—'The Cock and the Bull.'

Part Two

The Story of Le Fevre (curtailed), Sterne; Song— 'Brown Bess'; Song—'Admiral Benbow'; Naval anecdote; Song—'The Bundle of Proverbs'; The memorable words of Cardinal Wolsey; A Dozen Lines from Addison's Cato; Song—'I'm One of those Sailors who Thinks

Its no Lie'; Of an Intercourse with the World, Dr. Johnson; Song—'Young Sandy was Torn from his Alice's Side'; Poetical Translation from Ovid; Song—'I'm Little Bess the Ballad Singer'; Gray, Recitation; Song—'Tom Brisket and Flounder Nan.'

Lady Nugent goes to see him when he plays at Spanish Town. He reminds her of Dibdin, the famous English comedian, and she waxes melancholy over the thought that folly and extravagance have brought this gentleman to such a lowly state. The audience, she says, "were of all colours and descriptions: blacks, browns, Jews and whites."

By March 25th Lewis Dubois, first clarinet of the Kingston militia, takes a benefit with the French company. The bill is:

Shipwreck or Azemia, Arnold

Edwin .... Mr. Nau
Lord Atkinson .... Mr. Salentin
Alvan .... Mr. Remondet
Prospero .... Miss Tessier
Azemia .... Miss Francisqui
Fabrice .... Mr. Tessier

It has new scenery, machinery, and decorations. Tessier dances in the character of a savage. The opera commenced by a landing of Indians and concluded with a battle and comical dance of Indians. Between the second and third acts Mr. Dubois executed a concerto, followed by Mr. Bournon in a hornpipe. From this performance the gallant first clarinet received $280, which, we would say, was quite a neat little sum, but Mr. Dubois laments the fact in the public press that it was far insufficient to cover his debts; it left him out of pocket eighty-four dollars.

Well, sometimes there's no pleasing the French. And certainly there were times when the French didn't please their British hosts. We pick up the *Daily Advertiser* of March 23rd and read:

One Hundred Dollars Reward

Whereas a most gross, infamous and daring assault was committed by a Frenchman (supposed to be one of Mr. Tessier's Company from his having taken refuge behind the Scene) on the person of an inhabitant of this town, in the Theatre on Wednesday evening the 17th instant, and as every necessary legal process has been taken in order to bring him to justice, but without effect, the above reward will therefore be paid to any person or persons who will identify and bring forward to the Office of the Clerk of the Peace, the aforesaid Character, etc.

This reward was posted three times. While it might seem an isolated instance of assault, it was indicative of the feeling that was arising between the Jamaicans and their French guests. In June, 1809, Mr. Tessier of the company was released from the county jail where he had been confined for smuggling French passengers into the city. He was deported with orders never to return. . . . But that is getting ahead of our story. Here is Mr. Nau.

Mr. Nau announces his benefit for April 1st in *Jerusalem Delivered, a Grand Pantomime in Three Acts.* But like members of the old American Company, there's no accounting for temperament. The performance has to be postponed "on account of Miss Francisqui refusing to perform the character allotted to her." Can't you see her stamping her pretty little foot, and letting out a cascade of vitriolic French? Then Nau takes it all back—she didn't refuse to perform, she merely wanted a lot of back pay that was due her; and since she has a benefit shortly to come, etc. Peace settles down on the company.

Meantime, in Dallas' Long Room, Mr. Cussans slips in an entertainment called "The One by One Club."

But that rumble in the French company grew to alarming proportions. That, and the result of the assault. On April 14th the Grand Jury declared the theatre a public nuisance, "and as such that all performances by the company at present acting therein should be stopped." Little wonder that by June Mr. Touchmoulin of the company announces his intention "to leave this island with his family for St. Domingo, and declares he owes nothing."

These rowdy days also called a halt to Mr. Felix Byrne's ambitions. He, an island product, had believed that he surely would find support for his Boys' Boarding Academy, which he had hoped to open. But the pupils didn't come, so he had to go back to giving lessons and tuning musical instruments. He also had for sale a Chamber-Organ, Barrel-Organ, and Harpsichord.

All through the following year, 1803, J. P. Cussans seems to carry the burden of the attractions. He delivers his *Lecture on Hearts* while the Kingston court sat, and again at Spanish Town for the grand court there. Balls are given at these two towns and at Montego Bay and Falmouth, but apart from these, neither the newspaper nor Lady Nugent, who kept a fairly complete diary, finds any outstanding amusements to record.

In November Mr. Rannie, ventriloquist, offers the only exception, providing the island with a new form of divertisement. At the Mason's Lodge in Spanish Town, he makes his voice come "from closets, drawers, under tables, chairs, and from the ceiling." He also "causes the voice of a child to speak from the pocket of any lady or gentleman." The final sentence of his advertisement in the *St. Jago de la Vega Gazette* is priceless: "Mr. R. deems it necessary to inform the ladies and gentlemen of this town that he is the person named in the Encyclopaedia, who caused the great alarm that took place in Edinburgh a few years since, by causing a fish that was exposed for sale apparently to speak to its owner."

In 1804 Felix Byrne, whose career we have followed for some time, makes a venture in opening Harmony Hall Gardens. He provided pleasant, flower-bowered walks and a smoking room and four vocal performances each evening, and adequate refreshments. Each subscriber is given a pearl or silver ticket for himself and family. This is Kingston's own imitation of Vauxhall. Somehow, it didn't catch on. We soon find the auctioneer haunting the place. Death, too, robs Felix of his wife, Jane, in March, 1805. We note likewise on October 20th of that year, the death of John L. Woolls—evidently one of Stephen Woolls' sons.

Out in St. Elizabeth's Parish, at Lacovia Tavern, P. Rossi, formerly of the 20th Light Dragoons, tries to establish a rural Vauxhall. For a side line he teaches languages and music, military music especially. Those tourists who ride through Lacovia today might think pleasantly of Mr. Rossi's efforts and of the times when the militia held musters there and Rossi set out refreshments for them on the lawn, and how once this spot, now famous for its long Gothic tunnel of bamboos, was hilarious and hideous with Mr. Rossi's pupils practicing their military airs on oboes, slide horns, and bassoons.

A silence as of death settles on the Kingston Theatre. We hear nothing of it until in 1805 it is being used for quartering troops. Fear of a French invasion electrified the air and martial law was declared. The tension was lifted when Admiral Duckworth brought in a long line of prizes captured off Santo Domingo. And yet, at the time, Jamaica had further cause for rejoicing; Nelson's victory at Trafalgar set many a ball and dinner and illumination going. Rodney's glorious fight of 1782 was almost forgotten.

By 1808 J. Stewart, who had resided in the island twenty-one years, could sharpen his quill and, without a qualm or the slightest deviation from the facts, epitomize the island's amusements for that period:

There are no theatrical exhibitions in this island. About twenty-five years ago a company of the sons and daughters of Thespis came here. They had some years before migrated from North America, terrified and proscribed as they must have been by the fierceness of civil discord. But on peace being restored to that country, they returned to it; and have not since, nor have any others, visited the shores of this island. . . .

In Kingston there are occasionally tolerable concerts, the principal performers in which are French emigrants from St. Domingo; these unhappy people resorting, among other expedients, to this exercise of their talents, in order to obtain a livelihood. . . .

The want of public amusements and of amusing exhibitions in this island creates an eager and lively curiosity in the bulk of the people of all descriptions to see whatever has the appearance or promise of novelty in spectacles of the most trifling nature. Conjurors, sleight of hand men, dancers on the slack wire, exhibitors of wax-work figures, sometimes make their appearance here, and never fail to attract crowds of inquisitive people, to their great emolument, as they take care that the price of ad-mission should be consonant to the supposed wealth and munificence of the West Indies.[7]

CHAPTER XII

1808–1838

The Theatre Returns in Earnest—Kingston's Later Playhouses—Freedom Comes to Jamaica, and to the Reader

PICTURE, if you please, two groups of men talking of their dreams. The year is 1797. One group is in New York; the other in London.

The men in London are humanitarians. They dream, plan, and pray ardently for the day when England shall enact the legislation which will free every slave under the British dominion.

The other group consists of William Dunlap and Thomas Hodgkinson, active theatrical managers, and Lewis Hallam, erstwhile manager of the American Company of Comedians. Hallam is in his upper sixties. The second generation of the initial American theatrical dynasty, he is dreaming and planning of how it can further carry on the tradition of the Hallams. As for himself, he cannot do much more—his powers as actor and manager are fast waning and Death is to ring down his final curtain on November 1, 1808—but there is his son, Mirvan, who has been playing for some time on the American boards. Perhaps Hallam could get together a company for the West Indies. He might go back to Jamaica and open some of the theatres there. In Barbados, perhaps build a theatre. Mirvan could be put in charge as actor-manager.[1]

Of Hallam's dream, nothing came to pass.

Of the dream of the English humanitarians, much that was very definite and lasting eventually came to fruition. In 1808 the African slave trade was abolished; thenceforth Jamaica's supply of labor must come from the natural increase of her slaves. This legislation, aided by pressure from the abolitionists in England and the zealous preaching of a few missionaries in Jamaica, brought about a more humane treatment of the slaves. Despite this, a slave revolt broke out in 1803 in St. James's Parish, doing over £600,000 damage. The movement grew, however. Gradually Jamaican slaveholders became reconciled to their inevitable future.

In 1834 the slaves were freed, subject to an intermediate six years of apprenticeship, which was eventually shortened to four. These were bitter years. Apprenticeship was only a modification of slavery and brutal masters took advantage of it to wreak their vengeance on the least offender. It is estimated that in those four years, 60,000 apprentices received in the aggregate 250,-000 lashes and 50,000 other punishments by the tread mill, chain gang, and such other means of legalized torture.[2] Finally, on August 1, 1838, the 250,000 slaves in Jamaica were freed entirely. England reimbursed their owners to the grand total of £5,853,975. What it took the States four years of bloody war, England accomplished with the stroke of a pen. And to the gallery of its immortals it added the names of the men who had fought for this freedom—Clarkson, Wilberforce, Brougham, Stephen, Macaulay, Buxton, Allen—and, in Jamaica, Thomas Burchell, Walter Dendy, William Knibb, and James Mursel Phillippo. The unspeakable traffic in human flesh, that between 1656 and 1808 had brought upwards of a million slaves into the island, was ended forever.

The Theatre Returns

From the year 1806 on, Jamaica had her share of domestic troubles. The ferment of emancipation was working furiously. Now and then it broke out into slave revolts and into equally intense and much less warranted high-handed tactics by the planters and the Assembly which they controlled. . . . At the same time the ferment of Lewis Hallam's dream was also active. Although no Hallam was to lead it, and although the company did not hail from the States, the Jamaica theatre was revived —and from Barbados.

We recall (from way back in Chapter II) how a theatre building at Bridgetown, Barbados, was opened on January 1, 1812. It attracted stage folk from the other side of the Atlantic. Miss Eliza Fenwick, one of a famous theatrical family, had come to the Barbados Theatre from London in December, 1811. Her salary was six guineas a week. Four years later an offer was made her by the Jamaica Theatre for twenty guineas a week.[3] Jamaica was reaching out for talent. Already it had rolled up a reputation in the Kingston press.

The Kingston Theatre opened October 26, 1812, under the management of Messrs. Charles Manning, Jesse Reid, and Mrs. Elizabeth Shaw. Mrs. Shaw came up from Barbados. A Mrs. Shaw had made a Philadelphia appearance in 1794 as Lady Waitford in *The Dramatist* and played there until 1796. It may have been the same. Their first bill consisted of Home's *Douglas* with the farce of *Raising the Wind* for afterpiece. There was a special prologue and an address "written by a gentleman of Kingston" and spoken by Mr. Read in the character of Thespis, "attended by the Tragic Muse, with a dagger and bowl in her hands on one side, the Comic Muse on the other, with a character personifying Farce and a Harlequin personifying Pantomime, in the background."

The prologue, a contemporary stilted speech of fifty-four lines, began

> Blest be the Power, whose fostering hand
> Hath borne us safely to this gen'rous land.

After such a balanced bill and such a symbolic introduction of the muses, one would expect the Kingston critics to be completely disarmed. One, however, while acknowledging how starved the island has been for the theatre, "in a remote country like this, where the drama has for so many years been neglected and every necessary appendage thereto is obtained with great difficulty and numerous shifts are resorted to even to get up a single play," nevertheless, he felt called upon to judge the merits of the company. Mr. Manning in Glenalvon was "a first-rate actor on a provincial stage." Mr. Read in Young Norval played the part pretty enough—he is "a young player rising rapidly in dramatic merit." The character of Lord Randolph was sustained "by a young gentleman, Mr. Thompson, who apparently had never attempted so much before. Mrs. Shaw, as Lady Randolph, gave a degree of pathos and feeling to the part and Miss Shaw, as Anna, did all that was necessary."

In the farce of *Raising the Wind,* Miss Shaw personated antique virginity "as naturally as if she had in reality already arrived at that state of protracted purity." Mr. Hemming as Plainway mistook his part for that of a buffoon.

The last two items in the critique are significant:

The conduct of the audience on this occasion merits the highest enconiums; those disgraceful rows which on former occasions continually occurred in this theatre will, we trust, be witnessed no more.

The above night's receipts amounted to £438, besides which several persons obtained admittance through means of false tickets and a considerable part of the monies taken at the door, it is believed, was unaccounted for.[4]

While Kingston audiences had recovered from their rowdy ways displayed at the French theatre of a few years back, the temptation to cheat the box office was still too great to be resisted.

Our next note on this company is found in the *Jamaica Courant* of January 1, 1813, when it gives *The Honeymoon* and *The Jew and the Doctor* "under the patronage of the Corporate Body." Kingston, now being a full-fledged city, has no more need for a Master of the Revels. The casts run:

1813, January 1—*Honeymoon,* Payne

Duke Aranza .... Mr. Manning
Rolando .... Mr. Reid
Count Mountalban .... Mr. Louis
Juques .... Mr. Shaw
Lampedo .... Mr. DeLancy
Balthazar .... Mr. Morgan
Campillo .... Mr. Edwards
Juliana .... Mrs. Shaw

Zamora .... Miss Shaw
Volanti .... Mrs. Manning

Jew and Doctor, Dibdin

Abednego .... Mr. Manning
Changeable .... Mr. Reid
Bromley .... Mr. Morgan
William .... Mr. DeLancy
Thomas .... Mr. Edwards
Dr. Specific .... Mr. Shaw
Charles .... Mr. Lewis
Emily .... Miss Shaw
Mrs. Changeable .... Mrs. Shaw

Mrs. Manning in *The Honeymoon* is advertised as being her first appearance on this stage. Between the comedy and the farce she sang some songs. The prices were: Boxes, 13s 4d; Boxes for people of color, 11s 4d; Pit, 10s; Gallery, 6s 8d.

January 12—*She Stoops to Conquer*

Hardcastle .... Mr. Morgan
Young Marlow .... Mr. Manning
Hastings .... Mr. Louis
Tony Lumpkin .... Mr. Shaw
Diggory .... Mr. DeLancy
Servant .... Mr. Edwards
Landlord .... Mr. DeLancy
Mrs. Hardcastle .... Miss Shaw
Miss Hardcastle .... Mrs. Shaw
Miss Neville .... Mrs. Manning

This was followed by Garrick's *The Lying Valet.*
The season is well under way. Performances come along in regular succession. January 16th, *She Stoops to Conquer* with Dr. John Brown's *Barbarossa* as afterpiece;

January 22nd, Colman's *Mountaineers* and Coffey's *The Devil to Pay;* January 29th, *John Bull* and *An Irishman in London.* On February 15th is given for the benefit of the Mannings, *Lovers' Vows* and *The Jew and the Doctor,* with favorite songs; February 24th, Morton's *Cure for the Heartache;* and *Poor Soldier.* March 8th opens with Morton's *Speed the Plough* and Allingham's *Fortune's Frolic.* On March 10th comes Farquhar's old favorite, *The Beaux' Stratagem,* with Bickerstaff's *Sultan* for afterpiece. This last bill was given by request of the Colonel and officers of the 60th Regiment and the regimental band attended to play national airs.

Continuing March, we find *Tekel* and *Fortune's Frolic* on the bill for the 17th; *Poor Gentleman* and *Mock Doctor* for the 31st; *The West Indian* and *Wags of Windsor* for April 10th. Meantime Mrs. Shaw announces to the ladies and gentlemen of Spanish Town that she will shortly reopen the theatre there with *The West Indian* and *Who's the Dupe?* In Kingston the company continues. April 14th sees it put on "Monk" Lewis's *Castle Spectre* and Cross's *Purse;* and on April 24th, with *Hamlet* and *Love à la Mode,* Mr. Manning takes his benefit. He plays Hamlet. After the tragedy, Mrs. Manning dances a hornpipe and Manning offers two songs. He also makes a farewell address. He and Mrs. Manning and their child are departing for England. By December he is dead: "In England, shortly after his arrival, Mr. Charles Manning, formerly one of the managers of the company of comedians in Kingston."

The benefits commence and run with uninterrupted succession. Mr. Reid takes his on May 1st, with Morton's *Columbus;* and *The Village Lawyer.* The next night

Mrs. Shaw in *Castle Spectre* and *Purse*. Miss Shaw follows on the 8th with *The Road to Ruin* and Birch's
Adopted Child. On the 22nd, Mr. Shaw, evidently be-
lieving that women and children should come first even
in benefits, at last gathers the extra emolument with
Romeo and Juliet and *Padlock*. For Mr. DeLancy is
given *The Surrender of Calais* and *Two Strings to Your
Bow* on the 29th; Mr. Wolfe, whom we have not seen
in the bills, on June 5th with Colman's *Iron Chest;* and
Children in the Wood for afterpiece. Mr. Morgan on
June 12th selects Colman's *Blue Beard* and Betterton's
Barnaby Brittle. Miss Jones, whose name also is new to
us, chooses on June 26th, *The School for Scandal* and
The Spoiled Child. Then on June 28th, Mr. Reid elects
Wonder and *Padlock,* both old favorites with Jamaican
audiences. This benefit is given "by particular desire of
the Worshipful Grand Master, Wardens and Members
of the Provincial Grand Lodge of Ancient Masons." Mr.
Read favors them with a Masonic prologue.

Two more benefits and we are finished. For Mr. Lion,
another new name, on July 3rd, *The Point of Honour*
and *Richard III* and for Mr. David on July 16th, *Wild
Oats* and that hoary afterpiece *Catherine and Petruchio*.
With this the special performances come to an end.

There! You have been very patient, but we had to
get these down. To avoid your ennui I have deliberately
left out occasional one-night stands at Spanish Town.
You must confess that it has been an impressive run—
27 performances of which we have record and 45 plays
and afterpieces. No mean repertoire for a company drifting around the Caribbean Isles. Oh yes, I forgot to mention that Mr. Morgan and Mr. DeLancy also served as

scene painters.

The opening of the Kingston Theatre stimulated ambition in other parts of the island. In April officers of the garrison at Port Royal put on *John Bull* and Mrs. Centlivre's farce *The Ghost,* "for a benevolent purpose." This performance brought only praise from the critic of the *Jamaica Magazine.* He also reported that "the house was crowded with people of the first respectability, who departed wishing that an opportunity was often afforded them of spending an evening so rationally." [5] How *did* Port Royalers spend their evenings?

The desire for amusement even revived the assemblies. These decorous quarterly balls had just about expired in Kingston by 1813, but when a subscription list was handed round, it found ready acceptance.

By November, 1812, as we read in the *Royal Gazette* a subscription is being raised in Spanish Town for fitting up the Long Room, so that the comedians lately arrived might "perform therein as soon as they have lightened the purses of the inhabitants of the City."

The next time we hear from Spanish Town is in February, 1813, when *Poor Gentleman* and *Love à la Mode* are attempted by officers of the garrison assisted by the female part of the company of comedians. Meantime the company does come occasionally to the capital, so that Spanish Town is now quite a lively place.

On July 24, 1813, the Spanish Town Theatre opened in earnest. It was supported by the Theatrical Amateur Society of the capital, whose purpose was to raise funds to establish a regular theatre. Governor Fuller and his suite attended, together with several members of the Privy Council and the Assembly. The bills include *The*

Jew and the Doctor, Ghost, Love à la Mode, Pizarro, Garrick's *Guardian* and an old piece, *Harlequin Collector, Bold Stroke for a Wife, Isabella, How to Die for Love,* and several others. Miss Shaw of the company is assisting.

A New Company Appears

Readers of the *Gazette* of July 24, 1813, were apprized of the intelligence that Mr. W. Adamson, manager of the company of comedians at Barbados, is quitting that colony because he has received so little patronage, and is expected to come to Jamaica in two or three months. He will have with him Miss Wilmot of the theatres at Bath and London, and Mr. Smalley," both performers of considerable merit." This company has been playing in St. Thomas, St. Croix, and other islands. Barbados may have relented—or perhaps our newspapers are neglectful of the stage—for we do not hear of this company in Jamaica until 1816. It appears in Spanish Town. On February 1st, C. Kemble's *The Point of Honour* was given by a troupe whose names are new to us. The casts as reported in the *St. Jago Gazette* are:

Point of Honour, Kemble

St. Franc .... Mr. Louis
Valcour .... Mr. Hill
            with a favourite song of "Victory")
Durmiel .... Mr. J. E. Adamson
First Officer .... Mr. Cummins
Second Officer .... Mr. Harcourt
Zenger .... Master Murray
Bertha .... Mrs. Elliston
Mrs. Melfort .... Mrs. Hill

At the end of the play came a new comic song, "Irish Providence," by Mr. Adamson, a dance by Mrs. Elliston, and a song, "The Heart of a Sailor," by Mr. Hill. These were followed by the musical entertainment:

My Grandmother or The Talkative Barber, Hoare

Vapour .... Mr. Hill
Sir Mathew Medley ....Mr. Cummins
Souffrance .... Mr. Harcourt
Tom .... Master Murray
Dicky Gossip .... Mr. Adamson
Florella .... Mrs. Adamson
Charlotte .... Mrs. Elliston

The prices for tickets were back to the old rate—13s 4d for boxes, 10s for the pit, 10s for upper boxes, 6s 3d for the gallery. The feeling of the time is noticeable in an instruction: "No white person to be admitted to the upper boxes or gallery."

The following Tuesday the bill began with the popular opera:

Haunted Tower, Cobb

Lord William .... Mr. Hill
Lord De Courcy ....Mr. Hitchener
Adela ....Mrs. Hill
Lady Elinor .... Mrs. Elliston
Cicely ....Mrs. Adamson

Don Juan or the Libertine Destroyed

Don Juan .... Mr. Hill
Scaramouch .... Mr. Adamson

Of this performance we have a report from no less a personage than Matthew ("Monk") Gregory Lewis. He had come to Jamaica the previous year to look after his estates and spent some time traveling around the Island. His experiences and observations are related in

The Journal of a West Indian Proprietor:

I left Kingston at two o'clock in defiance of a broiling sun; reached Spanish Town in time to dine with the Attorney-General; and afterwards went to the play, where I found my acquaintance Mr. Hill of Covent Garden theatre performing Lord William in "The Haunted Tower" and Don Juan in the pantomime which followed. The theatre is neat enough, but, I am told, very inferior in splendour to that in Kingston. As to the performance, it was about equal to any provincial theatricals that I ever saw in England; although the pieces were by no means well selected, being entirely musical, and the orchestra consisting of nothing more than a couple of fiddles.[6]

Another week passes and Hill's company presents:

Duenna, Sheridan

Don Jerome .... Mr. Yates
Ferdinand .... Mr. Hitchener
Antonio .... Mr. J. E. Adamson
Carlos .... Mr. Hill
Isaac Mendoza .... Mr. Adamson
Lopez .... Master Murray
Father Paul .... Mr. Harcourt
Lorenzo .... Mr. Louis
Sancho .... Mr. Cummins
Starved Friar .... A Gentleman Amateur
Clara .... Mrs. Hill
Louisa .... Mrs. Elliston
Duenna .... Mrs. Stuart

The bill concluded with the laughable farce of

Midnight Hour or War of Wits, Mrs. Inchbald

Marquis .... Mr. Hill
General .... Mr. Yates
Sebastian .... Mr. J. E. Adamson
Nicholas .... Mr. Adamson
Mathias .... Mr. Harcourt
Ambrose .... Mr. Lewis
Julia .... Mrs. Elliston
Cecily .... Mrs. Stuart
Flora .... Mrs. Adamson

Just as the American Company of Comedians had its two Wignells, so this troupe had its two Adamsons—J. E. and W. It included Mr. Yates, a good comedian from the Theatre Royal Manchester, who made his American debut at the Park Theatre in New York on May 25, 1811, as Sir Willoughby Worrett in *Man and Wife.* An Adamson appeared in New York in *The Merry Wives of Windsor* on October 29th, 1816.[7]

The following Thursday the bill consisted of *The Castle Spectre* by M. G. Lewis—probably a compliment to his presence on the island—and the musical entertainment of *The Deserter.*

Mr. Hill and the company had apparently pleased the elite of Spanish Town, which begs for more. So we have two additional bills. The first began with Thomas Dibdin's opera, *The Cabinet,* never before presented in Jamaica. Prince Orlando was played by Mr. Hill, in which character he introduced several songs—"The Beautiful Maid," "Fair Ellen," "The Polacca," and "The Bird Duet." The cast ran:

Cabinet, Dibdin

Prince Orlando .... **Mr. Hill**

Count Curvosa .... Mr. Yates
Lorenzo .... Mr. Hitchener
Marquis de Grand Chateau ...... Mr. Harcourt
Peter Pullhard .... Mr. J. E. Adamson
Manikin ....Mrs. Elliston
Whimsiculo .... Mr. Adamson
Constantia .... Mrs. Elliston
Crudelia .... Mrs. Stuart
Curiosa .... Mrs. Adamson
Doralice .... Miss Brown
Floretta .... Mrs. Hill

At the end of the opera came a *pas seul* by Mrs. Elliston and then the farce:

First Floor, Cobb

Whimsey .... Mr. Yates
Monford .... Mr. J. E. Adamson
Young Whimsey .... Mr. Hitchener
Tim Tartlett .... Mr. Adamson
Fumish ....Mr. Cummins
Simon .... Master Murray
Frank .... Mr. Elliston
Landlord .... Mr. Harcourt
Mrs. Patty Pan ....Mrs. Stuart
Charlotte .... Mrs. Elliston
Nancy .... Mrs. Adamson

The last night of the season, February 27th, was a performance by desire of the Royal Saint Jago Lodge of Free and Accepted Masons "under sanction of the Grand Master." It opened with the celebrated romantic musical drama, "with appropriate new scenery, dresses, etc." of Desmond's *The Foundling of the Forest* and concluded with Millingen's *The Bee-Hive or Lots of Fun.*

Founding of the Forest, Desmond

Count de Vaubmont .... Mr. Louis
Longueville .. Mr. Hitchener (for this night only)
Florian .... Mr. Hill
Bertrand .... Mr. J. E. Adamson
L'Eclair .... Mr. Adamson
Gaspard .... Mr. Yates
Sanquine .... Mr. Elliston
Lenoir .... Mr. Harcourt
Bravo .... Mr. Cummins
Geraldine .... Mrs. Elliston
Rosabella .... Mrs. Adamson
Monica .... Mrs. Stuart
Unknown Female .... Miss Montford

Bee-Hive, Millingen

Captain Merton .... Mr. J. E. Adamson
Rattan .... Mr. Yates
Mingle .... Mr. Adamson
Joe .... Mr. Harcourt
Mrs. Mingle .... Mrs. Stuart
Emily .... Mrs. Elliston
Cicily .... Mrs. Adamson

Gone were the good old days when the Lodge marched to the theatre behind a military band and Masonic members of the cast and their wives recited Masonic odes and songs.

This was not the final appearance of Hill's company in Spanish Town, however; we find one more performance mentioned in the *St. Jago Gazette.* It is for June 17th, a melodrama in three acts called:

Magpie or The Maid, Cooke

Gerald .... Mr. Davids
Henry .... Mr. Louis

Everard .... Mr. Hitchener
Martin .... Mr. Harcourt
Malcour .... Mr. Yates
Bertrand .... Mr. Cummins
George .... Mr. Murray
Benjamin .... Mr. Adamson
Dame Gerald .... Mrs. Ford
Annette .... Miss Montfort

Apart from making the record of casts complete, our reason for listing these actors is to show what had been going on in the company. As "Monk" Lewis remarked in his *Journal:* "However various are the characters which actors sustain, I find their own to be the same everywhere. Although the Jamaica company did not consist of more than twenty persons, their green-room squabbles divided it, and we found one-half performing at Falmouth." [8] By this time Falmouth had become a great sugar port and the planters thereabout were growing richer and richer as the crops rolled in. It even had a newspaper—*The Jamaica Mercury and Trelawny Advertiser.*

The presence of part of the company in Falmouth is further sustained by the notice of the death of Mr. Jesse Reid, "late of the Theatre" of Kingston, who passed away at Falmouth on October 9, 1816. Three days following, in Kingston, after a short illness, died Miss Montfort, "late of the Theatre in this city, a young lady who promised to become an ornament to her profession."

The squabbles between the Thespians finally reached the magistrate. In October the Court of Common Council ruled that in the future Mr. Adamson of the new company could have the theatre for a week and then Mrs. Shaw of the old company the alternate week. This was rescinded in November by a ruling that permitted Mrs. Shaw to open her own theatre under her own management.

Among the punishments visited upon Matthew Gregory Lewis (doubtless for his sins) was to have to sit through a Kingston performance of his *Adelgitha*. The date in his *Journal* is March 4, 1818:

I was enabled to visit the Kingston theatre; the exterior is rather picturesque; within it has no particular recommendations; the scenery and dresses were shabby, the actors wretched and the stage ill-lighted; the performance was for the benefit of the chief actress, who had but little reason to be satisfied with the number of her audience; and I may reckon it among my other misfortunes on this ill-starred expedition, that it was my destiny to sit out the tragedy of "Adelgitha," whom the author meant only to be killed in the last act, but whom the actors murdered in all five. The heroine was the only one who spoke tolerably, but she was old enough and fat enough for the Widow Cheshire; Guiscard did not know ten words of his part; the tyrant was really comical enough; and Lothair was played by a young Jamaican Jew about fifteen years of age and who is dignified here with the name of "The Creole Roscius." His voice was just breaking, which made him "pipe and whistle in the sound." His action was awkward, and altogether he was but a sorry specimen of theatrical talent.[9]

Montego Bay

It was not to be expected that Montego Bay would be neglected in this revival of amusements and high times. January, 1816, sees the town invaded by Mr. Villallave who appeared in the old courthouse, Gedelia's, with his performing children. The little ladies dance on the tight rope; one of them, merely eight years old, even skips on the rope and performs in "an attitude never seen before." Mrs. V. assists, together with a tumbler known as "the celebrated Romanito." In the fourth act Mr. V. plays "with a stick, à la Breton." For this the lower boxes sold at 13s 4d a seat and the upper boxes for people of color, 10s. These Villallave tumbling shows run from the beginning of January until well into March. On several occasions they finish with a comic pantomime in which the Villallaves are assisted by Messrs. Pasquell, Floremondo, Romanito, Le Flor, and the two children, Venesianita and Little Indian. They had performed in Kingston, in 1812, with quite an encouraging patronage.

Shortly after this troupe gets under way at Montego, the ladies are favored with a ball. In February the anniversary of the installation of Cornwall Lodge is celebrated by a procession of the brethren to church, to hear a sermon by the Rev. D. W. Rose, rector of Hanover, and at five o'clock more than seventy of them sit down to dinner. Early in March the custos gives "a most splendid ball and supper to the inhabitants of the parish and numerous strangers collected from the different parts of the island." A brilliant assemblage of beauty and respectability, this was to celebrate the opening of the new courthouse, the present structure on the Parade. It was especially decorated for the occasion. One hundred and sixty ladies attended and several hundred gentlemen. At one A. M. came a collation, as usual at these balls, then the dancing went on until daylight broke across the Reading Hills.

Go down, you trippers to Montego Bay, go down to the Parade at dawn and see the ghosts of these revelers drifting out of the courthouse. . . . They lean over the balcony railing and call to their drivers. Boys run about rousing the dusky coachmen asleep on the carriage seats. Out into the cool air stray the ladies and gentlemen, their finery a little awry and crushed, their steps, perhaps, a little unsteady, their eyes blinking at the strong light. . . . And before Mr. Nathan's manager has taken down the shutters to his shop front windows or the morning's detail of police has marched past in their neat white tunics, or the country women, baskets of produce on their heads, have strutted down the lane to the market, the ghosts of these revelers have all faded into the morning light.

By July 4th comes the first assembly held in the new courthouse. Then, two days later the town is agog over an announcement that Mr. Hill will give a concert. It is to be in the assembly room of the courthouse, which the magistrates have offered him, and he is to be assisted by Mr. Maurice Pyke on the pianoforte. It was an elaborate program (which we have no intention of printing) and was so well received that Hill and Pyke gave two more concerts. Then the pair ride up the road to attend the Bachelor's Ball at Falmouth on August 24th. This was Race Week in Falmouth and high doings kept up night after night. When Hill and Pyke give their concert, they are assisted by the band of the 60th Regiment, stationed in town. Anyone riding through sleepy Falmouth today can scarcely believe that the town ever supported such giddy events. . . . However, step into the courthouse and see the ballroom with its crystal chandeliers and brocaded sofas, and even though this is not the original building (the one in which our events took place was destroyed by fire) yet you can readily understand why Falmouth can sleep peacefully on the memories of its merry past.

Kingston's Later Playhouses

Back on the south shore, Kingston was still preening itself on having been incorporated a city. This momentous event had come to pass in 1803. Almost immediately the city fathers began laying down rules and regulations for the theatre. In 1828 these were combined in one awesome document—"Ordinances and Bylaws relative to the Public Theatre and the Play Houses, and other Houses of Public Amusement, and for preventing disturbances and disorders therein." Ah, those rowdy Kingstonians! As early as 1807 the town had been impelled to do something about troubles in the theatre and again in 1812.[10] Now, anyone who made a rumpus during a play or around the theatre, if white or free colored, would pay from £20 to £50 fine or pass from ten days to three months in jail, and, if a slave, be given thirty-nine lashes and thirty days' hard work. No liquors were to be sold within the doors of the theatre. Kingston was determined that its theatre be respectable! Seven of its best citizens were put on the theatre committee to see that the ordinance was carried out.[11]

By this time the ramshackle old theatre on Kingston's Parade that had known the tread of Hallam and Henry had disappeared, probably having been destroyed by fire, and in its place was built another, the Theatre Royal, which was to serve the city for many decades. It was a brick structure in the old colonial style of architecture, with a wide indented portico supported by columns and reached by a handsome flight of steps. Having served for a century, it was torn down about 1900 and replaced by a more imposing structure, erected by the City Council. This building, in turn, was destroyed by the earthquake of 1907, after only a few performances. It was so shaken to pieces that it could not possibly have been repaired. For many years after that, since the city had no theatre building, operatic and dramatic companies were reluctant to visit the island, the only accommodation possible for their use being a small concert hall with poor acoustics.

While the townsfolk doubtless were anxious for another building, the government would not permit the municipality to spend the money to erect one. And little wonder—money had to be spent on more necessary repairs and cleaning up and building. Finally the Custos of Kingston, Colonel Charles James Ward, generously contributed the money for a theatre. It still stands today, bearing his name, and to those who have followed this account of the Jamaica theatre so far, it will be interesting to note that the location of the Ward Theatre is approximately the same site on which stood the theatre of Hallam and Henry.

Long before this time the trail that the American Company of Comedians had blazed between Harbour Street, Kingston, and Broadway, New York, had become an overgrown path. No longer did the States send down to the island for theatrical talent. Dramatically, Jamaica was isolated. Now and then some wandering troupe came to the island, played a few weeks, left a member or two behind in a graveyard, and then sailed away. Amateur theatricals were attempted from time to time; the Creole urge for mummery is bound to break out every so often.

From 1834 to 1838 came the final growing pains of Emancipation and yet the very year before that first date, both in Kingston and Spanish Town, local amateurs attempted most ambitious programs. The troubles of the time seem to have sobered some of the people. The riotous eating and drinking, of which we saw so much in a previous age, began to disappear. Society was being stirred by the ferment of decency. Even the Sabbath was being observed. An indication of the more sober attitude toward life generally and amusements in particular can be found in these amateur show bills. They are a definite return to the old classics that had been welcomed by Jamaicans half a century before.

In Kingston *Macbeth* is put on with relative success— and, also, much to the delight of the audience. Lady Macbeth was played by a local gentleman; Macduff had a squeaky voice that brought down hoots and catcalls from the gallery. But the highlight of the performance was when the tip of Mr. Bailey's nose was well-nigh shorn off "by the gigantic efforts of the Frisky Siward, who in his attempt to vanquish the illustrious tyrant, gave his *pas de deux* with such good will that it took effect on the proboscis of Mr. B." [12] That injured gentleman, however, bore it with the most perfect nonchalance. Later this amateur company played *She Stoops to Conquer*.

In January the next year, the Kingston Amateurs journey to Spanish Town to lighten with plays the labors of the Assembly of what the local critic dubbed "this singularly dull island." They chose that ancient classic, Thomas Otway's *Venice Preserved,* and were assisted by local warriors of the 56th Regiment stationed in the capital. These worthy grenadiers apparently put such zest into their lines and gestures that they fairly made the footlights jingle!

Final Exit

We could, were it not for the risk of becoming wearisome, continue this story of the Jamaican theatre down to our own day, for the stage in the Island never entirely died out. From time to time various visiting companies played with the assistance of local stage aspirants.

Once Kingston was reduced to being amused by an animal show. In this effort the parts of the animals were taken by local actors in lion, bear, leopard, and such other realistic skins, who accompanied their antics with equally realistic howls and roars. At the opening performance, one of the lions attained, surely, the uttermost flight of the ludicrous in all Jamaican theatrical history. Three of these noble beasts came onto the stage marching majestically and sufficiently realistic to startle the children in the auditorium. Suddenly the first lion sprang up on its hind legs and began to shriek in the best Jamaican (which can be very good) English, "Take it off! Take it off!" And the voice of the stage manager bellowed from the wings, "Get down on your four feet and keep on your skin." And the lion yelled back, "Keep it on? You come and put it on, and see how you like it." Thereupon the skin fell off and a man stood exposed to the gaze of the howling audience—in his underwear.

It seems that a scorpion, without evil intent, had decided to make its home in one shoulder of the lion's skin. When Mr. Levy, who was impersonating that particular beast, began gyrating around, the scorpion started to sting.

Mr. Levy's departure from theatrical life was swift and final.[13]

Although we have no such impelling excuse for leaving the stage as Mr. Levy, nevertheless we take this opportunity—and now make our exit.

FOOTNOTES AND BIBLIOGRAPHY

Chapter I

1. Jamaica View'd. By Captain Hickeringill. London, 1661. Page 1.
2. Historic Jamaica. By Frank Cundall. London, 1915. Page 291.
3. This account is at the end of Wood's *Laws of Jamaica,* published in London in 1716, a copy of which is in the West Indian Reference Library of the Institute of Jamaica.
4. Calendar of State Papers, Colonial Series. America and West Indies, 1685–1688. Edited by Hon. J. W. Fortesque. London, 1899. No. 981.
5. Quoted in *The Governors of Jamaica in the Seventeenth Century.* By Frank Cundall. London, 1936. Page 130.
6. Council Minutes (MSS) 1692–1695. Pages 47–48.
7. The Fool's Opera or The Taste of the Age. Written by Mat Medley. London, 1731.
8. Scarlett is an old Jamaica name. A Captain Francis Scarlett came out with the first expedition. He served as member of the Assembly for St. Andrew in 1680–1 and returned to England, where he died. His nephew, William Scarlett, of the Inner Temple, inherited his estate and moved to Jamaica. It was evidently from this William Scarlett that Tony borrowed lawbooks.
9. Major General William Selwyn, colonel of the 22nd or the Cheshire Regiment, arrived in Jamaica in January, 1702, as Governor and died April 5th of the same year. Jamaica was not too healthy a place in those days. The Assembly voted £2500 to be presented his widow, and in August £2000 were appropriated for his heirs at law and £100 to the captain of the man of war that carried Madame Selwyn home to England. Colonel Thomas Handasyd of the 22nd Regiment, afterward

Brigadier General, was appointed Lieutenant Governor in 1702 and Captain General and Governor in Chief in 1705. The Thomas Nichols that Tony Ashton mentions must have been the one who was Clerk of the Council in 1690.

10. Anthony Ashton. By Watson Nicholson. South Haven, Michigan, 1920. Page 50.
11. Description of the Island of Jamaica. By Richard Blome. London, 1678. Pages 17 and 25.
12. Historic Jamaica. By Frank Cundall. London, 1915. Page 16.
13. A Voyage to the Islands Madera and Jamaica. By Sir Hans Sloane. Vol. I, page xi.
14. Chronological Outlines of Jamaica History. By Frank Cundall. Kingston, 1927.
15. Acts of the Assembly Passed in the Island of Jamaica from 1681 to 1737. London, 1738.
16. A New and Exact Account of Jamaica. By Charles Leslie. Edinburgh, 1739.
17. The Importance of Jamaica. London, 1740.
18. The British Empire in America. By John Oldmixon. London, 1741. Second edition, Vol. 2, page 416. This theatre, by the way, is not mentioned in the first edition of 1708. Perhaps the Spanish Town theatre of 1682 was gone by this time. Oldmixon evidently got his later information from a local correspondent.
19. A New History of Jamaica. By Vice Admiral Edward Vernon. London, 1740.
20. Caribbeana. Vol. V, page 132.
21. Council Minutes. November 1727—October, 1730. MSS. Page 9.
22. The Longs of Jamaica and Hampton Lodge. By R. M. Howard. London, 1927. Vol. I, page 474.
23. Charlotte Cibber's unfortunate romance with Richard Charke is related in that lady's *Narrative of the Life of Mrs. Charlotte Charke, Written by Herself,* London, 1755. She and Richard, after six months' acquaintance, were married in St. Martin's Church, London. Both were young and indiscreet. Shortly afterward he took to wandering off with other girls and Charlotte passed most of her time tracing her spouse "through the Hundreds of Drury." Occasionally, however, he deigned to

call on her. Their daughter Kitty became Mrs. Harman of the American stage. Charke early rolled up a reputation for himself as a violinist. Not alone did he accept Henry Moore's invitation to come to Jamaica, but the rascal borrowed £100 from Moore's agents in London in order to pay the debts of his lady love whom he intended sending for his pleasure to Jamaica. Charlotte refers to her as "Mrs. Sally K...g, one of the Ladies of the Highest Irreputable Reputation at that time in or about Covent Garden." Evidently Mrs. K. never sailed for the island. Charke died after he had been there a year and a half. Charlotte, after a checkered career, died in 1759.

24. Memoirs of an American Lady. By Anne Grant. New York, 1901. Page 133.
25. The Dramatic Records of Sir Henry Herbert, Master of Revels 1623–1673. By Joseph Quincy Adams. New Haven, 1917.
26. Annals of the English Stage. By Dr. Doran. London, 1888. Vol. II, page 62.
27. Gentleman's Magazine, 1766. Vol. 36, pages 33–4.
28. *Ibid.*
29. The Philadelphia Stage from the year 1749 to the year 1855. By Charles Durang. Philadelphia, 1837.
30. *Ibid.*
31. In his *Memoirs* (Vol. II, Page 96–7) Tate Wilkinson, patentee of the Theatres Royal at York and Hull and for many years a wandering player, relates a merry incident of Moody's arrival in England. The date was some time in June, 1759. "Mr. Moody arrived at Portsmouth from Jamaica, and in his hand led from the lucky bark (that wafted him safe to England) a lady to whom he paid due attention, a Mrs. Osborne. She was a sensible woman, and had not lost time while abroad, as her waist was not one of the most slim." She played in *The Mourning Bride;* by the fifth act had to quit, as her time was about due, and she was carried to the state-bed where she was delivered of a "brave chopping heir." Wilkinson continues: "I called the next day to inquire after her health and found the lady dressed and sitting at a table, perfectly well, shelling peas for her dinner. In a few days we had a merry christening; I was one godfather, and think my friend Moody was a god-

father, or some kind of a father—which, he knows best."

32. Annals of the New York Stage. By George C. D. Odell. Vol. 1, pages 68–9.

33. It may be a coincidence of names—and then, again, it may not—that in 1757 a schooner, the *Charming Sally,* was rented as a tender to His Majesty's ship *Wage,* stationed at Port Royal. According to the Council Minutes, the Government paid £108/6/9 for the hire of the *Charming Sally* from January 14th to March 19, 1757.

Chapter II

1. A History of the American Theatre. By William Dunlap. New York, 1832. Page 17.

2. The Philadelphia Theatre in the 18th Century. By Thomas Clark Pollock. Philadelphia, 1933. Page 6.

3. The strange name Jago, however, is not foreign to early Jamaica records. Although I have been unable to find any of that name in our period, yet in 1675 a John Jago married Dorothy Hunter. Perhaps the Jago of the Murray and Kean company was a descendant of these two.

4. Journals of the Assembly 1745–56. *Vide* also A History of Printing in Jamaica by Frank Cundall, Kingston, 1935.

5. It was the American Revolution that brought both David Douglass and his printing partner, William Aikman, to Jamaica. Originally from Scotland, the Aikmans settled in Charleston and at the outbreak of the Revolution came to the island with other Loyalists. By 1779 Douglass and Aikman were "Printers to the King's Most Excellent Majesty for Jamaica and Its Dependencies," and began issuing the *Jamaica Mercury and Kingston Weekly Advertiser,* which from 1780 on was known as the *Royal Gazette.* William Aikman also ran a book and stationery store in King Street. He died in 1784 at the early age of thirty-five. Several books bear the imprint of this firm: *Observations on the Dysentery of the West Indies* by Benjamin Moseley, M.D., 1780; *A Brief History of the Late Expedition Against Fort Juan* by Dr. Thomas Dancer, 1781; *A Short Dissertation on the Jamaica Bath Waters,* also

by Dancer, who was physician at Bath and later Island botanist; *Elements of Free Masonry Delineated* by William Moore; and *Thoughts on the State of the Militia of Jamaica* by Alexander Dirom. In 1782 they began printing their Almanac and Register.

6. The British Empire in America. By John Oldmixon. London, 1708. Vol. 2, page 127.
7. Caribbeana. London, 1741. Vol. 1, page 37.
8. George Washington's Diaries, 1748–99. Edited by J. G. Fitzpatrick. 4 vols. New York, 1925. Page 25.
9. History of Barbados. By Sir Robert Schomburgk. London, 1848. Page 250.
10. In addition to Barbados, other Caribbean islands enjoyed the theatre at an early date.

In the Danish West Indies at Christiansted in 1771 was the Bass-End Theatre, where, according to the *Royal Danish American Gazette,* planters and their families watched the Leeward Islands company of comedians perform *King Lear, Richard III, The Mock Doctor, The Virgin Unmasked,* and such other popular plays of the day. Frederichsted also had its theatre. *Vide The Danish West Indies Under Company Rule.* By W. Westergaard. New York, 1917. Page 248.

Antigua's first theatre was established by a party of amateurs and opened on January 17, 1788, with Otway's *Venice Preserved.* The orchestra was composed of the band of the 69th Regiment then stationed on the island, and the funds from this performance were devoted to the erection of a Free Masons' Lodge. Thereafter visiting companies occasionally put in for a few weeks' run. They were usually assisted by local amateurs. One of Antigua's native sons became the well-known eccentric "Romeo Coates," who was an attraction in London. *Vide Antigua and the Antiguans,* 2 vols. London, 1844. Pages 211–2.

St. Lucia's Theatre Royal was not established until December, 1832, when some English and French amateurs, aided by a company from Martinique under direction of Mons. Charvet, gave performance two or three times a week for six months. The company again visited the island in 1834. *Vide St. Lucia: Historical, Statistical and Descriptive.* By Henry H. Breen.

London, 1844. Page 270.

11. Boston Gazette, May 8–15, 1738.
12. Only three copies of the *Jamaica Courant* within the range of these dates are known to exist, and they offer no theatrical information. The *Kingston Journal,* started a year after Hallam landed, is missing in its earlier numbers. The *St. Jago Intelligencer* of Spanish Town, begun in 1757, is equally missing or uncommunicative.
13. Governor Henry Moore gave permission to Douglass to play in Albany for a month in the summer of 1769. Hallam, Henry, Miss Cheer, and Woolls were in the cast. *Vide Players of a Century: A Record of the Albany Stage.* By A. P. Phelps. Albany, 1880.
14. This is found in a petition sent the Assembly on November 19, 1783, by one "Edward Becher, only son of Hannah Becher, wife of William Jenkyns, Esq., formerly Hannah Becher, of the parish of Kingston . . . widow. . . . That by this indenture made at the island of Jamaica . . . the 4th day of May, 1753 . . . the said William Jenkyns and Hannah his wife, did fully, clearly and absolutely grant, bargain, sell . . . except the old messuage formerly called the Old Play-house in Harbour-Street there."
15. Memoirs of a Life Lived Chiefly in Pennsylvania. By Capt. Graydon. Page 76.
16. *Ibid.* Pages 76–8.
17. Dunlap. Page 81.
18. Poems Chiefly Written in the West Indies. By Bryan Edwards. Kingston, 1792.
19. Biographical Notes of Members of the Assembly of Jamaica, 1663–1837. By John Roby. 1837.
20. This data is found in the handwriting of John Philip Kemble, an intimate friend of John Moody. *Vide The Life and Letters of John Paul Jones.* By Mrs. Reginald de Koven. New York, 1913. Pages 12–3.
21. John Paul Jones: Man of Acton. By Philip Russell. New York, 1927. Page 24.
22. Sheridan's Jamaica Monthly Magazine. September, 1833. Page 174.

23. The Charleston Stage in the 18th Century. By Eloa Willis. Columbia, S. C. Page 56.
24. Seilhamer held that both Miss Cheer and Miss Wainwright were engaged in the West Indies, but a letter from Dr. Alexander Garden of Charleston to Lieutenant Governor David Colden of New York tells of their arrival in Charleston and gives their source as London.
25. Thomas Augustine Arne, 1710–78, was a well-known composer who made his early reputation by writing the music for Fielding's *Tom Thumb* and Addison's *Rosamunda;* later he composed the score for Milton's *Comus* and Cowper's *Judgment of Paris.* He is best remembered as the composer of "Rule, Britannia." He and his brother and sister were engaged for a time at the Drury Lane Theatre. Arne and his wife also played in Ireland. Others of his score were for *Thomas and Sally, Love in a Village,* and *A Trip to Portsmouth.*
26. "The following is a particular and authentic Account of the melancholy Accident which happened on board the Brig Dolphin, commanded by Capt. John Malbone, of this town, viz. Last Wednesday night she arrived off Point Judith, from Jamaica and when within about five Miles from Land, at half after ten o'clock the same Night, a Negro Boy went down between Decks, amongst the Rum where there stood several Puncheons of Water, and (as he says) with an Intention to draw some Water, but mistook, and broached a Case of Rum; at the same Time the Door of the Lantern, in which he carried the Candle, being open, and the Candle falling into the Rum, set it on Fire; This so affrighted the Boy, that he neglected to stop the Running of the Rum, and in less than half a Minute the Head of the Cask flew out, and the Flames were immediately communicated to fifteen Casks more, all between Decks, so that all possible Means used to extinguish it proved entirely ineffectual; the Vessel was all in Flames in a very few Minutes, and consequently reduced twenty-six Persons, being the Number of People, including Passengers, on board, to a Distress and Horror that must be left to the Reader's Imagination;— among many of them subsisted the tender and endearing Connections of Husband and Wife, Parent and Child, Brother and

Sister, etc., between whom the merciless Flames were now
effecting a cruel and inevitable Separation; and it was with the
utmost Difficulty that a Soul on board saved his Life.—There
were eleven Passengers, viz.—Mr. John Henry, Mr. William
Brooks Simson, Mr. Nathaniel Green, Mrs. Storer, Mrs.
Henry, Miss Ann Storer, Mrs. Frances Storer, Miss Maria
Storer, Miss Sarah Storer, and Mr. Henry's two Children,
one sixteen months and the other four months old; five of whom
perished in the following Manner, viz. Mrs. Storer, Miss Sarah
Storer, and Mr. Henry's two Children being in the Cabbin,
were suffocated with the Smoke before the two small Boats
could be got out, they being thrown over with the utmost Difficulty, not having any Thing ready to hoist them: Mrs. Henry
was upon the Deck, with her Sisters, and might have been
saved with them, but overcome with maternal Love and Affection on having her Mother cry out, *The Children,* oh the
Children, she ran and threw herself headlong down the Companion, into the Flames, and was there instantly consumed.
The Remainder of the People, to the number of twenty-one,
got ashore with Difficulty, in the two small Boats, not without being wet in landing; some of them, the same Night, with
Trouble and Fatigue, got up to the House of Mr. Silas Niles,
who received them with great Humanity, and afforded them
all the Assistance in his Power, as did also the Rest of the
Neighbours.—The Vessel burnt till eight o'clock the next Day,
when she sunk.

The above Brig belonged to Messrs. Evan and Francis Malbone, of this Town, was upwards of 200 Tons Burthen, was
allowed to be the best Vessel belonging to the Colony, and was
returning from the first Voyage, with a rich and valuable
Cargo, and had got within three or four Hours Sail of this
Harbour when the above Misfortune happened. The Vessel
and Cargo were valued at Four Thousand Pounds Sterling,
and the Effects of the Passengers at Two Thousand Pounds
Sterling.

Last Saturday a Collection was made at the Sabbatarian
Church, and Yesterday at the other Churches in Town, for
Relief of the unfortunate Passengers, who are all Strangers

8. In Old St. James's. By Joseph Shore and John Stewart. Kingston, 1911. Page 55.
9. Sloane. Vol. I, page cxvii.
10. Stewart. Page 182.
11. J. H. Harvey Clark in the *Gleaner,* March 6, 1937.

Chapter VI

1. The differences in complexional degrees were as follows: A *sambo* is the offspring of a black woman by a mulatto man. A *mulatto* is the child of a black woman by a white man. A *quadroon* is the offspring of a mulatto woman by a white man. A *mestee* is that of a quadroon woman by a white man. The offspring of a female mestee by a white man, being above the third in lineal descent from the negro ancestor, was white in the estimation of the law and enjoyed all the privileges and immunities of His Majesty's white subjects. All the rest—mulattos, quadroons, or mestees—were considered by law as mulattos or persons of color. A *creole,* whatever his position or color, is a native, so one spoke of white creoles, colored creoles, and black creoles. *Vide Jamaica, Its Past and Present State.* By James M. Phillippo. London, 1843.

2. Incidents of sickness in the company abound. Such as this: "Kingston, July 21st. The continuance of Mr. Henry's Indisposition having unfortunately deprived Mr. Wignell of his assistance he hopes the public will accept of the unavoidable alterations [i. e., in the cast of *Measure for Measure*] in the characters, Angelo by Mr. Wignell and Claudio by Mr. Godwin. . . . August 4th, The tragedy of the Orphan of China, with the entertainment of the Maid of the Oaks, to have been performed this evening for the benefit of Mr. Morris, are unavoidably postponed until Thursday the 9th instant on account of the indisposition of Mr. Hallam. . . ." The old fever, we know, came back on many of these gentlemen and ladies of the stage when they returned to the cooler atmosphere of the States.

Chapter VII

1. Pennsylvania *Gazette*, December 8, 1766.
2. Journal of the Assembly. Vol. 7, pages 532 and 653.
3. Odell. Vol. I, page 224.
4. Retrospections of America. By John Bernard. New York, 1887. Pages 135–6.
5. The exploits of Three-Fingered Jack so captured popular imagination that they rolled up a bibliography of no fewer than sixteen items, including plays and pamphlets. The original account was given by Dr. Benjamin Moseley—who wrote the prologue for the first performance of the American Company of Comedians at Kingston—in his "Treatise on Sugar."

   Jack was a lone bandit, whose arsenal consisted of a famous obi, a cutlass, and two guns. So successful were his raids that the negroes and some of the whites believed he possessed supernatural power. Jack was said to have been inspired to take revenge on Europeans by his mother, who was treacherously taken in West Africa and brought to Jamaica as a slave by a ship's captain whom she had succoured when he was shipwrecked. Landed in Jamaica, Jack slew his sentinels and captured the captain and took him as prisoner to a cave near Mount Lebanus in St. Thomas-in-the-East. From this hideout he made successful forays on the countryside until the Governor, John Dalling, was requested by the Assembly to offer an award for his capture. He was finally cornered and killed by two negroes and a small boy on January 27, 1781.

   An extensive account of Three-Fingered Jack and his bibliography, written by Frank Cundall, is found in the *West Indian Committee Circular* for January and February, 1930.

Chapter VIII

1. Neither the first nor second edition of this play is listed in Cundall's *Bibliographia Jamaicensis*. While puzzling over this, I happened to find, in The Players' collection, a manuscript copy of *Orvidus or the Columbian Father*, "a serious dramatic Pastoral; Compiled and Adapted to the Stage by J. H. 1786.

Altered and Revised, 1788 and re-named *The Convention or the Columbian Father.*" I suspect this also was John Henry's work.
2. The Independent Journal or The General Advertiser, January 18, 1786.
3. Dunlap. Pages 106–7.
4. Columbian Magazine or Monthly Miscellany, February, 1800.
5. Dunlap. Page 81.
6. Odell. Vol. I, page 293.
7. Columbia Herald, May 20, 1786.

Chapter IX

1. Sloane. Vol. I, page xlix.
2. Long. Vol. II, page 348.
3. *Ibid.* Vol. II, page 424.
4. The Music and Musical Instruments of Jamaica. A lecture by Astley Clark. Jamaica, 1913.
5. Jamaica Song and Story. Collected and Edited by Walter Jekyll. London, 1907.
6. Sketches of Character. By I. M. Belisario. Kingston, 1837.
7. Journal of a West Indian Proprietor. By M. G. Lewis, London, 1834. Page 53.

Chapter X

1. By 1800 there were only twenty churches in the island serving a population of 400,000, an aggregate of 19,000 to each parish served by one rector. This averaged one church in each 560 square miles. The Church of England rector with such a potential congregation on his hands could do little toward teaching religion to slaves or bettering their position even if the planters had wanted these services. By 1816 his burden was eased when a curate was assigned each parish. In January, 1813, five *tons* of Bibles were sent out to Jamaica to be distributed to the inhabitants.

Missionary work among the blacks was begun by the Moravians in 1754. The Wesleyans started their work under the personal direction of Dr. Coke in 1789, and the Baptists came in 1813. At present Jamaica is a swarming ground for every conceivable type of sect, sane and "crazy." A thorough picture of the state of religion at the beginning of the nineteenth century, is found in the Rev. J. M. Phillippo's *Jamaica, Its Past and Present State,* London, 1843. Today Jamaica contains about 1000 churches, chapels, and mission stations.

2. Journal of the Assembly. Vol. 5.
3. Petition to the Prince Regent, December 10, 1811.
4. Supplement to the *Cornwall Chronicle,* Saturday, July 15, 1786.
5. Long. Vol. II, page 279.
6. Columbian Magazine, or Monthly Miscellany. May, 1800.
7. Lady Nugent's Diary, London, 1907. Page 174.
8. Marly or A Planter's Life in Jamaica. Glasgow, 1828. Page 111.
9. Supplement to the *Cornwall Chronicle.* June 10, 1789.

Chapter XI

1. History of the British West Indies. By Bryan Edwards. London, 1818. Vol. III, page 50.
2. Manners and Customs in the West Indian Islands. By J. B. Moreton. London, 1790. Page 34.
3. Samuel Arnold, 1740–1802, was composer to Covent Garden. ⸻ he produced his opera *The Maid of the Mill.* ne organist and composer to the Chapel Royal. ⸗ in Westminster Abbey.
4. James Fannin was one of those rare examples of a good printer in a provincial town. He conducted a printing-house at Montego Bay from 1776 to 1807, producing the *Cornwall Chronicle* from 1781 to 1806. Two years later, retiring to England, he died there. Several books bear his imprint.
5. Edwards. Vol. V, pages 88–9.
6. Columbian Magazine, or Monthly Miscellany. May, 1800.
7. Stewart. Pages 176–7.

Chapter XII

1. Diary of William Dunlap. 3 vols. New York, 1929. Page 162.
2. Jamaica, Its Past and Present State. By Rev. J. M. Phillippo. London, 1843. Pages 171–2.
3. The Fate of the Fenwicks. By A. W. Wedd. London, 1927. Page 170.
4. The Jamaica Magazine, February–June, 1812.
5. *Ibid.* Page 212.
6. Lewis. Page 165.
7. Odell. Vol. II. Page 226.
8. Lewis. Page 171.
9. *Ibid.* Page 363.
10. The rowdiness of Kingston audiences was almost proverbial. When Don José de Villallave and his company played in Kingston, he threatened to leave the island on account of a gang of rowdies assaulting his clown and other members of the company and demolishing a great part of the scenery and fixtures. (*Royal Gazette,* March 28–April 4.) Before Manning, Reid and Mrs. Shaw opened the legitimate theatre, they drew up and submitted to the magistrates a code of regulations for the purpose of keeping order at the theatre. (*Royal Gazette,* September 19–26, 1812.)
11. Appointments of Committees in Common Council, 1832.
12. Sheridan's Jamaica Monthly Magazine. October 1833. Page 302.
13. Planter's Punch, 1930–1.

OTHER BOOKS CONSULTED

Anderson, Izett and Cundall, —Jamaica Negro Proverbs and Say-
    Frank   ings. London, 1927

Blome, Richard   —Description of the Island of Ja-
                            maica. London, 1678

Bridges, George Wilson   —Annals of Jamaica. London, 1828

Carmichael, Mrs. —Domestic Manners and Social Conditions of the White, Coloured and Negro Population of the West Indies. London, 1833

Chetwood, W. R. —A General History of the Stage. Dublin, 1749

Cundall, Frank —Aborigines of Jamaica. Kingston, 1934

Cundall, Frank and Pietersz, —Jamaica Under the Spaniards. Jos. L.   Kingston, 1919

Dallas, R. C. —History of the Maroons. London, 1803

Dancer, Dr. Thomas —The Medical Assistant. London, 1919

Doran, Dr. —Annals of the English Stage. 3 vols. London, 1888

Duperly, Adolphe —Daguerian Excursions in Jamaica. Kingston, 1844

Firth, C. H. —The Narrative of General Venables. London, 1900

Ford, Paul Leicester —Washington and the Theatre. New York, 1911

Greenwood, Isaac J. —The Circus. New York, 1898

Hakewill, James —A Picturesque Tour of the Island of Jamaica. London, 1825

Hill, Richard —Lights and Shadows of Jamaican History. Kingston, 1859

Hill, Richard —The Picaroons. Dublin, 1869

Hornblow, Arthur —History of the Theatre in America. 2 vols. Philadelphia, 1919

Ireland, J. N. —Records of the New York Stage. New York, 1866

————— —Importance of Jamaica. London, 1740

James, Reese D. —Old Drury. Philadelphia, 1932
———— —Journal of the Institute of Jamaica. 1892–1899
———— —Jamaica, As It Was, As It Is, and As It May Be. London, 1835

Kidd, Joseph B. —Illustrations of Jamaica. London, 1840

Leslie, Charles —A New and Exact Account of Jamaica. Edinburgh, 1739

McMahon, Benjamin —Jamaica Plantership. London, 1839

Nicholl, Allardyce —The Development of the Theatre. New York, 1927
"   " —A History of the Early 18th Century Drama. New York, 1925
"   " —A History of the Late 18th Century Drama, New York, 1927

Ogle, Sir Chaloner —The Tryalof. London, 1743

Quinn, Arthur Hobson —History of the American Drama from the Beginning to the Civil War. New York, 1923

Roby, John —Members of the Assembly of Jamaica. Montego Bay, 1831

Sonneck, O. G. —Early Opera in America. New York, 1915

Sturges, Joseph and Harvey, Thomas —The West Indies in 1837. London, 1838

Williams, James —A Narrative of Events Since the First of August 1834. London, 1837

INDEX

Abolitionists in Jamaica, 315
Absentee landlordism, 249
Academy for oratory, etc., 224
Actor-Boys, 240
Adamson, J. E., 326, 327, 328
Adamson, W., 323, 324, 325, 326, 327, 328, 329
Adamson, Mrs. W., 324, 327, 328
Adcock, Mr. and Mrs., 38
Addison, 37
Adelgitha, Lewis, "Monk," 330
Adopted Child, The, Birch, 321
Adventurers, English, 4
Æsop in the Shades, Garrick, 114
African tribes (Jamaica), 233
Agreeable Surprise, The, O'Keeffe, 219, 261, 263, 264, 265, 267, 270, 271
Aikman, William, 28, 87, 99, 120, 275
Albany, N. Y., 221
Albemarle, Duke of, 5, 12
All for Love, Dryden, 145
Allen, Andrew Jackson, 221
Allen, E., 62, 77, 79, 80, 81, 82, 84, 85, 209, 215, 221
Allen, Mrs. E., 209, 216, 221
Almanac for the Year of our Lord, 1751, 33
American Company of Comedians, 54, 62, 70, 76, 77, 83, 88, 91, 93, 101, 148, 157, 159, 163, 187, 188, 191, 195, 199, 204, 208, 209, 210, 214, 215, 217, 220, 225, 248, 250, 254, 280, 284, 295, 298, 314, 326
Anatomist, The, Ravenscroft, 30, 147
André, Major, 272
Angel, Frederick, 19

Anglo-French War, 250
Angolas, 239
Annapolis, Md., 43, 54, 189, 215
"Annie Oakleys," 197
Apology, Mrs. Phillips', 22, 26
Apostles' Battery, 28, 171
Apprentice, The, Murphy, 99, 172
Aradas, 239
Arms of the King, 280
Army (British) theatricals, 19
Arne, Dr., 50
Arnold, Dr., of London, 285
Art Work, 140
Ashton, Richard, 9
Ashton, Tony, 8
Assembly, The, 12, 16, 33, 47, 70, 71, 102, 129, 138, 170
Assembly Room: Ranelagh House, 290, 296
Augsburg, Germany, 284
Author, Foote, 150, 250
Azemia, or *Shipwreck*, 308

Bacon, 109, 110, 112, 113, 144
Bagg's Tavern, Kingston, 65
Bailey's nose, 335
Baines, John, 19
Balcarres, Lord, 299
Ballard, Thomas, 136
Ball dress, 259
Balls, Refreshments at, 258
Balloon Ascension, 305
Baltimore, Md., 189, 209, 216, 223, 253, 275
Bands, Regimental, 278
Baptists, 249
Barbados, 35, 36, 47, 90, 275, 316
Barbados Comedians, 323
Barclay Street (N. Y.) Chapel, 221

Barbarosa, Brown, 320
Barber of Seville, The, Mrs. Griff-
ith, 307
Barnaby Brittle, Betterton, 321
Barnard, John, 21
Barracks illumination, 277
Barretts, The, of Cinnamon Hill, 74
Basle, Peace of, 300
Bath of St. Thomas the Apostle, 13
Beaux' Stratagem, The, Farquhar,
179, 185, 202, 270, 271, 279, 320
Becceley, Mrs., 38
Beckford, Peter, 16
Beckford, William, 116, 140
Bee-Hive, The, Milligen, 327, 328
Beef Market, Montego Bay, 268
Beekman Street Theatre, New York,
43, 48
Beggar's Opera, The, Gay, 80, 202,
271, 294
Belle, 38
Belle's Stratagem, The, Mrs. Cow-
ley, 159, 160, 164, 178
Benefits, 83, 84
Bentley, 209
Bernard, 278, 285
Bernard, John, 191
Betterton, playwright, 321
Bevil, Young, 46
Bickerstaff, playwright, 79, 99, 113,
120, 144, 145, 147, 149, 159, 200,
202, 279, 320, 321
Biddle, Charles, 194, 212, 216, 222
Biddle Family, 52
Biffari, Mons., 298
Bignall and West, 222
Bird Catcher, The, 197
Birds, Trained, 284
Birch, playwright, 320, 321
Birmingham, 195
Birthday, His Majesty's, 188, 279,
280
Bitti, Alexander, 19
Blacksmith, The, O'Keeffe, 306
Bligh, Captain William, 298
Blue Mountains, 58

Bold Strike for a Wife, Mrs. Cent-
livre, 79, 181, 197, 323
Bonynge, Young, 65, 66
Boston, 150, 208, 222
Boullay, Mons., 297
Bounty, The, 298
Bournon, 308
Bradford's Concert Room, 268
Brass Ankle girls, 232
Breadfruit Tree, 298
Breakfast, Second, 258
Brelet, 306
Bridgetown, Barbados, 35, 36, 37
Bridgetown Theatre, 316
Brissot (France), 281
Bristol (England) Public Library,
86, 210
British islands, 283
Broadway, New York, 2, 30
Broken Bridge, The, 197
Brooke, Mrs., playwright, 213, 271
Brothers, The, Cumberland, 106
Brown, Dr. John, playwright, 320
Browne, Commodore, 17
Browne's Tavern, 217
Buccaneers, The, 123
Bucks Have At Ye All, 185, 196,
205, 207
Buck's Ramble, The, 154
Bullock, Hon. William, 297
Burchell, Thomas, 315
Burgoyne, General, playwright, 149,
216
Burke, Michael, innkeeper, 217
"Buskin and Sock," 264
Busy Body, The, Mrs. Centlivre,
111, 213
Butchers' John Canoe, 241
Byrne, Felix, 285, 301, 304, 310, 311
Byrne, Mrs. Jane, 311
Byrne's House, 268

Cabinet, The, Dibdin, 326
Callender, Samuel, commissary, 24
Calliope, 283

Calphrey, Eliza, 29
Cameron, Miss Margaret Cheer, 49
Camp, The (songs), 227
Campbell, Major General Archibald, 89, 157, 190
Canoe (or Cannu), John, 240, 241
Cape François (Santo Domingo), 171, 281, 282
Carey, playwright, 85
Caribbean Isles, 321
Caribbean Sea, 1, 88, 163
Carleton, Mary, 9, 124
Carolina, 11
Cassada Bread, 136
Cassino, 260
Castle Spectre, The, Lewis, 320, 321, 326
Catherine and Petruchio, Shakespeare, 82, 93, 168, 194, 221, 222, 223, 321
Cato, 223
Cawdell, playwright, 146
Cedar Street, Philadelphia, 1
Centlivre, Mrs., playwright, 49, 79, 82, 110, 112, 121, 144, 151, 152, 181, 197, 199, 202, 212, 213, 271, 272, 279, 322, 323
Chances, The, Fletcher, 202, 204
Chapel Street Theatre, New York, 43, 48
Chapter of Accidents, A, Miss Lee, 147
Charke, 20
Charke, Charlotte, 47
Charleston, S. C., 32, 34, 38, 43, 49, 55, 182, 193, 215, 223, 225, 232, 251, 252, 275, 283, 302, 304
Charleston Theatre, 43
Charleston Theatre in the Eighteenth Century, Miss Willis, 224
Charming Sally, 30
Cheats of Scapin, The, Otway, 167
Cheer, Miss, 48, 83, 150, 151, 154, 155, 160, 163, 164, 178, 180, 181, 182, 183, 216
Chesapeake Bay, 163

Chestnut Street Theatre, Philadelphia, 218, 298
Chew-stick (Gouania domingensis), 137
Children in the Wood, 267, 321
Choleric Man, Cumberland, 93
Christmas—of Negroes, 239, 241, 242
Christmas—to slaves, 225
Christmas holidays, 247
Christmas "Set Girls," 242
Chronicle, The, 157, 199, 203, 205, 216, 252
Chrononhotonthologos, 185
Church of England, 249
Church-street, Kingston, 285, 288
Church Street Theatre, Montego Bay, 269, 300
Cibber, playwright, 22, 146
Cibber, Colley, 20
Cibber, Mrs. Charlotte, 20
Circus, 303
Citizen, The, Murphy, 79, 93, 182, 183, 202, 223
City Council's theatre, 334
City Tavern, Charleston, S. C., 225
Clandestine Marriage, The, Colman the Elder, 202
Clark, Miss, 51
Clarkson, Mr. and Mrs., 38
Claypole, James, 140
Cleone, Dodsley, 194, 195
Cobb, playwright, 324, 327
Cockfights, 274, 275
Coffee growing, 15
Coffee houses, 263
Coffey, playwright, 32, 98, 202, 320
Cokaine, playwright, 116
Colbeck Castle, Old Harbour, 131
Colman the Elder, playwright, 144, 153, 201, 202, 217, 256, 326
Colman, Junior, playwright, 37, 108, 265, 266, 267, 320, 321, 322
Columbian Magazine, 26
Columbus, Morton, 320
Columbus, Christopher, 3

Company of Comedians from London, 34, 47
Company of Comedians from Virginia, 31
Comedy of Errors, The, Shakespeare, 270, 271
Comus, Milton, 147
Concerts of music, 208, 272, 273, 278, 291, 303
Concanen, playwright, 45
Conchas, 239
Concubinage, 125, 126, 127
Congos, 239
Congreve, playwright, 84
Connu, John, 239
Conscious Lovers, The, 46
Constant Couple, The, Farquhar, 153, 178
Constantine House, 130
Continental Congress, 92
Contrast, The, 275
Contrivances, Carey, 85
Cooper, Thomas A., 220
Cornwall Chronicle, 75, 77, 85, 86, 161, 194, 209, 210, 215, 227, 251, 270, 271
Cornwall, County of, 76
Cornwall Gazette, 274, 293
Cornwall Lodge, 331
Cornwallis, Lord, 163, 170
Coromantyn tribe, 228, 236, 238
Cortes' company of tumblers, 293, 297
Cotingham, James Henry, 257
Cotta drum, 236
Cottas, Cutting the, 230
Countess of Salisbury, The, Hartson, 106, 112, 172, 176
Country dance music, 261
Courant, Jamaica, 14
Court of Momus, 205
Covent Garden Theatre (London), 51, 101, 179, 192
Cowley, Mrs., playwright, 108, 159, 178
Crasto, 265

Creole Blacks, 231
Creoles, 128, 134, 143, 228, 246, 254, 257, 260, 334
Cries of London, The, Roberts, 84
Crisp, playwright, 145
Cromwell, 4, 74
"Crop-over" dance, 235
Cross, 262, 263, 265
Cross Purposes, O'Brien, 79, 203, 221
Crugers Wharf, New York, 43, 47
Cuba, 1, 3
Cubenas, 228
Cudjoes, 228
Cuffees, 228
Cumberland, Duke of, 186
Cumberland, playwright, 93, 106, 187, 195, 196, 201, 203, 279, 320
Cummins, 323, 324, 325, 327, 329
Cunningham, Henry, Governor of Jamaica, 18, 19
Cure for the Heartache (song), 320
Curtis (tight and slack rope dancer), 288, 289
Cussans, J. P., entertains, 307, 308, 310
Custos of Kingston, 334
Cymbeline, Shakespeare, 177, 203

Daily Advertiser (Kingston), 284, 285, 293, 302, 305, 309
Daily Advertiser (New York), 219
Dallas's Lodging House, 300
Dallas's Long Room, 285, 288, 310
Daly, Hyacinth J., 72
Dancer, Dr. Thomas, 14, 169
Dancer, Mr. (actor), 119
Dancing, 209, 237, 238, 257, 260
Dancing Schools, 103, 104, 197
Daniell, William, 29, 33, 42
Daphne and Amintor, Bickerstaff, 149
Darling, Colonel, Governor, 88, 89
Dauney's (Mrs.) Long Room, 255, 274
Davids, 328

Dawson, 197
De Barthe, 300
de Castillo, Sir James, 131
de Grasse, Admiral, 90, 163, 164,
    170, 171, 174, 212
De Lancey, 318, 319, 321
de Lantagnac, Adhamar, 24
De Poincy, 300
Decorations, Floral, 260
"Decoy" in St. Mary's, 131
Delancy, Colonel, 272
Demerara, 90, 163
Dendy, Walter, 315
Dennis, Thomas, 21
Depard, Colonel Edward, 171
Derby, Lieut. Hyacinth Richard, 29
Dermot, 54, 62, 77, 79, 80, 82, 83, 84,
    105, 106, 108, 109, 110, 111, 113,
    149, 150, 151, 153, 154, 155, 158,
    159, 160, 165, 166, 167, 168, 172,
    173, 175, 176, 177, 178, 179, 180,
    181, 216
Descriptive Account of the Island of
    Jamaica, Beckford, 116
Deserter, The, Henry, 151, 203, 326
Desmond, playwright, 328
Deuce Is in Him, Colman the Elder,
    144
Devil to Pay, The, Coffey, 32, 98,
    202
Devil upon Two Sticks, The, Foote,
    98, 112, 159
Diana, sloop, 225
Diary of George Washington, 36
Dibdin, Charles, 152, 279, 287, 308,
    326
"Digging Sings"—of slaves, 238
Diligence, brig, 9, 11
Dinners, 137, 138
"Dish of Mr. Foot's Tea, A," olio,
    75
Distressed Mother, The, Phillips,
    145
Ditters' Favourite Symphony, 269
Divorce, Jackman, 179
Doctor's Cave Beach, 72

Doctor's Last Examination, The,
    203
Dodsley, playwright, 173, 179, 184,
    194, 195, 199, 200, 202, 211
Dogs, Trained, 284
Dominica, 89, 90
Donaldson, William (poet), 45
Don Juan, Delphine and Oulton,
    306, 324
Douglas, Home, 93, 183, 194, 203,
    213, 223, 279, 316
Douglass, David, 21, 28, 33, 39, 42,
    47, 48, 53, 54, 57, 62, 87, 120, 148,
    169, 171, 175, 189, 224, 225
Douglass, David, Jr., 29, 292
Douglass, Mary, 29, 72
Douglass, Mrs., 43, 62
Douglass and Aikman, 175
Dragoons' Riding School, 305
Dramatic Fête of T. Wignell, 204,
    205
Drax, Charles, 17
Drinking, 135, 137
Drums—of slaves, 235
Drunken Man, The, Hippisley, 189
Drunken Peasant, The, 167, 223
Drury Lane Theatre (London), 9,
    51, 192
Dryden, playwright, 145, 187, 189,
    198
Du Bourg, Mlle., 298
Du Casse, 7
Du Metz, 300
Du Moulin, Peter, 300
Duenna, The, Sheridan, 99, 106,
    121, 202, 203, 227, 325
Dubois, Lewis, 308
Duckworth, Admiral, 312
Dueling, 125
Duke and No Duke, Cokaine, 116
Duke of Gloucester (Williamsburg,
    Va.), 1
Duke of York (in Richard III), 48
Dumm's Long Room, 254
Duncomb, David, 108
Dundo, 236

Dunlap, William (historian), 32, 218, 314
Durang, John, 121, 209
Durang, Miss, 209
Dutch, The, 90

East Indian, The, 220
Ebos, 239
Edinburgh, 311
Edward, Bryan, 45
Edward and Eleonora, Hull, 179, 186, 201, 202
Edwards, 318, 319
Egleton, Henry, 6
Eidsphusikon, 286
Eighteenth century, 169
Elements of Free-Masonry Delineated, The, 175
Elliston, 328
Elliston, Mrs., 323, 324, 325, 326, 327, 328
Eloise, Miss, 307
Emancipation, 139, 231, 235, 247, 335
Emigres (French), 283
England, 90, 208, 218
England, Lord Chamberlain of, 21
English Merchant, The, Colman, Jr., 108
Entertainment miscellany, 286, 287
Entertainments of Rosina, 227
Epilogue, Joe Haines's, 159
Essay on the Bilious or Yellow Fever of Jamaica, 33
Essequibo (British Guiana), 90, 163
Estates, 130
Eton Club dinner, 297
Etonian Steward, 297
European musical instruments, 237
Evans, pianist, 292
Exigencies of Jamaican life, 249

Fair, May Day, 14, 15
Fair Penitent, The, Rowe, 184, 188
Falconi, Signor, 305
Fallotica, Signor, 289, 293

Falmouth (Trelawny), 85, 163, 254, 310, 329, 332
Falstaff, Sir John, Humours of, 165
Family visitations, 139
Famine threatens Jamaica, 198
Fannin, James, 293
Fantocconi, The, 286
Farquhar, playwright, 32, 158, 178, 179, 185, 187, 202, 271, 320
Fawcett, playwright, 45, 192
Fearon, Thomas, Chief Justice, 131
Feasts, 137
Female Fruitgatherers, The (dance), 197
Female Pedlar, The (dance), 194, 195, 197
Fenwick, Miss Eliza, 316
Ferry Inn, 67
Fielding, playwright, 22, 113, 172, 176, 197, 201, 279
Fireworks, 169, 293
First Floor, The, Cobb, 327
Fleance (Macbeth), 48
Fletcher, playwright, 121, 204
Fleury, Miss, 303
Flora, or Hob in the Well, Colley Cibber, 32
Floremondo, 331
Florizel and Perdita, Shakespeare, 164, 166
Foods, 134, 135
Ford, Mrs., 329
Foote, playwright, 98, 105, 112, 150, 159, 229, 253, 272, 279
Foreign refugees: types, 299
Forrest, Edwin, 221
Forrest, George, 145
Fort Charlotte, 277
Fort Frederick, 213
Fort George, 213
Fort Omoa, Nicaragua, 109
Fortune's Frolic (song), 320
Foucard, Mons., 297
Foundling of the Forest, Desmond, 327, 328
Fox Chase, The (song), 263

France, 90
Francisqui, Miss, 303, 306, 307, 308, 309
Francken, Henry Andrew, 21, 190, 191, 292, 297, 298
Freedmen, 127
Freemasons, 174, 175, 185, 207, 221, 321
Freemasons' Hall, Jamaica, 45
Freemasons' Lodges, 284, 311
French "Set Girls," 246
French Theatre at Kingston, 305
French Wars, 299
Front seat placeholders, 142
Furies in ballet, 306
Furnishings, 133
Furniture, 132

Gamester, The, Mrs. Centlivre, 82, 147, 199, 202, 212
Garden patches of slaves, 229
Gardens of Harmony Hall, 311
Gardner, Mrs., 150, 151, 210, 250, 251, 252
Garrick, playwright, 77, 79, 94, 98, 114, 119, 145, 149, 157, 158, 166, 183, 185, 196, 202, 204, 271, 319, 323
Garth, General, 157
Gay, playwright, 80, 202, 271
Gazette, The Jamaica, 103, 114, 116, 118, 148, 156, 177, 261, 263, 266, 267, 268, 323
Gazette, The Royal, 187, 292
General Assembly of Pennsylvania, 208
General Description of the West Indian Islands, Singleton, 40
Genii, The, Woodward, 106, 109, 110, 153, 159
Gentle Shepherd, The, Ramsay, 202, 227
George II, 16
George III: his recovery, 276
George, Nancy, 33

German Princess, The, 124
Ghost, The, Mrs. Centlivre, 110, 121, 322, 323
Girls, "Blue," 244
Girls, "Brown," 243
Girls, "Red," 243, 244
Godwin, 54, 93, 97, 98, 99, 103, 107, 109, 110, 120, 144, 146, 147, 149, 150, 152, 154, 155, 157, 158, 159, 160, 165, 166, 168, 169, 172, 175, 177, 182, 186, 194, 195, 196, 197, 215, 223
Godwin, Mrs., 153, 158, 166, 167, 173, 197, 215, 223
Gold Coast negroes, 228, 239
Goldsmith, playwright, 79, 256, 319
Gonne, (silversmith), 199
"Good Hope," 131
Goodman, Richard, 53, 54, 56, 94, 97, 99, 105, 106, 109, 110, 111, 113, 144, 145, 146, 147, 149, 150, 151, 153, 154, 155, 158, 159, 160, 165, 166, 168, 169, 172, 173, 175, 176, 177, 178, 180, 181, 182, 183, 216
Gouania domingensis (chew-stick), 137
Governor's dances, 258
Graham, Robert, of Gartmore, 127
Grand Court, 270
Grand Master, Provincial, 185
Grand Masters in parade, 246
Great Britain, 225
Grecian Daughter, The, Murphy, 166, 173
Green Bay, 173
Gregoire (France), 281
Grenada, 89, 90
Griffin's Tavern Feast, 305
Grove Hill, 198
Guadaloupe, 174
Guardian, The, Garrick, 323
Guardians Outwitted, The, Mrs. Centlivre, 152
Guenin, Mons., 297
"Guiney Birds," 232

Haiti, (Santo Domingo), 4, 246
Half-Way Tree, 68
Hall, Jasper, 130
Hallam, Adam, 38
Hallam, Lewis, 21, 28, 29, 34, 38,
    66, 87, 91, 93, 97, 98, 99, 104, 105,
    106, 108, 109, 111, 113, 118, 141,
    144, 145, 147, 148, 150, 151, 153,
    158, 159, 160, 164, 165, 167, 168,
    169, 172, 175, 177, 179, 180, 181,
    182, 183, 184, 188, 208, 211, 216,
    218, 219, 223, 253, 284
Hallam, Master of the Revels, 118,
    161, 190
Hallam, Mrs. Lewis, 38, 43, 44, 216
Hallam, Miss Helen, 38
Hallam, Lewis the Younger, 38,
    113, 114, 175, 314
Hallam, Mirvan, 114, 314
Hallam, Miss Nancy (or Ann), 38,
    48
Hallam, William (of Paddington,
    England), 29, 56
Hallam's Troupe of English Actors,
    34, 38
Halls of Tryall, The, 74
Hamilton, Mrs., 42, 94, 98, 99, 108,
    109, 146, 147, 149, 150, 154, 155,
    158, 159, 160, 168, 172, 173, 175,
    176, 177, 178, 179, 181, 216
Hamlet, Shakespeare, 79, 109, 144,
    145, 320
Hamley, Colonel William G., 69
Handcraft products of slaves, 229
Hanover Parish, 15, 194, 207, 274
Hanson, Francis, 6
Harbour Street (Kingston), 2, 30,
    41, 63, 99, 119
Harbour Street Theatre, 224, 290
Harcourt, 323, 324, 325, 326, 327,
    328, 329
Harlequin Collector, 106, 144, 145,
    166
Harlequin Friday, 213
Harman, Mrs. Catherine Maria,
    45, 47, 48

Harmonica, The, 290
Harmony Hall, Charleston, S. C.,
    223, 224
Harmony Hall, Kingston, 278
Harper, 200, 201, 211, 212, 216, 222
Harper, Mrs., 200, 201, 211, 212,
    216, 222
Harris (limner), 103
Harrison, Mrs. Sarah Baldwin, 72
Harrison, Thomas, playwright, 92,
    113
Hartson, playwright, 106, 172, 176
Haughton, 211
Haughton, Miss, 211, 212
Haughton, Miss H., 211
Haughton, Miss M., 212
Haunted Tower, The, Cobb, 324
Haydn's Favourite Overture, 268
Haymarket Theatre (London),
    192, 253, 256
H-d-e, Mr., 11
Headdress snatching, 274
Heart of a Sailor (song), 324
Hebrews, 143
Heiress, The, Burgoyne, 216
Hemming (musician), 199, 204, 227,
    255, 318
Henry VIII, 20
Henry, John, 51, 52, 53, 56, 62, 77,
    79, 80, 81, 84, 100, 118, 122, 141,
    148, 150, 151, 153, 155, 159, 180,
    189, 199, 200, 203, 211, 212, 215,
    216, 218, 220, 222, 223, 225, 253,
    284, 298
Henry, Mrs. Ann, 52, 56
Henry, Maria, 53
Hennsant, 303
Herbert, 191
Herring, Hon. Oliver, 297
Hibbert, Thomas, 130
"Hibbert's House," 130
Hickey, William (diarist), 65
High Life Below Stairs, Townley,
    93, 111, 175, 186
Hill, 323, 324, 325, 326, 327, 328
Hill, Mrs., 323, 325, 327

Hill, playwright, 116
Hippisley, 189
Hispaniola, 4
History of the American Stage Before the Revolution, Seilhamer, 91
Hitchener, 324, 325, 327, 328, 329
Hoadley, playwright, 119
Hodgkinson, 220, 314
Hogg, John, 52
Holland estate, 16
Hollander, the Young Magician, 206
Home, playwright, 93, 183, 194, 203, 213, 279, 316
Honduras, 185
Honey Drum, 137
Honeymoon, The, 318
Hood, Admiral Sir Samuel, 171
Horse Racing, 12, 13
Housefurnishings, 130
Houses, Great, 130, 131
How to Die for Love, 323
Howe's Thespians (Philadelphia), 121
Hughes, George, 54, 62, 77, 79, 80, 82, 83, 84, 97, 99, 102, 155, 156
Hughes, Mrs. Katharine, 157, 170, 184
Hull, playwright, 179, 186, 201, 202
Humours of Mother Cole, The, 203
Humours of Sir John Falstaff, 181
Hunter, Robert (Governor General), 19
Hunter's Quay, 59
Hurricanes, 90, 116, 198
Hyde, Miss, 45
Hyet, 59
Hynes, 262, 265

Illumination, Montego Bay, 276
Immigration, 193
Incent, 306
Inchiquin, Earl of, 7
Indentured servants, 4
Indian dances, 308

Inkle and Yarico, Colman the Younger, 37, 265, 266, 267
Insolent Carpenter, The, 197
Invasion, 177, 178
Irish Man in London, An, 320
Irishman of the Stage, 27
Irish Providence (song), 324
Irish Widow, The, Garrick, 77, 79, 145, 157, 158, 203
Iron Chest, The, Colman the Younger, 321
Irvings of Ironshore, The, 74
Isabella, Garrick, 196, 323
Island, The, 274

Jack-in-the-Green, 245
Jackson, Colonel, 3
Jackson, Henry, 211, 267, 268, 269
Jacobite Rebellion, Second, 27
Jago, 33
Jamaica, 2, 7, 10, 15, 20, 21, 27, 35, 37, 44, 48, 49, 61, 74, 88, 89, 92, 95, 102, 109, 113, 121, 124, 142, 170, 171, 174, 176, 188, 190, 208, 216, 224, 227, 247, 248, 250, 255, 256, 263, 275, 283, 301, 312, 315, 316, 323
Jamaica Courant, 15, 318
Jamaica Gazette, The, 60, 62, 224
Jamaica Magazine, 322
Jamaica Mercury and Trelawny Advertiser, 28, 87, 329
Jamaica Theatre, The, 1, 43, 187, 248
Jamaica troops, 89
Jamaican Miniatures, Mrs. Phillips, 26
Jamaican missionaries, 315
Jamaican women, 258
Jamaica's dramatic isolation, 334
Jane Shore, Rowe, 77, 182
Jealous Wife, The, Colman the Elder, 155, 156, 163, 217, 256
Jenks, Captain Sam, 73
Jephson, playwright, 110, 113

Jerusalem Delivered (pantomime), 309
Jew and the Doctor, The, 318, 320, 323
Jewelry fashions, 259
Jew Outwitted, The, Cumberland, 195, 196, 219
Jews in Jamaica, 127
Jodrel, Paul, 9
John Bull, 320, 322
John Street Theatre (New York), 1, 50, 189, 208, 209, 222, 252
Johnson, 54, 61, 62, 77, 79, 80, 83, 84
Jones, Hon. James, 72
Jones, Miss, 321
Jones, John Paul, 45, 46
Jones, Rev. William, 91
Journal and Weekly Advertiser (Philadelphia), 83

Kean, Thomas, 33
Keith, Sir Basil, Governor, 64, 88
Kenshaw, 28, 42
Kensall, Edward, 19
Keyting, 11
Kidd, Mr. and Mrs., 223
King and the Miller of Mansfield, The, Dodsley, 81, 106, 173, 179, 184, 199, 200, 202, 211, 267
King Henry IV, Shakespeare, 165, 181, 186
King, Thomas: his sons, 18
King's Arms, The, 119
King's House (Spanish Town), 188, 258, 304
Kingston, 1, 2, 10, 11, 16, 18, 23, 24, 27, 38, 47, 48, 49, 54, 64, 68, 76, 85, 90, 92, 95, 104, 109, 113, 122, 131, 140, 141, 157, 161, 162, 163, 165, 169, 173, 175, 194, 199, 204, 209, 211, 226, 242, 250, 254, 260, 272, 276, 278, 280, 283, 285, 288, 295, 312, 317, 318, 322
Kingston Amateurs, 335
Kingston animal shows, 336

Kingston apathy in 1800, 302
Kingston audiences, 318
Kingston equipages, 142
Kingston Grenadiers, The (song), 167, 168
Kingston Parish Church, 48, 272
Kingston Playhouses, 333
Kingston population 1775, 68: 1790, 283
Kingston Privateers, The, Pillon, 160, 161
Kingston subscription concerts, 286
Kingston Sunday markets, 229
Kingston Theatre, 41, 62, 67, 302, 316, 322, 330
"King Store" (Kingston), 41
King-Street, 99, 119, 120
Kirk, Miss, 176, 177, 178, 208
Knibb, William, 315
Knight, William Powers, 294
Knowles, Charles, Admiral, 47
Koo-koos, or Actor-Boys, 240, 241

Laconia musters, 311
Lady Cured, The Dumb, Fielding, 172
Lafayette (France), 281
Lake (dancer), 209
la Plass, 7
Lard Bay, 72
Larke, 201, 204
Larke, Mrs., 200, 201, 204
La Rosa, Signor (tumbler), 180, 181, 182
Law of Lombardy, The, Jephson, 110, 113
Lawes, Sir Nicholas, Kt., 14, 15, 25
Lawrences of Running Gut, 74
Lecture on Heads, 162, 163, 187, 189, 194
Lecture on Hearts, 207, 310
Lectures in Philadelphia, 208
Lee, Miss, playwright, 147
Leeward Islands, 36
Le Flor, 331
Legrand, 307

Leigh, Mrs., 39
Les Amis des Noirs, 281
Leslie, Charles, 17
Lethe, Garrick, 114, 119, 121, 185, 196
Lewis, Hon. John, 297
Lewis, Matthew Gregory ("Monk" Lewis), 243, 320, 324, 326, 329, 330
Libertine Destroyed, The, 324
Light Dragoons, 20th Regiment, 72
Ligon, Richard, 37
Liguanea (Kingston), 17
Liguanea Plain, 10, 58
Lilliputian Camp, The, 153
Lilly, Colonel Christian, 10
Linart, Lawrence Westenzon, 19
Linco's Travels, Garrick, 149, 164, 166
Lindsay and Wall, 189
Lion, Mr., 321
Lionel and Clarissa, Bickerstaff, 145
Liquors of Jamaica, 135, 137
Littleworth, Mayor of, 14
Liverpool Prize, The, Pillon, 161
Liverpool Theatre Royal, 209
London (England), 21, 192, 285
London Merchant; or the History of George Barnwell, George Lillo, 32
London Theatres, 225
Long, Edward (historian), 67, 70, 128, 135, 257
Long, Mrs. (Lady Rosehill), 49, 217
Long, William, 95
Long Room (Spanish Town), 322
Long Mountain, 57
Louis (actor-singer), 318, 319, 323, 325, 326, 328
Love, Mrs., 44
Love à la Mode, Macklin, 145, 187, 222, 320, 322, 323
Love in a Village, Bickerstaff, 106, 144, 159, 200, 227, 285

Lover's Vows, 320
Lucea, 162, 208, 277
Lugg, John, 86
Lugg's Great Room, 75
Lyar, The, Foote, 106, 251, 272
Lying Valet, The, Garrick, 94, 98, 203, 204, 209, 319
Lyon, Isaac: his Tavern, 277
Lyttelton, Governor, 233

"Mabiales," 246
Macbeth, Shakespeare, 120, 121, 335
Macklin, playwright, 145, 187
Madden, 113
Madeira wine, 137
Mad Poetess, The, 252
Magpie, The, Cooke, 328
Mahon, 211, 262, 265, 266, 267, 270, 271, 272, 286, 292, 297
Mahon, Mrs., 262, 265, 266, 267, 268, 287, 292, 297
McTaggart, William, 271
Maid, The, Cooke, 328
Maid of the Mill, The, 99, 209, 227
Maid of the Oaks, The, Burgoyne, 149
Maidstone, John, 200, 201, 203, 211
Malone, 38
Man and Wife, Colman the Elder, 107, 326
Manning, 316, 317, 318, 319, 320
Manning, Mrs., 319, 320
Mantica Bahia, 72
Market Day, 229, 230
Marks, 33
Maroons, 4, 15, 97, 232, 249
Marry or Do Worse, 36
Martha-Brae, 162, 207, 215, 224
Martial law declared, 16
Martinique, 89, 171, 172
Maryland Assembly, 189
Masonic benefits, 112
Masonic oration, 168
Masquerades (Jamaican), 228

Master of the Revels, 26, 28, 160, 190, 261, 263, 297
Mattocks, Mrs., 66
Mayor of Garratt, The, Foote, 279
Meal-times, 134
Measure for Measure, Shakespeare, 149
Medley, Mat, 8
Melmoth, Courtney, playwright, 189, 202
Melpomene, 283
Memoirs of Mary Carleton, 124
Merchant of Venice, The, Shakespeare, 30, 38, 40, 54, 113
Merchant's Pocket Companion, 33
Mercury, The, 92, 96, 99, 100, 102
Merry, Mrs. (Mrs. T. Wignell), 218
Merry Wives of Windsor, The, Shakespeare, 97
Messiah, The (oratorio), 225
Mestees, 126, 143
Metchler, 224
Metchler, Mrs., 53, 201
Methodists, 249
Michaut, Mons., 298
Midas, O'Hara, 81, 84, 121, 202
Militia muster, 170
Millar and Carnaby Band, 304
Mill'd dollars, 61
Miller, 38
Milligen, playwright, 328
Milton, playwright, 147
Mimos, 9
Minnahs, 238
Miranda, 50
Miranda Hill, 22, 73
Miss in Her Teens, Garrick, 183, 271
Miss Out of her Teens, 224
Mistress of the Revels, 25, 26, 41
Mock Doctor, The, Fielding, 113, 172, 176, 197, 201, 320
Momford, Miss, 328
Momus, Court of, 205
Moncrief, playwright, 45

Monsieur Tonson, Moncrief, 45
Montague, Rt. Hon. Lord Charles Greville, 157, 186
Montego Bay, 49, 53, 74, 85, 86, 100, 131, 141, 157, 161, 162, 163, 193, 194, 196, 199, 205, 209, 210, 211, 213, 214, 215, 221, 222, 223, 226, 233, 249, 250, 253, 267, 274, 276, 285, 293, 300, 304, 310, 330, 331
Montego Bay Theatre, 72, 76
Montfort, Miss, 329
Montgomery, T. C. (surveyor), 23
Montreal, 221
Montserrat, 41, 90, 163, 170, 174
Moody, John, 26, 29, 31, 42
Moore, 33, 147, 149, 150, 152, 160, 161, 163, 164, 166, 167, 168, 172, 173, 175, 177, 178, 179, 181, 182, 183, 184, 185, 186, 209, 216, 221
Moore, Hannah, playwright, 93, 198
Moore, Sir Henry, Lt. Governor, 20, 26, 47, 140, 190
Moore, William (printer), 34
Morales, Isaac, 50, 98, 99, 101, 107, 145, 146, 147, 149, 150, 153, 154, 155, 158, 160, 165, 166, 167, 168, 172, 173, 175, 176, 177, 178, 179, 180, 181, 182, 183, 216, 262, 264, 265, 266, 291
Morant Bay, 13, 97
Moravians, 249
Morgan, 118, 120, 124, 144, 318, 319, 321
Morgan, Sir Henry, 9
Morris, Owen, 28, 39, 44, 62, 77, 79, 80, 81, 82, 84, 94, 97, 99, 105, 106, 107, 108, 109, 110, 111, 113, 144, 145, 146, 147, 149, 150, 151, 153, 154, 155, 158, 159, 165, 166, 167, 168, 169, 172, 173, 175, 176, 177, 178, 179, 180, 181, 183, 187, 191, 200, 201, 211, 212, 215, 218, 220
Morris, Mrs. Owen, 39, 44, 56, 62, 77, 79, 81, 82, 83, 84, 94, 1c6, 107, 110, 111, 113, 145, 146, 147, 149,

151, 153, 154, 155, 157, 158, 159, 160, 166, 168, 169, 172, 175, 176, 177, 178, 179, 180, 182, 184, 188, 200, 201, 203, 211, 212, 215, 218, 220, 253

Morris, Mrs. Owen (Second), 44

Morriseau (refugee musician), 300

Morton, playwright, 203, 320

Moseley, Dr. Benjamin, 63, 169

Mountaineers, The, Colman the Younger, 320

Mount Diabolo, 85

Mourning Bride, The, Congreve, 84

"Mrs. Allen" (drink), 65

Much Ado About Nothing, Shakespeare, 157

Muilman, Henry, 22

Muligin, Miss, 262

Mulattos, 126

Mundingoes, 239

Murphy, playwright, 79, 93, 99, 106, 145, 149, 166, 172, 173, 182, 183, 202, 214

Murphy, Hon. Thomas, 297

Murray, Master Dicky, 33, 323, 324, 325, 327

Murray, Patrick, 19

Murray, Walter, 32, 329

Murray and Kean (comedians), 30, 31, 32, 35

Music at dances, 261

Musical instruments of slaves, 235, 236, 237

Musical Lady, The, Colman the Elder, 201

Muster, General (1782), 168

My Grandmother, 324

Nassau, 88

Nassau Street Theatre (New York), 48

Nathan's Store, 77

Nau, Mr., 307, 308, 309

Negro dances, 238

Negro manners, 257

Negro parades, 242

Negro songs, 238

Nelson (British military governor), 89

Nelson (singer), 198, 262, 265, 267

Nelson's victory celebrated, 312

Nevis, 41, 163, 170, 190

New American Company of Comedians, 54, 223

Newgate, 4

New Orleans Theatre, 298

Newport, R. I., 222

New Year mummeries, 247

New Year's Gift, A, 166, 168

New York, 34, 43, 47, 189, 208, 216, 221, 222, 254, 272, 304, 305

New York City Tavern, 252

New York Mercury, The, 48

New York Theatre, 32

Nicaragua, 107, 109

Nichols, 11

Nicholson, Mrs.: her Lodging House, 119

Northern Colonies, The, 47, 51, 59, 163, 170, 189, 190, 304

Northern Liberties Theatre, 224, 301

Nugent, Lady, 304, 308; her diary, 69, 259

Obeah Man, 118

Obi, Fawcett, 192

O'Brian, Rev. Dr. (chaplain), 299

O'Brien, playwright, 79, 203, 221

Ogé, George (of Paris), 281

Ogé, James, 282, 283

Ogé Rebellion, 282

Ogle, Sir Chaloner, Admiral, 130

O'Hara, playwright, 81, 84, 121, 202

O'Keeffe, playwright, 145, 212, 214, 261, 263, 264, 265, 267, 270, 271, 278

Old Harbour, 131, 271

Old Maid, The, Murphy, 106, 145

Oliphant, Mrs., 265

Ombres Chinoises, Les, 286

Orange-street (Kingston), 286

Orphan, The, Otway, 32, 112, 185
Orphan of China, The, Murphy, 149, 214
Osborn, Mrs., 33
Othello, Shakespeare, 118
Otway, playwright, 32, 112, 114, 167, 185, 335

Pachebel, John Michael, 19
Padlock, The, Bickerstaff, 79, 113, 147, 262, 264, 279, 321
Painting and etching, 139
Panic in real estate, 250
"Pantaloon in the Suds," 196
Papaws, 239
Paplay's Store, 60
Parade, The, 69, 292, 300
Parade Playhouse, 299
Parish of Hanover, 277
Parish of St. Andrew, 256
Park Theatre (New York), 220, 326
Parker, 54
Parker, Sir Peter, 174
Pasquell, 331
Passion Week, 202
Patch, Samuel, 108, 265, 266, 268, 270, 297
Paul, John, 46
Peeping Tom of Coventry, O'Keeffe, 279
Penn, 4
Pennsylvania, 199, 208
Pennsylvania Packet, 91
Pensacola (Florida), 163
Pepe, Signor, 296, 297
Percy, Hannah Moore, 93, 198
Performances, Occasional, 312
Pests, 249
Peters, Mary, 28
Petit, Mons., 297
Phelps, 262, 265
Philadelphia, 28, 32, 34, 44, 47, 51, 54, 188, 208, 218, 220, 224, 226, 254, 272, 275, 298, 301, 304

Phillips, Teresa Constantia, 22, 23, 24, 41
Phillipps, James Mursel, 145, 315
Philosophical Society, American, 169
"Pickaninny Christmas," 235
Picture of a Playhouse, or Bucks Have at Ye All, 84
Pieck benefit, 296
Pillon, playwright, 160, 161
Pinnock, 212
Pizarro, 323
Planters, 129
Plate, china, glass, 133
Playbook (Kingston), 93
"Point, The," 163
Point of Honour, The, Kemble, 321, 323
Polly (schooner), 199
Polygamy among slaves, 230
Pool, Thomas, 207
Poor Gentleman, The, Colman the Younger, 320, 322
Poor Soldier, The, O'Keeffe, 212, 214, 227, 271, 320
Popette, Miss, 306
Portland Parish, 15
Port Royal, 2, 6, 9, 10, 11, 16, 58, 89, 121, 123, 138, 170, 173, 174, 191, 211, 250, 322
Porto Rico, 4
Pratt, 147
Price, Sir Charles, 131
Prince Edward (Richard III), 54
Princess-street, 102
Printers' ticket offices, 263
Pritchard, Betty Green, 10
Privateeering, 16
Privy Council of Jamaica, 304
Prologues, 113, 203
Providence, 49
Publius Horatius, 51
Puppeteers in the West Indies, 35, 36
Purse, The, Birch, 320, 321
Pyke, Maurice, pianist, 332

Quacos, 228
Quadroons, 126
Quaker, The, Mrs. Centlivre, 151,
272, 279
Quakers, 249
Quamins, 228
Quaos, 228
Quashebas, 144
Quashies, 228
Quateron, 143
Queen Anne, Reign of, 16
Queen Street Theatre (Charleston),
1, 43, 49, 50
Quin, Miss, 262, 264, 265, 268, 284
Quinteron, 143
Quondam Theatre, 267

Raising the Wind, 317
Ramsay, playright, 202
Ranelagh House, 67, 156, 170, 173,
184, 283, 290
Rannis (ventriloquist), 310, 311
Rattles, of the slaves, 237
Ravenscroft, playwright, 147
Raynard, Mrs. Anna Hallam, 62,
64, 98, 99, 105, 107, 108, 110, 112,
113, 145, 146, 147
Raynard, John (organist), 48
Read, Jesse, 316, 317, 318, 319, 327
Reading Hills, 199, 301
Recruiting Officer, The, Farquhar,
32, 158, 187
Refugees' concerts, 300
Refugees, French, 297
Regiment, Sixtieth, 320
Register Office, The, Morton, 203
Reign of Terror (France), 283
Remondet, 300, 306, 307, 308
Reprisal, The, Smollett, 106, 153,
159, 176
Restoration, in England, 4
Retrospections of America, Ber-
nard, 191
Revels, Master of the, 20, 21, 26
Revolutionary War, 2, 28, 114, 122,
188, 189

Rhode Island, 226
Richard III, Shakespeare, 54, 152,
172, 186, 224
Richmond, Va., 222
Richmond Hill, 215, 226
Rigby, Mr. and Mrs., 38
Rio Cobre, 69
Rivals, The, Sheridan, 109, 153, 256
Road to Ruin, 321
Roberts, David Benjamin, 54, 62,
77, 79, 81, 82, 83, 84, 85, 147, 186,
201, 203, 216, 262, 264, 279, 287,
288, 295, 296, 298
Robertson, George (artist), 140
Robespierre (France), 281
Robinson Crusoe, 213, 227
Roby, James (historian), 86
Rodgers, 255
Rodney, Admiral, 89, 90, 170, 173,
174, 212
Rodney–de Grasse battle, 293
Rodney Memorial, 90, 288
Rodon, Hon. John, 72
Roman Father, The, Whitehead,
51, 107
Romanito, 331
Romeo and Juliet, Shakespeare, 62,
150, 321
Rose, John, of Cottersbrook, 18
"Rose Hall," 131
Rosehill, Lady, 49, 217
Rosehill, Lord (Maryland), 49
Rosina, Mrs. Brooks, 213, 222, 270,
271
Ross, Rev. D. W., rector of Han-
over, 331
Ross, Hercules, Esq., 157
Rossi's Lacovia Tavern, 311
Rowe, playwright, 93, 182, 183, 184,
194, 203, 213, 223, 279, 316
Rowley, Admiral, 190
Royal Convert, The, Rowe, 36
Royal Empire Society (London),
261
Royal Gazette, The, 28, 152, 154,
160, 174, 269, 271, 272, 322

"Royalists," 246
Royal Saint Jago Lodge (Freemasons), 327
Royalty Theatre, 284
Rule a Wife and Have a Wife, Fletcher, 121
"Rule Britannia," 157, 176
Ryan, Dennis, 223, 225

Saba, 40
Sailor's Return, The, Bickerstaff, 120
Saint Andrew's Lodge (Freemasons), 284
Saint Patrick's Lodge (Freemasons), 284
Sale, 144, 146, 147, 149, 150
Salentin, 308
Salimen, George Edward, 292
Salomon, Mons. (flutist), 262, 266, 268, 269
Salt Pond Hills, 173
San Juan de Nicaragua, 89
Sanitation in old Jamaica, 133
Santo Domingo, 7, 171, 246, 281, 282, 286, 292, 310, 312
Saunders, Hyman (conjuror), 59, 94, 95, 205, 253
Savanna-la-Mar, 162, 207, 273
Savannah (Georgia), 223, 283
Savannah, The, 89, 103
Scandal Club, The, 168
Scarlett, 10
School for Fathers, Bickerstaff, 97
School for Scandal, The, Sheridan, 147, 175, 202, 211, 219, 222, 253, 267, 321
School for Soldiers, Henry, 151, 203
School for Wives, The, 220
Schroeter, Ensign (scene painter), 272, 280
Scorpion, The, 336
Scotch reel, 259
Scott, 33
Scott, J. (organist), 303

Scott, Hon. George, 297
Scott, Hon. John, 297
Scott, Michael, 241
Seilhamer, George O. (historian), 91, 188, 223
Selwyn, Governor, 10
Sequira's Dancing Room, 286
Servant Mistress (opera), 303
Servants in Jamaica, 132
"Set Girls," 243, 244, 245, 246, 247
Seven Ages, The, Shakespeare, 154
Sevilla Nueva, 3, 5, 6, 8
Shadows of Shakespeare, Pratt, 147, 152, 159, 202
Shakespeare, playwright, 38, 54, 62, 79, 93, 97, 108, 109, 113, 120, 144, 149, 150, 152, 154, 165, 166, 168, 172, 181, 186, 194, 203, 221, 222, 223, 224, 321
Shakespeare's Heroes, 27
Shaw, 318, 319, 321
Shaw, Miss, 317, 319, 323
Shaw, Mrs. Elizabeth, 316, 318, 319, 329, 330
She Stoops to Conquer, Goldsmith, 79, 97, 256, 270, 271, 319, 335
She Would and She Wouldn't, Cibber, 146
Sheep Shearing, The, Shakespeare, 166
Sheridan, playwright, 99, 106, 109, 121, 147, 153, 175, 202, 203, 211
Shipwreck, or Azemia, Cumberland, 106, 203, 308
Shirley, Sir Anthony, 3
Siege of Damascus, The, 187
Sierra Leone (Africa), 300
Sills, The, of Providence Plantations, 74
Singing of Negroes, 142
Singleton, 38, 40
Sir Courtly Nice, Crowne, 36
Six Clerks Office, 9
Sixteen-Mile Walk, 136
Sixty-second Regiment, 29
Skeating Duet, The, 265

Skerrett, Captain, 277
Slack Rope Tumblers, 278
Slavery's toll in Jamaica, 316
Slave Market, 74
Slave revolts, 249, 250, 315
Slave trade abolished, 88, 315
Slaves apprenticed, 315
Slaves freed, 1834, 315
Slaves' dance music, 234
Slaves' dances, 234
Slaves' musical instruments, 236, 237
Slaves' provisions, 233
Sleight of hand, 206, 278
Sloane, Sir Hans, 5, 13, 135, 136, 228, 234, 236, 239
Smalley, 323
Smith, William, 21, 28, 263
Smiths, The, 42
Smith's Village, 69
Smock Alley Theatre (Dublin), 256
Smollett, playwright, 106, 159
Solario (*Merchant of Venice*), 54
Songs of Negroes, 238
South Carolina Gazette, 50, 55, 224
South, The (States), 121, 283
Southwark Theatre (Philadelphia), 43, 50, 54, 56, 221, 226
Spaniards, 3, 96, 143, 171
Spanish Fryar, The, Dryden, 145, 187, 198
Spanish Town, 3, 5, 11, 12, 13, 16, 18, 29, 33, 46, 49, 69, 70, 71, 76, 79, 85, 90, 95, 107, 121, 130, 141, 161, 169, 173, 187, 193, 208, 217, 226, 227, 232, 250, 270, 271, 272, 278, 279, 280, 296, 304, 308, 310, 321, 323, 326
Spanish Town Amateurs, The, 335
Spanish Town balls, 258, 259
Spanish Town Cathedral, 303
Spanish Town players, 270
Spanish Town Road, 70
Spanish Town Theatre, 5, 87, 320, 322
Speed the Plough (song), 320

Spencer, Thomas, 14
Spoiled Child, The, 37
Spoilt Child, The, Bickerstaff, 321
Sports and Pastimes, 14
St. Andrew's, 15
St. Ann's, 162, 274
St. Ann's Bay, 3, 85
St. Ann's Parish, 6, 17, 29
St. Catherine's, 29
St. Cecile, Ode to, Dryden, 189
St. Clair (refugee musician), 300
St. Croix, 41, 323
St. Elizabeth's Parish, 311
St. Eustabius, 163
St. Eustatius, 41, 90
St. Jago de la Vega Gazette, 3, 47, 296, 311, 323, 328
St. James's Assembly dance, 255
St. James's Church (Bristol), 226
St. James's Musical Society, 254
St. James's Parish, 86, 194, 204, 207, 274, 315
St. Just (singer), 303
St. Kitts, 41, 90, 163, 170
St. Lucia, 90, 171
St. Michael's Church (London), 225
St. Philip's Church, 50
St. Thomas, 192, 323; Parish, 13, 16
St. Vincent, 89, 90
Stag Dinner toasts, 276
Stamitz's Third Symphony, 268
Stanton, Colonel, 13
States, The, 214, 216, 222
Sterlings, The, of Content, 74
Stevensons, The (portrait painters), 140
Stewart, J. (historian), 312
Storer, Mrs., 51
Storer sisters, 51, 122
Storer, Miss, 56, 62, 98, 99, 105, 106, 107, 109, 110, 111, 113, 147, 149, 150, 151, 153, 154, 155, 158, 159, 160, 172, 173, 175, 177, 178, 179, 181, 182, 183, 184, 186, 200, 201, 204, 214, 227

Storer, Miss Fanny, 53, 201, 216, 224, 227
Storer, Miss Maria, 73, 77, 79, 80, 82, 84, 200, 201, 216, 224, 227
Storms at Jamaica, 248, 249
"Stokes Hall," St. Thomas, 131
Stone, John, 71
Stratagem, The, 111, 158
Stuart, Mrs., 325, 326, 327, 328
Sugar colony, 4
Sugar in 1795, 249
Sugar-cane munch, 142
Sugar-canes of the South Seas, 298
Sugar Plantations, 74
Sultan, The, Bickerstaff, 320
Supreme Executive Council of Pennsylvania, 189
Surrender of Calais, The, Colman the Younger, 321
Suspicious Husband, The, Hoadley, 119

Talkative Barber, The, 324
Talking fish (Edinburgh), 311
Tambourines, 237
Tamworth Grammar School, 9
Tars of Old England, The, 176
Taylor, Simon, 16, 33
"Teak Pen," Clarendon, 131
Tekel, 320
Tempest, The, Shakespeare, 108
Temple Hall, 15
Templeman (slack-wire tumbler), 189
Tessier, Augustus, 305, 306, 307, 308, 309
Tessier, Miss, 306, 308
Thalia, 283
Theatrical Candidates, 105
Theatrical Club, 270
Theatrical Fête, 263
Theatre audiences, 142, 143
Theatre, New (Montego Bay), 77, 199, 200
Theatre revived, 1806, 316

Theatre Royal, Covent Garden (London), 151
Theatre Royal (Kingston), 333
Theatre Royal (Manchester), 326
Theatre, Spanish, 8
Theatres closed, 310
Theatres: customs, 141
Theatres, Earliest, 32
The Journal of a West Indian Proprietor, Lewis, 325
Thespians, 249, 329
Thespians, Military, 114, 120, 121, 150, 185, 272
Thespis, Daughters of, 312
Thomas and Sally, Bickerstaff, 97, 120, 202, 227
Thompson, playwright, 186, 256, 278, 317
Three-Fingered Jack, 191, 192
"Thro' the Wood, Laddie" (song), 167
Tobago, 90, 163
Tom Cringle's Log, Scott, 69, 241
Tom Thumb, Fielding, 279
Tony Lumpkin in Town, O'Keeffe, 145
Tortula, 41
"Touchwood, Lady Francis," 44
Touthemoulin (musician), 300, 310
Towers, John, 12
Towne, Dr. Richard, 36
Townley, playwright, 93, 111, 175, 186
Traffic rules, 188
Tragedy of George Barnwell, 36
Trelawny, 250, 274
Trelawny, Governor, 130
Trelawny Parish, 194, 207
Tremaine, John, 33
Trinity churchyard (New York), 48
Trip to Brighthelmstone, A, 177
Trip to Dover, A, 167
Trip to the Jubilee, A, Farquhar, 178
Triumph of Genius, Cawdell, 146

True and Exact History of the Island of Barbados, Ligon, 37
Trumpet Tree, 237
Tuke, Miss, 44, 216, 219, 220
Tulipano (opera), 303
Tumbling and Sword Dancing, 32
Turk's Island, 90
"Twelfth of April, The," 196
Two Constantias, The, Garrick, 202
Two Friends (slaveship), 46
Two Strings to Your Bow, 321
Tyler, Royall, Major, 275

Ullman (exhibitor), 284, 286
Union Street (Montego Bay), 73
Upton, Robert, 30

Valton, Peter (organist), 50
Van Backman, Mrs., 269
Venables, 4
Venetian, The, 278, 285
Venice Preserved, Otway, 45, 114, 335
Vere, Jamaica, 20
Vernon, Vice-Admiral Edward, 18, 19
Versailles, Peace of, 90
Vice-Admiralty Court, 190
Village Lawyer, The, 320
Villallave, 330
Villallave children, 330
Villallave, Mrs., 331
Ville de Paris (warship), 174
Villegrain, 306, 307
Villeneuvi, 303
Villeneuvi, Mrs., 303
Vintner Trick'd, The, Yarrow, 144, 262
Virgin Unmasked, The, Fielding, 113
Virginia, Crisp, 145
Virginia Company of Comedians, 167
Virtue in Danger, 168
Visiting Families, 139

"Vivat Respublica," 209
Volunteers, The, 107

Wags of Windsor, 320
Wainwright, Miss, 50, 56, 62, 64, 79, 80, 82, 83, 84, 94, 98, 105, 107, 109, 110, 111, 112, 145, 146, 147, 149, 154, 155, 158, 160, 166, 167, 169, 172, 173, 175, 176, 177, 178, 179, 181, 182, 183, 216
Walker, Mr., of Barbados, 36
Walker, W., Grand Secretary (Freemasons), 174
Walpole, Horace, 22
War of the Spanish Succession, 16
Ward, Colonel Charles James, 334
Ward Theatre (Kingston), 334
Washington, General, 163
Washington, George, 36, 193, 218
Washington, Lawrence, 36
Waterman, The, Dibdin, 279
Water Street Theatre (Philadelphia), 34
Ways and Means, Colman, 279
Wax candles, 132
Weldon, 266, 270, 292, 296
West Africa, 228
West Indian Lady's Arrival in London, A, Miss Cheer, 155, 163
West Indian, The, 37, 45, 81, 187, 201, 278, 320
West Indies, 2, 34, 57, 228, 313
West Indies' Players, 32
Westmoreland, 90, 274
Westmoreland Parish, 116
Weston, 212
Wexford Wells, 45
Whidahs, 239
Whitehead, playwright, 107
Whites, 128
Who's the Dupe? Mrs. Cowley, 108, 320
Wickstead, Philip, 140
Wignell, Thomas, 57, 77, 78, 79, 80, 82, 84, 94, 98, 99, 105, 107, 175, 180, 200, 204, 205, 207, 218, 220

Wignell, William, 62, 64, 79, 80, 82, 83, 84, 94, 98, 99, 106, 108, 109, 110, 111, 112, 113, 144, 145, 146, 147, 149, 150, 151, 153, 155, 158, 159, 165, 166, 167, 168, 172, 173, 175, 177, 179, 182, 183, 200, 201, 202, 203, 211, 212, 298
Wild Oats, 321
Williams's Long Room, 204, 206
Williamsburg, Va., 30, 31, 34, 38, 40, 54, 148
Willis, Miss, 224
Wilmot, Miss, 323
Wilson, Miss Jane, 304
Wilsone's St. Cecilia (songs), 227
Windward Islands, 207
Winter's Tale, Shakespeare, 166
Witches' Dance, The, 267
Wives Metamorphized, The, Coffey, 32
Wollmer, John, 16, 272
Women actors, 28
Wonder! An Honest Yorkshireman, A, 62
Wonder! A Woman Keeps a Secret, The, Mrs. Centlivre, 49, 144, 181, 271, 321

Woodham, Charles Somerset, 33, 34
Woodward, playwright, 106, 109, 153, 154
Woolery, Edward, 256
Woolery, Frances Burnet, 256
Woolls, Stephen, 50, 51, 62, 94, 98, 99, 105, 106, 107, 108, 110, 112, 113, 144, 145, 146, 147, 149, 150, 151, 153, 154, 155, 158, 160, 165, 166, 167, 168, 172, 173, 175, 176, 177, 178, 179, 180, 181, 182, 200, 204, 212, 215, 220, 221, 227
Woolls, Master Thomas A., 98, 106, 112, 150, 153, 154, 159, 165, 167, 172, 280
Woolls, Mrs. Thomas A., 280
Worlidge, John, 71, 72
Worn, Mr., 112

Yarrow, playwright, 144, 262
Yates, 325, 326, 327, 328, 329
Yellow Jack, 137, 138
Yorktown, 163, 170
Young Florentine, 301

Zara, Hill, 116
Zoffany (artist), 140